The Unbeaten Track

ARTHUR TARNOWSKI

The Unbeaten Track

with a Foreword by
BARBARA WARD JACKSON
and
Preface by DOUGLAS BADER

HARVILL PRESS, LONDON

ISBN 0 00 272362 X

© Arthur Tarnowski 1971

Made and Printed in Great Britain by
William Collins Sons & Co. Ltd.
London and Glasgow
for the publishers Harvill Press Limited
30a Pavilion Road, London S.W.1

1st April 2016

Dear Amaryllis,

To the handicapped of all nations

"To Journey, to witness - in heart's
freedom and wonderment,
to reach out across far horizons
beyond the murkey confines of
Parochial mediority -

'tis to LIVE, 'tis to LOVE"

My fathers wrote these words for me in a
book he gifted to me as I set out on my travels.
This book is the most meaningful gift I have
to give. I am incredibly grateful to have
you in our lives. These moment we share
are magical. Thank you.

With Love,

Lucian and Tiea
AKA 'The monkeys'

Acknowledgements

The account of the Expedition of necessity is abridged, and leaves out mention of many incidents and much valuable technical advice, services and assistance rendered to the Expedition and its objects; in particular my grateful thanks are due to Dr Arthur Hanslip, Jean Claude Luyat and Vishnu Mathur, who took part in the earlier stages of the Expedition and rendered valuable technical services to it as doctor, photographer and cameraman respectively. It was especially due to Vishnu Mathur that several travel films were made on the Expedition and subsequently shown on BBC television.

The success of the Expedition was in great part due to the indomitable cheerfulness and devotion to the task before us shown by Jocelyn Cadbury and Julian Ingram.

To the Reader's Digest I owe a very deep debt. From Mr James Monahan I received invaluable help and guidance in the course of the Expedition, and without the constant help of Mr Anthony Burton-Brown who undertook the onerous task of shaping and editing this book it would never have been written.

My thanks go also to the governments and officials of the countries in which we travelled for the hospitality and the facilities they so generously extended to us; to the doctors and nurses of the hospitals and institutions we visited who gave us so much time and encouragement and above all I acknowledge my debt to Amte who brought our hopes to realization.

But the Unbeaten Track Expedition would never have set out without the enthusiasm of the members of the sponsoring committee, amongst whom I would especially like to thank Sir Robert and Lady Jackson, Mrs George Villiers and Lady Peake.

Finally, among the persons and foundations who helped the Expedition financially or in kind are the following:

The Automobile Association; Boots Pure Drug Co. Ltd.; Bosch A. G.; The British Motor Corporation; British School of Motoring Ltd.; The British Steamship Navigation Co. Ltd.; Ella Lyman Cabot Trust; Miss Dorothy Cadbury; Mr Lawrence Cadbury; Mr Paul S. Cadbury; Mr Norman A. Cadbury; Cadbury Bros. Ltd.; The Dunlop Co. Ltd.; Feeney and Johnson Ltd.; Mrs Ismini Fitch;

Mark Fitch Fund; Gray, Dawes, Westray & Co. Ltd.; Calouste Gulbenkian Foundation; Kodak Ltd.; The Lucis Trust; Matheson & Co. Ltd.; Nippon Kogaku K. K.; Pneumatic Tent Co. Ltd.; The Reader's Digest Foundation; Mr David Rockefeller; Shell International Petroleum Co. Ltd.; Mr Adlai Stevenson; Sir Dorabji Tata Trust; The World Rehabilitation Fund, Inc.; Zimmer Orthopaedic Ltd.;

It is their confidence and generosity which enabled this project to be mounted and carried through successfully and so I wish to thank every one of them not only in the name of the Expedition they had made possible, but also on behalf of those handicapped in Asia who have been helped as a consequence of their generosity.

Contents

Foreword 12

Preface 13

Prologue 15

1 Childhood in Poland 20

2 The German and Russian Occupations 28

3 We escape 46

4 London and the Travel Bug 61

5 Polio 81

6 A Goal in Life 99

7 The Expedition sets out: Turkey and Persia 121

8 In remote Nuristan 145

9 Courage and Fatalism in India 162

10 'Chief Fool' at the Holi Festival 184

11 Thailand 194

12 Japan and the House that Toichiro built 212

13 The Armanath Pilgrimage: a Climb of 12,000 feet 223

14 I am exorcised in Ceylon 241

15 Fansa, Melkote and other Indian Rehabilitation Projects 256

16 Anandwan: Amte's Miracle 279

17 Sandhi-Niketan: the End of the Track 301

Colour Illustrations

On the Amarnath Pilgrimage *frontispiece*

On the way to Malamchi, Nepal *facing page* 18

Blon with his wife and daughter 18

Nepalese peasant 228

Sowing the first crop at Somnath 237

Harvesting chilis in Kashmir 237

Crippled beggars 260

Amte and his family 269

'Gift of Labour' 269

Mealtime at Anandwan 288

The beginnings of Sandhi-Niketan 305

Black and White Illustrations

Between pages 72 and 73

Dukla
Zaleze
Countess Wanda Tarnowska
Arthur, 5 years old
With Sheikh Ali in Iraq
In Bali
Preparing a paddy field
Village market

Between pages 136 and 137

Trying to raise funds
A stop in Eastern Turkey
A game of 'Jirit'
Nuristan step-ladder
Grape harvest in Afghanistan
The author in Ghazni

Between pages 168 and 169

Taj Mahal
Gol Gumbaz mausoleum in Bijapur
Details of the Channakesava temple in Belur
The King's Balance in Vijayanagar
Kandariya-Mahadeo temple in Khajuraho

Between pages 200 and 201

Sadhus
Local festival in Rameshwaram
Pushkar Fair
Jain pilgrims in Satrunjaya
Snake charmers at Molar Bund
Villagers by a wayside station
Maruti
Ratanam

Foreword

There are two stories in this book. The first concerns the courage of a young man who, stricken by polio and desperately handicapped, refused to accept the tragedy as an end to his vision of a useful life.

The second is a demonstration that courage is a necessary but not sufficient response to the disaster of becoming physically handicapped. Without resources, without modern instruments and methods of rehabilitation, all the courage in the world will not let the lame man walk again and set about the task of regaining his life and independence.

Throughout the world, there are thousands upon thousands of maimed human beings who could repeat Arthur Tarnowski's 'miracle' if they had the means and the help. His whole story is, in the last analysis, a plea to the rich, the comfortable, the active and the unhandicapped to see that courage and assistance are matched not only for a fortunate minority but for all the world's handicapped people.

BARBARA WARD JACKSON

Preface

Having started to read this book I was quite unable to put it down until I had finished. It is the story of a Pole, Arthur Tarnowski, of good family, brought up in the luxury of a Polish country estate, surrounded by loyal servants and villagers who for generations had lived on the estate and were virtually part of the family.

When the author was nine years old Adolf Hitler's Nazis invaded and occupied Poland. The author describes calmly and without exaggeration the cruelty and the meanness of the Germans and the bitterness and humiliation of the Poles. As a boy he joined with his mother in the dangers and excitement of resistance to the occupying forces, first German and then Russian. It is difficult for the reader to decide which was the more ruthless. He and his mother finally escaped and settled in England, by way of Italy and France. He completed his education in London during the course of which he became fascinated by the East.

At the age of twenty-four he travelled across Europe, the Middle East, India and the Far East. He did this in the cheapest way, not only because he had no money but because he was determined to live like the ordinary folk in the countries through which he passed. In Singapore he contracted polio which left him paralysed from the waist downwards.

This is the story of his fight against this disability. He won it and as a result of his experiences during his trip through the East he was determined to try and assist others with incurable diseases throughout the Near East and South-East Asia. His real interest lies in India.

The author writes fluently and his powers of description are uncanny and graphic. As you read the book you are carried along by Tarnowski's own thoughts and emotions; you can smell the stench and squalor of the places he visited; you can sense the hopelessness which the fatalistic religions of the East impose on the sick.

The Unbeaten Track is an inspired title for a tremendous story. I hope it will be widely read.

DOUGLAS BADER

Prologue

ON the far horizon, the rising sun was tinting with crimson the snows of the high Himalayas. It was 6 a.m., and I felt ravenously hungry.

'Hey, surely that porridge must be smoked enough by now?' I called.

Pinuri, our head porter and guide who had been up for the past hour, was filling the shepherd's hut where we had camped for the night with clouds of acrid smoke.

'Coming, Sahib,' he said, whistling cheerfully as he spooned the steaming concoction into mugs. The porridge tasted wonderful, despite the grit. We wolfed it down, and followed it with tea, stewed black, as dark as the cauldron that simmered over the open fire.

The old woman who owned the hut came down the ladder from the garret where she had been sleeping, scratching her bottom energetically. Pausing a moment to review the scene, she cleared her throat, and spat from between her toothless gums.

'Pinuri, how much should I pay her?' I asked. Local custom allowed the traveller to seek a night's rest in any hut, but the owner always charged something.

'Three rupees plenty,' Pinuri replied. I handed over the money, and calculated that the charge came to fourpence a head. But two scraggy goats had shared our lodgings, together with a cockerel which had crowed most of the night from a wicker basket a few inches from my head. Perhaps the charge was quite reasonable, after all. The old woman tucked the coins away inside her bodice. She watched with an expressionless face as we checked our kit, and prepared to move off.

We travelled light. Apart from our sleeping bags and a few warm clothes, we had only brought torches, cigarettes for the porters, and various basic foodstuffs that we knew would be unobtainable in the hamlets. Even so, two days out from base camp in Kathmandu, Nepal, each of our five porters was shouldering sixty pounds.

The prospect of the mountain before us was daunting as we zig-zagged up the stony path. Pinuri took the lead, climbing with the ease of a mountain goat. Every so often he would break into song, to be answered by the high-pitched yodelling of another Sherpa towards the rear, whom we had nicknamed America Wallah. Uncle Sam's popularity was due to a pair of U.S. Army mountaineering boots and a windcheater which America Wallah had acquired on a previous Himalayan climb and of which he was immensely proud. As their voices echoed from mountain to mountain in the clear air, I felt glad to be alive.

We stopped for lunch on a grassy ledge, overhanging a valley deep below, but Pinuri would not let us rest for long.

'Must go, Sahib. Must reach next sheep hut before night.'

After another hour's hard climbing, I heard mutterings behind me.

'My God, Arthur, this is killing me. How much farther?'

Julian Ingram, my companion and the expedition's mechanic, was finding it hard to keep up. A few weeks previously, he had been sitting behind an office desk. He was puffing and blowing hard.

'Cheer up, Julian,' I answered. 'It levels off quite soon.' From my vantage point I could see that Pinuri had stopped ahead, and was pointing vigorously to some huts clinging to the flank of the mountain, a little below the path. The huts looked even more ramshackle than the previous night's 'hotel'; I wondered uneasily why he was stopping. By the time the rest of us had caught up, Pinuri was sitting on the ground outside one of the hovels. As we approached, I saw at a glance that the man he was sitting alongside was severely disabled, his legs bent and contracted in a rigid position.

I could also see from the look on their faces that they were wondering: what was I, a fair-haired, white 'Englishman' doing in this part of the world? Why was I being carried on the back of a Sherpa? They probably thought I was lazy.

'Hey, Sahib,' Pinuri greeted me excitedly, 'you ask me find man no walk. No legs like you. Man here.'

It was quite true. Eight years previously, I had lost the use of my own legs through polio. My lower extremities were paralysed;

whenever the going was too rough for my wheelchair, I had to be carried. One of our main purposes while on this expedition was to find others who had suffered a similar disability. So wherever we went, I made a point of asking if there were any disabled people in the locality.

Now the Sherpa who had been carrying me placed me on the ground, and Julian heaved me out of the conical basket, or *bora*, in which I had been riding. The assembled group looked on without a flicker of interest or surprise as I tucked my legs into a comfortable position with my hands.

'Pinuri, please ask him his name and age.'

While they were talking, I looked at their pathetic hovel, bare of furniture of any sort, except for their two brightly polished brass cooking pots, their most valuable possessions. Apart from some turnip peels drying in the sun a few feet away, there was nothing to be seen. From the look on their faces I felt I knew the story, even before Pinuri began to translate.

'He says his name Blon of Tamang people. This wife Sailee, this daughter. Age he not know.'

Despite Pinuri's rudimentary English, we gradually pieced together the story. Blon had once managed to eke out a precarious living, working in the fields. But about seven years ago, over the space of two days, his left arm and both legs had become totally paralysed.

'He say Lama come to pray, chase it away,' Pinuri added. 'But Lama no help.' Pinuri was obviously enjoying his new role as translator. Julian, on the other hand, was visibly shaken. 'But why doesn't someone call a doctor?', he asked me quietly.

'Because the nearest doctor would be back in Kathmandu. And even if they could find one prepared to make the two-day trek, what would they pay him with?'

To make sure, I checked with Pinuri, who confirmed that the nearest doctor was in fact in Kathmandu. I worked it out that even if Blon had been fit and earning, the doctor's fee would represent a whole year's wages. But now Blon could barely drag himself about painfully on his bottom.

'When did they last eat?' I asked Pinuri.

'Three days ago. But Sailee says today they eat.' he added, pointing towards the turnip peels. Evidently they could not afford whole turnips. Sailee and the daughter went out regularly to look for work, labouring in the fields for two rupees a day. But there had been no work now for two months, and they were reduced to begging in the village. 'She just come back from village,' Pinuri said. 'For five days nobody give her anything.'

'What a life,' Julian murmured, looking up towards the majestic span of the Himalayas. 'What hope have they got?'

'None at all, this side of a miracle.'

Pinuri was urging us to get going again. As I thought of some way to say good-bye, some word of comfort to these people in their barren, hopeless situation, I could only think of those words from Virgil's *Aeneid* Una salus victis nullam sperares alutem. 'The only peace for the damned lies in hoping no more.'

I had faced this moment of departure many times before. It had defeated me every time. What could I say? Blon was not unhappy, but resigned to fate, to his lot in life, his *karma*. There was nothing to say. I merely looked at him full in the eye, hoping that in some way I would pass on to him some of my own faith and hope.

The path grew steep again. As I looked back at the huts I could see Blon lying where we had left him. Suddenly America Walla started cursing me from below. 'No move, Sahib. Me fall.'

'Sorry, America Wallah.'

Obviously it was getting tricky, even in American boots. I sat as still as I could in the lurching basket, hanging on to the sides with my hands. I thought again of Blon, condemned to a slow and miserable death. Surely *something* could be done? Surely there was something that even I, with my own disability, could do for such people, even on a modest scale. But what? That was the problem we still had to solve.

The sun was now setting, and the temperature falling sharply. I began to worry a little as to whether we were going to make it to the next hut. The thought of camping out in a temperature of eight degrees below zero centigrade was alarming. I grew more worried when I realized that we had to cross a series of torrents. The water gushed down with such fury that it sent up a cloud of spray on to the paths. The spray was freezing, and the paths and narrow log bridges were becoming dangerous.

The stars were out by the time we reached the last bridge. In the dim light I could just see a swollen torrent about forty feet below, and the outline of the hut on the far bank. Julian was the

The author being carried in a basket on the way to Malamchi, Nepal

Blon with his wife and daughter outside their hut

first across, bouncing over the narrow plank bridge. But instead of carrying straight on, he turned, cupped his hands round his mouth, and shouted back. His words were lost in the roar of the water, so I waved to him, signalling that he would have to come-back.

'Hey, look out,' he muttered. 'That plank is dead lethal.'

It was a nasty situation. The slightest movement on my part could send America Wallah and myself down into a very cold bath. I could control everything except my legs.

'Julian, I think you had better strap me down.'

Taking a long piece of string, Julian wound it round and over my legs, dangling over the side of the conical basket, strapping them down firmly.

'There, that should do the trick,' he said, finishing a tight knot. 'Off you go.'

America Wallah heaved me up, and put one foot gingerly on to the plank to balance himself. Then, taking dainty steps like a ballet dancer, he crossed swiftly to the far side.

CHAPTER I

Childhood in Poland

*

THE world into which I was born was a happy world. But that world was already dying, and was destined not to survive my adolescence. I was born on the 7th of January 1930 in Dukla, a large house in southern Poland, on the foothills of the Carpathian mountains. Both my parents belonged to Polish landowning families. My mother had known my father since childhood; the two families were related, and frequent guests at each other's estates. They were married shortly before the First World War. My sister Sophie and brother Stanislas were born during the latter part of the First World War. My parents separated in 1933 and from that time until the outbreak of the Second World War my mother and I lived together at Dukla.

I was a happy child. My older brother and sister were away much of the time studying abroad, and I was left to my own devices. I had a tutor and governesses; after struggling with my lessons, we would take a break in mid-morning, and I would let off steam by tearing up and down the long corridors on my tricycle, bells tinkling to warn the servants to retreat to a safe distance.

I was never lonely, for there was always so much going on at Dukla. Visitors were frequent, and we never sat down to luncheon without guests – distant members of our large family, artists, politicians, statesmen, intellectuals, men of letters. From an early age my mother encouraged me to join in, provided that I behaved properly, and since the conversation was frequently conducted in French or English, I had ample opportunity for practising these languages. Afterwards I sometimes offered to conduct them over the place, fervently hoping, as we processed down the stately corridors, that they would ask me for details of some distinguished Tarnowski ancestor, scowling down from his portrait on the wall. Proudly I would relate how this was Jan Tarnowski, Hetman (Commander-in-Chief), whose dates were 1488 to 1561, and who served under King Zygmunt I and King Zygmunt-August. In 1521 he had led Polish troops to assist King Louis of Hungary against the invading Turkish armies; in 1531 he won the battle of Obertyn against the Volovians (his major victory); and in 1535 he beat the Russians at the battle of Starobudy. He also fought successfully against encroaching Tartar hordes.

The house, with many guest rooms, always stood open to welcome distinguished visitors both from Poland and abroad. It held treasures brought back from grand tours over the generations. Renaissance paintings, tapestries, marble busts, oriental carpets, crystals and other *objets d'art* graced its sombre interiors, objects often chosen for their beauty rather than high value or artist's renown. Patronage of this nature entailed an incidental bonus, inasmuch as it was more likely to bring recognition to a talented artist as yet unknown, than the frenzied biddings for well known names, where art objects are sought after and acquired more because of their price-tags and the prestige they are supposed to confer on the owner than for their artistry and aesthetic merit.

Outside, a riot of colour burst from the shrubberies and herbaceous borders. Beyond the lawns and gardens spread a mile-long park, with millennial oaks and lindens heavy on the bough, marked with ponds where I used to shoot wild duck and row a caique. Carefully raked alleys, vaulted over by the weather-beaten lindens, led over the park and cut between the ponds over bridges flanked by wrought-iron trellises.

My mother loved the park, flowers and house, and her taste in arranging and embellishing these surroundings never failed to draw the visitors' delighted recognition. I remember once the distinguished French authoress, Rosa Bailly, came to stay for a few days at Dukla. I was attracted by the kindly gentleness and intelligence of her expression, flattered by her attention and the serious questions which she put to me despite my six years.

I took her on a guided tour, for once eager to tell her the little I knew of the personalities and deeds behind the ancestral portraits whose stiff gaze normally provoked me to thumb my nose at them when nobody was looking. 'Look! Till recently this frieze was covered with plaster. Mummy discovered it when a bit of plaster fell off. So she had all of it removed, and the fresco was restored. It's probably by an Italian master of the seventeenth century. And this portrait is of Hetman Tarnowski. Everybody in

Poland learns about him from history books. He was the brilliant Commander-in-Chief of the Polish armies in the reign of King Zygmunt in the sixteenth century.' And so we went from room to room, the excitement of my comments enhanced all the more by her good-natured interest.

The following day I joined her on a walk around the park. Madame Bailly was visibly moved by the carpets of flowers that set off so discreetly each other's hues and shapes, and beyond the ornamental lattices, statuary and the backdrop of the house. 'This,' she said, 'is like entering the carefree world from A Thousand-and-One Nights . . . a world whence all trace of ugliness and decay has been banished. Yet fables are apt to be shattered so rudely . . . ' I felt cross and a little frightened. 'But Dukla is not a fable! It has stood here for very, very long and always will.' 'Of course,' she smiled indulgently.

Later Madame Bailly was to write about Dukla. I read her description against the background of the strident syncopated phrases of Hitler's speech, blaring out over the radio: ' . . . in the same manner as she maintains the park, the countess adorns the walls, decorates and beautifies her rooms. There is nothing around her untouched by the charm of her genius. Having enclosed life in the castle, she transmogrified a mediaeval fortress into a jewel, where "everything is harmony and beauty – luxury, quietude and bliss".

'A vision of broken crystals, torn pictures, frenziedly trampled furniture flits through my mind. In this way in the east of the country Polish mansions were lost by the hundred, palaces which in those semi-wild areas constituted replicas of our French castles and hearths of culture. I dare not think of the Lady of this palace. I fear to draw on her the tragedy lurking in nearby forests; or even closer in her own orchard, if I can imagine her in the glare of conflagration, as Parisians saw Madame Lamballe.'

As it turned out, her words were almost prophetic. Yet if the gathering storm was being discussed, nobody expected it to overwhelm the world of Dukla, with its six foot walls and its proud oaks that had withstood so many wars and tempests.

In the flush of recently won independence after a hundred and fifty years of foreign domination my tutor's patriotism, like that of most Poles, was exacerbated to the point of chauvinism. Mr Wajda would assure me with quiet conviction, 'If each Pole kills at least three Germans before being overcome, we shall win.' His arithmetic was simple for this was roughly the ratio of the two populations. Germany and Russia were the enemy lands, which had to be hated with a passion equalled only by the love of one's own fatherland.

I remember my shock during a geography lesson when Mr Wajda unfolded a particularly large map of Poland and the adjoining countries. I took one long look at the frontier that meandered in intricate loops and wriggles around the country. 'But Mr Wajda,' I gasped, 'how am I to fit my love on the one side of this line and start my hate immediately on the other? What if I forget one of these squiggles and love some enemy territory? What would they do to me, Mr Wajda?' 'Don't worry about that,' he replied. 'It's the principle that matters!'

I liked Mr Wajda. Despite his overweening patriotism and his habit of dividing the brotherhood of man into those who were right and those who were wrong, he was good fun and possessed a knack of instilling interest into the lessons of arithmetic, history, geography, Polish language, Latin and the other subjects he taught me.

There were others concerned in my education and early days, whose precepts pulled in a different, less bigoted direction. Miss Peggy was my English governess. Plump, ruddy cheeked, wearing hearty tweeds, brogues and thick stockings, Miss Peggy personified to me the British Empire about which she spoke with such vibrant eloquence. She reflected the Empire still at the height of its power, tough, confident and all fair-play. I was fond of her though I feared her discipline and sharp rejoinders. In preparation for the life of an English public school, she initiated me into English literature, starting with Kipling. I was due to follow my brother at Downside, but the war put paid to that.

The character-building and somewhat spartan discipline of self-control nurtured by Miss Peggy were the great foundation stones of the English system of education at the time, a system much beloved of the Polish nobility.

Madame Rolland, my French governess, on the other hand, brought the sparkle and *l'esprit de la belle France*, with her culture and refinement. She had taught me French almost from the time that I had first learned to speak Polish, and later I was to go through most of the Bibliothèque Rose with her, together with classics of travel literature, which stirred my awareness of different lands and peoples across the globe. Having been in the family for so long, dear Madame Rolland was more like a second mother to me. She had been governess to my mother in her teens and had then guided my sister and brother. She was an integral part of the family, and those bonds were to prove stronger than all the trials and misery of the looming international conflict, for she remained the faithful companion throughout the war and its aftermath.

Mr Machnowski was not strictly a tutor but a companion. This however did not lessen the influence he exerted over me. He was a painter, an artist of remarkable aesthetic sensitivity. My mother felt that the companionship of a person capable of experiencing and communicating beauty would exert an influence at least as valuable as that of the more orthodox classroom instruction. In fact, Machnowski possessed an uncanny gift for perceiving beauty, especially in seemingly small and common things which a less sensitive eye would have passed unnoticed. Moreover he had the gift of sharing his perceptions with a natural, cheerful spontaneity that was never precious or boring. The sweep and liberalism of Machnowski's views was too pervasive and far-reaching to leave room for narrow parochialism, political or cultural.

I learned most of all from my mother. She taught me that true nobility does not depend on the external show of wealth and position, but rests in the heart, in service and self-command. When she was about twenty, a terrible epidemic of cholera broke out in the area of Wysock where her family estate was. Little treatment was available at the time, inoculation hardly even thought of. In the villages of the region people were dying in large numbers, and the fear of contagion was such that the healthy shunned cottages where anyone was sick. In consequence such families had great difficulty in obtaining food and basic necessities. Laden with food, medicines and other provisions, my mother would go on horseback, visiting the cottages, tending the sick and dying without a moment's hesitation. People loved and blessed her, but they welcomed her visits without particular surprise since care and protection from the *dwor* (estate) in times of danger or calamity was regarded as almost natural.

So often the type of life which I was born into, which for centuries had formed my family background, is regarded as merely a matter of ease and privilege. No doubt it involved that too. But wealth and privilege were accepted as something natural; something that had been part of a way of life for too many generations to be held as objects for further ambition and lust. It involved patronage in the field of arts and learning, representing the country abroad, providing leadership, especially in times of national danger. Amongst the virtues, rectitude, honour, self-command and above all courage were regarded as the worthiest and inculcated from earliest days.

My mother's beauty and charm were well-known. She was above medium height, with a beautiful complexion, fine features, and soft auburn hair that never faded or greyed even during our later years of trial. She was witty, graceful and sensitive; few could resist her charm, not even the famous Panicz.

Panicz, or 'The Lord' as he was nicknamed by the terror-stricken people of the area, had gained a well-deserved notoriety for his exploits, his killings, highway robberies and cunning elusiveness. In the early thirties he led a group of desperadoes, all with prices on their heads and photographs marked 'Wanted' in police stations. The reward offered for the capture of Panicz was very high but, even though it represented a fortune to a villager, nobody was foolhardy enough to have a go. Panicz was a good-looking man in his thirties, thickset, with strong rough features, a droopy moustache like a Mexican *bandido's* and large blue eyes with a steely glint to them that carried his utter fearlessness and ferocity. He also had a great sense of humour and liked sending notes to the police, suggesting periodic increases in the price on his head.

Early one evening my mother was travelling by car with a cousin to a grand reception in his castle. As the car sped through a forest road, suddenly the chauffeur braked hard and the car lurched to a halt. 'It's Panicz and his gang. God have mercy on us!' he cried out. Several men surrounded the car, guns at the ready. Chewing a primrose, Panicz strode nonchalantly over and flung open the rear door where my mother was sitting, glittering in pearl necklaces, diamond and ruby tiara, rings and bracelets. 'Oh, Panicz! What an unexpected pleasure. I always wanted to meet you,' she smiled at him. Panicz's manner shed some of the swagger. 'Oh, it's you, Countess! Good evening. I too wanted to meet you.' he said, eyeing the jewellery. 'Splendid! Now we have both had our wish granted, you must step in for a chat. Kupisz,' she called the chauffeur, 'hold the door for Mr Panicz and then fetch us some brandy from the boot.'

While his men lounged about by the trees, Panicz sat a trifle self-consciously, sipping the Napoleon brandy. 'Do tell us of your feats. That last raid on the bank was terribly daring.' My uncle looked on silently, watching with obvious anger and distrust. But Panicz was soon put at ease; he loosened his ammunition belt and propped up his rifle by the seat. Twirling his moustaches between mouthfuls of brandy, he recounted some of his remarkable stories with his usual zest and humour. Not to be outdone for hospitality, he ordered his men to pick some of those orange mushrooms in which Polish forests abound in early autumn, and roast them on a spit over an open fire. With lashings of butter they tasted delicious. A couple of hours later Panicz left for the deep forest, shaking my mother's hand warmly. 'Countess, if you ever need anything, just let me know. I know how to be a gentleman. And you can always travel through my domain in these forests in complete safety.' 'Thank you Panicz,' my mother replied. 'These forests are actually mine, so I'll feel doubly safe!' They laughed.

My mother frequently travelled about the country visiting relatives or on business, and often she would take me along. Nothing thrilled me more. The joy of experiencing new visits and places was enough to dispel all tiredness. If the trip involved an all-night journey, I would lie with my feet on the chauffeur's lap and my head on my mother's, watching the stars pass as the car sped along twisting roads. Some of my most vivid memories of my earliest childhood are of glimpses plucked along those dusty roads. The sombre contour of a hill spiked with dark silhouettes of slender pines and firs, rigid and a little ominous like bewitched sentinels in the twilight; rough and gnarled boughs suddenly thrust overhead against the blue of the sky, tensed and writhing like the dragons locked in combat on the Ming vases in the hall at Dukla; the harsh rockface, truncated by roadmen's pickaxes, that protested numbly at its disfigurement with little sharp angular shadows and bright exposed veins in the dazzling sunlight.

We spent most of our summer holidays abroad, usually on the French coast. Days were divided between swimming and basking on warm sands and visiting surrounding places of interest. I remember one day while in Normandy – I must have been six at the time – when with my mother and Madame Rolland we went to visit Mont St Michel, which was then only approachable over a causeway at low tide. My mother, who shared my passion for exploring, didn't need much coaxing to come with me up the stairway that spiralled on and on to the top of the highest tower and descended deep into the vaults of murky dungeons. Oblivious of time, we not only missed all food that day, but the last bus to the mainland. Luckily a fisherman was waiting to pick up stragglers in a predicament such as ours, and agreed to row us back despite the rising storm. The waves kept bursting right into the boat, so we had to keep bailing the water out for dear life.

CHAPTER 2

The German and Russian Occupations

*

THAT whole world was shattered by the Second World War. I was nine years old when war was declared in 1939. We were staying at the time at Zaleze, another of our family homes, some sixty miles to the northwest of Dukla.

The terror of war impressed itself on me from its very first day as the peace of countryside air was shattered by the angry whine of German Stuka planes. During the twelve days before their armies reached Zaleze, the planes commanded the skies and often swooped down to machine-gun the civilian population; in a near-by village three people, including a child, were killed. Once when I was out in the fields with a friend, we had to dive into a ditch as one of them came low towards us.

'When I was last in London,' my mother said, 'everybody there was telling me that the Germans would never dare attack us, because our allies would make short shrift of them.' But except for Warsaw which held out for two months, the Polish defences had crumbled within a fortnight. Hitler had ordered the total destruction of the Polish army and air force. Without the aid from Britain and France, which we had hoped for and expected, his orders were carried out to the letter. Poland fell, after a brief but valiant resistance.

We soon experienced the terror of the Nazis at first hand. One of the first extortions was to impose a crippling tax, in kind, on peasants and landowners alike. This was a constant worry to my mother, and she frequently visited Rzeszow to see the Nazi officials.

Often I used to come along for the ride. I remember once how I was sitting with the coachman, in the main street of Rzeszow. All Polish residents had been thrown out of the street, their houses commandeered by German army personnel; the German army now lived there, often with their families, shopping in well-stocked stores reserved for them. We were waiting for my mother to finish her business, which I knew wouldn't take longer than absolutely necessary, for she hated having to go to these places.

We soon heard terrible shouts coming from behind a bend farther up the street. 'What's going on?' I asked the coachman in a frightened voice. When I looked at him I noticed that he was as white as a sheet. He turned towards me and muttered gruffly that he did not know and that we'd better stay quiet. With that he sat in frozen silence on his box, staring straight ahead.

Then round the corner I saw a pathetic procession approaching us. Men, women and children, of all ages, all ragged and pitifully thin, were being herded along like a flock of goats by Nazi guards. As I looked out of the open coach, I saw an elderly man stumble, and fall in the gutter. Immediately, he was set upon by one of the guards, shouting and cursing, and pushed back into line with the bayonet. As blood started to trickle down his arm, I turned away, sickened at the sight. But that was not all. Looking down from their windows and balconies, I saw some of the German officials, often with their wives and children, cheering, egging on the guards, jeering at the Jews who were being led out, after months of starvation in the ghetto, to their execution.

The scene left an indelible impression on me and I remember how I described it that evening to my mother at home. We were sitting together on the bed in my room, but I was restless, haunted by the sight of that procession, those people walking like spectres from a nightmare beyond the reach of the most horrific dream. My understanding boggled at the contrast between the handsome, clean-limbed appearance of the SS guards – young, healthy men, none of them more than about twenty – and the bestiality of their behaviour. 'Surely such men should *look* like monsters, as well?'

She looked at me sadly and pensively.

'Man's attitudes and beliefs,' she said, 'are moulded by the society in which he lives. By the pack, in other words. When a country is gripped by an evil creed like Nazism, precious few are strong enough not to run with the pack, especially when they are bombarded the whole time with pressure to conform – from newspapers and the radio right down to their next door neighbour.'

She paused for a moment looking out at the peacefulness of the park.

'The trouble is that the world is not divided between the good and the bad. These abominable doctrines are held, these atrocities are committed by otherwise normal individuals.'

The Nazis trusted no one; and rightly so, for the whole of Poland was being rapidly organized into a complex network of resistance. As a counter measure, and also to ensure that the mounting exactions of farm produce were delivered, they billeted their staff with many of the larger landowners. Our own 'guest' at Zaleze was a fat, slow-witted but reasonably affable Rhinelander called Lorer. In fact, Lorer proved an excellent, if unknowing, screen for the Resistance activities in which we were engaged. Lulled with amiable conversation, his attention distracted by generous helpings of pork (for which he had an insatiable appetite), he failed to notice that the house had become a meeting place for the underground fighters. Frequently partisans were hidden there; the wounded were nursed back to health, keeping as quiet as they could when Lorer was near. His mouth stuffed with pork, Lorer would merely grunt that another German train carrying troops and equipment to the eastern front had been ambushed. Little did he realize how frequently the plans for the ambush had been drawn up under his nose. At one point an important consignment of money, amounting to some two and a half million zlotys, was being transmitted from the Polish government in exile in London for the Resistance. As usual in such cases the sums were passed from cell to cell within the Resistance towards their final destination, usually in Warsaw. When this particular consignment reached Zaleze, my mother had to take it another hundred and fifty miles, to a cousin of ours, Zamoyski, whose estate was near Lublin, to the north-east. But how? All our cars had been confiscated long since; even if we succeeded in acquiring a car, the roads were dotted with German check-points.

Suddenly my mother thought of Lorer. Of course! She told him that she had to consult Cousin Zamoyski about estate business. But it was out of the question to go alone, unescorted. 'Would you accompany me, as the matter is most urgent?' She asked him, turning on the full force of her famous charm. Lorer fell for the bait immediately. 'Of course I would be delighted,' he replied. 'Since I am a German official, we shall have no trouble.'

Finding a car, however, was less easy. The two or three taxis remaining in Rzeszow were literally falling to pieces through lack of spares. So our friends in the Resistance stole a German car, and surreptitiously transferred its engine into one of the battered taxis. When the taxi roared into the drive, Lorer's jaw dropped. 'But you can't expect me to demean myself by getting into *that*! Besides, it will break down before we reach the gate!' 'Ah, Herr Lorer, don't judge from appearances,' my mother replied. 'The engine is excellent. Wonderful pre-war German manufacture!' Lorer was finally coaxed into the taxi and sat beside my mother at the back.

All went well at first, and they passed several road blocks without difficulty. But then, at the approach to a bridge the taxi driver pulled up sharply, confronted by rifles. 'Everybody out,' barked the officer in charge. 'I have orders to search all non-military traffic.'

My mother wound down her window with quiet deliberation. Without saying a word, she put her index finger to her lips, and pointed to her bulging tummy. She had turned the money belt round to the front, to allow her to sit more comfortably.

When the officer hesitated, looking sheepish and confused, Lorer's old style gallantry came to the rescue. 'Officer, I am a Party member. Kindly let us proceed on our way!' The officer saluted. He had no option but to let the car pass.

It was evening when they arrived, tired and dusty after their long drive. But when Cousin Zamoyski saw my mother, he paled visibly. As soon as the essential courtesies of introduction were over, he drew her aside, while Lorer craned his neck to admire the mansion's facade.

'I'm sorry, Wanda, but you can't stay for more than a few minutes,' he whispered earnestly. 'Some of our friends have just been arrested. I am expecting the Gestapo at any minute!'

Arrest, torture and execution were only too common for those implicated in Resistance work, and so my mother decided to return immediately. 'Very well. But hide the money. Here – quickly!'

'Herr Lorer, we must return now,' she called across the courtyard. 'We've settled the estate business so we needn't waste any more time.'

But Lorer was looking forward to a comfortable night's rest, and protested that it was much too late to start back. My mother looked at him seriously.

'Herr Lorer, I am in the grips of wanderlust. We just have to go.' She looked at him disarmingly, her mouth twitching with humour. Lorer threw up his arms in despair, moaning 'Lorer, du bist verrückt!' ('Lorer, you must be crazy!')

Lorer was eventually recalled. In 1942–3, we had a far less pleasant guest at Zaleze, a Gestapo officer by the name of Captain Kruge. Unlike Lorer, Kruge never stayed with us; he merely liked to come and relax in the house and its grounds, and to go shooting birds in the pheasantry. Frequently he brought his wife and five-year-old son with him. It was an odd set-up, because his wife was deeply religious and a remarkably good person. She would talk to my mother deploring the Nazis and weeping bitterly over the crimes perpetrated by her husband. 'God will punish us terribly. What will become of Germany? Our people have gone mad.'

Meantime her husband would take the boy around the estate. I watched them once, from a distance, as they approached a chicken run. To my horror, I saw the boy lift up his foot and squash several newly-hatched chicks. I heard the father's reaction ringing round the yard: 'Good! You'll grow up to be a real tough man,' he said, clapping the boy on the shoulder.

During this period the population throughout Poland was being ground down by levies, hostage-taking, and above all, mass deportations. My mother was continually being asked to intercede with the Germans on behalf of local able-bodied men to prevent their being sent as forced labour to Germany. Whole villages were being depopulated for slave labour. She achieved the impossible, bribing, cajoling, claiming that they were essential for work on our estate; it is no mean tribute to her skill and courage that during the German occupation not a single man was deported from Zaleze or the neighbouring villages for slave labour.

The Nazis were also bent on the cold-blooded extermination of all Poles of the Jewish faith. Intercession on their behalf almost invariably proved unavailing, and also exposed those who dared to try this to the risk of death themselves or deportation to a con-centration camp, branded as a 'Jew lover'. My mother took the risk a number of times. On the whole, her efforts proved in vain: but she found that she could help a little when the Nazis began to assign the Jews to work on various construction jobs on the estates. To the Jews starving in the ghetto, such work meant food, if only meagre rations. But if they were directed to an estate like ours, food, clothes, medicines and so on would be passed to them in quantities when the guards' attention was distracted.

Whenever Kruge came, he would take a malicious pleasure in asking if there were any Jews working; if so, he would stand over them and torment them in whatever manner his evil mind could devise. One day my mother and I were walking with Kruge, who was dressed in mufti, through the estate. A bedraggled, starved boy of about eleven ran up to my mother and asked her for food. Kruge looked sharply at the boy, his eyes narrowing. Before my mother could tell him to run off, Kruge had grabbed the boy, lifting the skeletal frame so that their eyes were level. 'You're a Jew, aren't you?' he hissed. The child grew deathly white and squirmed. Letting go with one hand Kruge reached for his revolver. My mother sprang forward and seized his hand as it closed around the butt. Kruge, taken aback, let go of the boy and glared at my mother. Wrenching free of her grasp he turned the pistol and levelled it at her. I stood frozen to the ground as she stood there without flinching, looking him straight in the eye. Slowly, Kruge replaced the revolver in the holster.

Our relations with Kruge were now strained to breaking point. In fact, the fury of the Nazis was turning upon the entire population. Their war machine was being sabotaged only too effectively. Members of the Resistance continued to come and go from Zaleze; we were naturally apprehensive that this would come to the attention of the Gestapo. But our luck held. We took care to leave the track leading to the estate in a state of disrepair, so that after a shower of rain it became a virtually impassable quagmire. My mother's perfect command of German also helped. Maybe the Germans weighed the consequences carefully before eradicating estate owners from whom they exacted substantial quantities of produce. Nonetheless, we were badly shaken when, early in 1943, a particularly brutal-looking Gestapo officer paid us the first of several visits. I gathered soon enough, from my mother's icy expression and ill-concealed anguish, that something really bad was afoot. When we were alone one evening (after a particularly long visit) she told me how they were blackmailing her. It was simple enough: if they ever received evidence of Resistance activity at Zaleze, I was to be tortured to death before her eyes.

Her awful predicament and inner distress were apparent to me. As a patriot, her duty was clear, however agonizing the consequences, and I did my utmost to support and reassure her. I was only twelve, but I was proud of her. We had a long talk that evening; I believe we both had tears in our eyes.

Far from backing out of Resistance work, my mother became further involved. As the war drew on I, too, was frequently asked to act as look-out boy, whilst meetings were being held at Zaleze, or when Resistance fighters were leaving on hazardous missions. I distributed the weekly journal, which they printed on secret printing presses around the country, to the members of the Resistance in Zaleze, bringing them their copies stuffed under my clothes.

I was always given a warm welcome by my 'subscribers'; the news that I brought told of Nazi reverses on all fronts, of how fellow partisans had ambushed German trains, convoys, and blown up bridges and other military objectives. But as our guerrilla raids proliferated, so the aggressors' sullen repression grew in intensity. Posters appeared on walls and hoardings in Rzeszow, as in other towns throughout the country, listing the names of hostages that were rounded up to be shot if there were any further acts of sabotage. Soon enough stickers would be pasted across saying that the threat had been carried out. I remember one day somebody who had just come from Rzeszow saying that a new poster had just been pasted up including the name of a fifteen-year-old boy. Before the paste was dry, the lad's mother had been caught scribbling: 'Let the young blood flow, rather than a patriot's arm waver at the sacred duty.' She had been shot dead on the spot. A couple of days later I passed the place. The poster was splattered with blood; a sticker had been added, announcing that her son had been executed together with some thirty other hostages.

The final weeks of the German occupation, in July 1944, were marked with unparalleled terror. No one was safe; as the Russian Army drew nearer, the carnage reached an unprecedented scale. But our luck held; perhaps the Gestapo gave up hope of acquiring the evidence that would spell out my death.

To a fourteen-year-old like myself these were wild and turbulent days, as the two giants rolled over the country gripped in a merciless contest. It was all grimly exciting. There usually was plenty of action on the spot, but we were severely hampered by a shortage of arms, particularly rifles and semi-automatics. My own pistol and shotgun were useful enough at short range; but I needed a rifle, and was determined to acquire one.

One day a lone German corporal came cycling into the farm-yard at Zaleze, dismounted, and demanded that we hand over a cart and a pair of horses. I looked covetously at his rifle, slung nonchalantly over his shoulder, as I called the stableman. Telling him to harness a good pair of horses, I started chatting amiably to the German, who spoke fair Polish with a marked Silesian accent. Various alternatives for an ambush raced through my mind, as I assured him passionately of my wholehearted support for the war against the Russians. On the pretext of hurrying the stableman, I excused myself for a moment, and slipped inside the cottage of a trusted retainer, Bronek, a member of the Resistance. It didn't take me long to convince Bronek, and another reliable Resistance man, that we should lay our ambush about a mile away near a wood, so that later no suspicion could fall on Zaleze. I hurriedly passed them my shotgun and a supply of buckshot cartridges. As the stableman harnessed the horses for the German, the two men slipped out behind, and took up positions behind one of the linden trees lining the drive. There was no other exit; the German corporal was trapped. As he was about to drive off, I shook him warmly by the hand, and slunk off across the fields towards the fateful spot, eager to get as close as possible to my men without attracting the corporal as he rode ahead of me. As I watched him approach the spot, I felt a pang of remorse; having planned his death so cold-bloodedly, I had shaken his hand. But just as he was coming within shotgun range, he swerved violently and drove off at an angle across the fields. I swore in anger and frustration.

Bronek opened fire, but the German jumped off the cart and ran for his life. As I lay watching thwarted in a field some four hundred yards away, I suddenly realized that we had come under fire ourselves from a German patrol. Bullets were whining past, far too close for comfort; several rifles had opened up from across a stream. The three of us ran zig-zagging towards the wood, and dived for cover. Just as I was about to fling myself again into a hollow, I felt a sharp pain in my arm, and realized that I had been nicked by a bullet.

For several hours we lay low in the wood in case the Germans came after us. My injury was only superficial; as I bandaged up my forearm with a strip of my shirt, I heard the dull thud of gunfire drawing rapidly nearer, till the shells whined overhead to burst farther west. 'The Russians must be pretty close now,' I said. 'Let's make a dash back to Zaleze.' 'Look!' cried Bronek as we reached the outer courtyard, 'Russians!' It was true. As I swung round, panting from the exertion, I saw a scruffy Russian soldier galloping down the linden avenue towards the house. I quickly dodged back into my room by a back entrance, and began feverishly to pack my more treasured possessions. Minutes later, when I had just returned from taking them to safety in one of the remoter attics, I passed by Madame Rolland's room. I noticed that for the first time she was listening openly to her radio – an offence punishable by death under the Nazis. The voice of the BBC reporter came over loud and clear as he described the scene of a French town that had just been liberated by the Allies. In the background, we could hear the joyful shouting of the people in the streets. For a moment, we stood listening rooted to the spot. 'Of all the rotten luck! To think this is supposed to be *our* day of liberation. . . . ' she sighed.

Naturally we were glad to see the back of the hated Nazis. Under different circumstances, their retreat would have been the cause of the same wild excitement. However, most of us realized that the Russian advance represented no liberation, but merely the exchange of one form of aggression for another. As I watched from my bedroom window, another Russian arrived at full gallop in a horse-drawn cart. Glumly I remembered their reputation, and began to pack away more of my possessions.

Suddenly the two Russians burst in. Hastily I stuffed the keys of my trunk into my pocket, and stood up. To my astonishment, they ignored me completely, and proceeded to ransack the room, opening drawers and cupboards, rummaging about, tossing clothes and ornaments carelessly on the floor. They were evidently in a trigger-happy mood, and so I watched, powerless to protest. Food and drink seemed to be at the top of their list. They calmly drank the water-glass in which I had preserved some eggs; one of them picked up my pencil eraser and bit into it thoughtfully, leaving a deep toothmark (I still have the eraser to this day).

The initial pillage continued for a whole week. Down in the kitchen, I saw the maid bravely 'frisk' them when she gave them food, retrieving whole canteens of knives, forks and spoons from their pockets and boots. Nothing was immune from their insatiable appetites.

Nearly all of them wanted to see my mother. 'Where is the Countess? What does she look like?' they kept asking. When they finally saw her, they stared with unconcealed curiosity, like children on their first outing to a zoo. To do them justice, they were courteous enough, but obviously rather disappointed. She was human! Not only human, but tall and beautiful and very, very poised. They made up for it in the harness room, where they found some riding whips. 'Ah, these are what you use to lash the people with!' they commented sourly.

One of the first things we noticed about the Russians was their lack of organization. They spread westwards like the proverbial hordes from Asian heartlands, which in past ages had pushed and plundered across these lands. Their equipment was makeshift, to say the least. The wheels on their carts squeaked and wobbled. Their trucks, originally provided by Uncle Sam, had their US stars painted over to look like the Communist emblems, but were rattletraps through careless handling and poor maintenance. Admittedly these looked better than the Russian ZIS lorries which were all patched up with bits of wire. But only a little better.

Horses were naturally high on their list. Having already lost most of our cattle, pigs and chickens, we were determined to save as many of our more valuable riding horses as possible. At one stage, when a particularly villainous troop of Russians were seen heading our way, we brought our Arab stallions up into the house, coaxing them up the back steps, through the back entrance and into a guest room that had been spread with a deep litter of straw to give the parquet some protection. That saved them for quite a time; when a Russian sergeant tried to steal them, he found to his anger and dismay that the stallions refused to be led out through the low door by anybody except their groom. 'You know the trick?' the groom said to me when the sergeant had given up the unequal struggle. 'They become as docile as lambs when I give them a drop of vodka!'

In contrast to the Germans, who tended to act as part of one huge machine, the Russians were unpredictable. About two weeks after the pillage began, a Russian officer came galloping into Zaleze, and came up to my mother with a broad grin on his face.

'Here, take these,' he said, handing her several packets of tea. 'For you.' Without waiting for thanks, he turned and galloped away again. Tea had been totally unobtainable for years, and his gift was much appreciated.

On another occasion, as I was walking in the park, a jovial quartermaster emerged from a shed with a dozen bars of Russian chocolate – 'Here, have a feast! I bet you haven't tasted this for some time!' When I rushed back to my room to enjoy the chocolate, which was unobtainable during the war, I stumbled on a drunken soldier snoring on my bed. Riled by the 'intrusion', he jumped up and whipped out his revolver, swaying on his feet and scowling. I rushed out again, to enjoy my chocolate elsewhere.

Large numbers of Russian troops were always encamped around Zaleze. At first the stay of any particular unit was brief, lasting two or three days, before they would move on westwards to the front-line, or, battle-weary, be sent east to rest. The quicker they came and went, the more they looted, intent on grabbing even the most useless things. But the rate of this 'turnover' slowed down with each passing week. Early in September 1944 an entire regiment came for almost three weeks. By this time we had shed most of our initial diffidence, and had learned how to cope with the mercurial but basically easy-going temperament of Soviet soldiery.

I spent much time with them bartering fruit for tea, chocolate and other unobtainable delicacies. And sneaking in with my heart pounding I began to pinch arms from their tents or quarters. But more often than not I would just sit and chat. They intrigued me enormously, especially as most people spoke about them using such blank, collective terms as 'the enemy', 'the Reds', 'Rusky', 'the occupants'. This seemed to cast them in a monolithic mask of evil, to be faced with equally set hatred. Curiosity prompted me to try and lift this veil a little and to glimpse what lay beneath. The longer a Soviet unit remained, the better the opportunity I had for closer acquaintance. Far away from their homes and families, they were usually only too glad to talk about themselves.

During the warm, indolent summer evenings I would join a group of them and we would lie sprawled on the trodden grass by the tents, and they would brew tea. Somebody would strum a balalaika, singing quietly, the nostalgic words telling of deep forests, golden cornfields swishing in the wind, and the expectant face of the loved one. They would roll strong, acrid tobacco in carefully torn bits of newspaper, licking it profusely to make it stick. Often they'd offer me one, and I'd try to smoke like an old habitué, only to cough and splutter. 'Ochen krepkaya Russkaya mokhorka, takaya khorosha!' ('Very strong Russian tobacco, *so* good!') they would laugh, thumping me on the back. So I'd try to recover my composure, sipping hard at the scalding tea, poured into mess-tins or discarded food cans.

I became particularly friendly with Petya, who came from a village in the Omsk area of south-western Siberia. He was a sergeant-major, a *starshina*, as he was called whenever rank was used. Despite being quite tall, he was so broad and muscular that he looked squat. He had the ungainly, shuffling gait of a rustic and a broad, open face, the rotundity of which was broken by the verticals of unruly strands of hair falling over his forehead, and the horizontal of a wide, fleshy mouth.

Despite such gawky demeanour, Petya was something of a natural philosopher, a romantic of marked sensitivity. Our friendship began quaintly enough one day when I remarked rather sourly that the Russians, who camped all over the park, had trampled down my 'secret garden'. This actually was a patch at the far end of the park, which I had turned into a private retreat, and I went there whenever I wanted to be alone. I had let weeds and flowers grow there, till the place was like a jungle.

Petya perked up, as soon as he heard this. 'Secret garden, what secret garden?' he asked.

'Oh nothing, just a corner of the park,' I shrugged indifferently. But Petya was visibly interested. 'I too had a secret garden when I was a boy,' he said. 'The fields of our *kolkhoz* were surrounded with deep forests, stretching for hundreds of miles. In one spot at the edge of it, away from paths, birch-trees grew around a water-hole fed by an underground spring. The undergrowth was particularly thick there, and I encouraged it more by swiping pocketfuls of fertilizer from our kolkhoz, to spread it over weeds, flowers and all.'

His hands were clasped round his booted legs as he sat gazing into the distance, smiling to himself. 'What, fertilizer?' I exclaimed excitedly, all reticence gone. 'I too used to pinch fertilizer for mine. You should've seen the nettles and bracken! I bet you never clapped eyes on bigger!'

Petya laughed delightedly. 'Except in mine! With all that fertilizer I wasted there! What else did you have in yours?' 'Oh, blackthorn, bramble and other scrub,' I replied. 'Also wild flowers, primrose, crawfoot, forget-me-nots, night-shade. . . . '

'Same here,' said Petya, 'and lots of violets, come June. Spring comes late in Siberia, but when it does burst out, it makes up for everything with unbelievable beauty and intensity. I had a mongrel dog, Byelka, in those days. During the long, warm June evenings, with Byelka scampering at my bare heels, we used to race across the fields to my garden. At first I used to snare hares there, but later I didn't want to harm anything. They'd often lie low there, waiting for the night to nibble the young corn. I'd lie on the soft moist grass by the pool and listen to the breeze. I'd watch skeins of wild geese heading high for the lakes and rivers up north. The lowering sun would tint the wafer-thin bark flaking off the birches, and as the dapple leaf shadows quivered over the filmy bark, it seemed as if it had come alive, the crimson life-blood throbbing in them. I would almost close my eyes and let the light filter the same hues through my eyelashes, dreaming my eyelids to be birch-bark slewing to the sun, and myself part of all the secret gardens in the world. For to live and put forth in a way is to seek eternity.'

I felt I had known Petya for years. 'How absurd . . . the ferns and violets of Omsk and Zaleze, places half across the world, to have forged an understanding between us.' I said reflectively.

Petya shrugged his shoulders, munching a blade of grass. 'Why absurd? It's the same earth, the same life!'

'Ah, but it's not that simple. You're a Red, a member of an invading army on the rampage. And I am a Pole, a landowner to make matters worse. We're supposed to be enemies.'

Petya laughed heartily, his golden teeth flashing. 'Supposed to be, yes! But are we? No. Why? Because we talk together, we find that we've got families, hopes, fears, childhoods and much else besides secret gardens in common.'

I stuck to my guns.

'Look here,' I said. 'Two days ago your secret police arrested Ludwig, one of our men from the Resistance. He had a fine record for fighting the Germans. Apparently he's being tortured now. All he's done is to be a good Pole. And what of his wife and children?'

'No doubt that's awful. My two elder brothers got killed in action fighting the Germans. Some days ago my best friend got mowed down in an ambush set by your Resistance men. What had he done? Look, I've still got his photograph.' He pulled from his breast-pocket a tattered photo of a proud family group sitting in front of a cottage. 'Those are his parents sitting in the first row, and there's my friend with two of his children perching on his knees. The younger three are clutching his wife's skirt.'

I felt myself blush as I stared confusedly at the simple, happy family picture. Petya dispelled my embarrassment with a guffaw. 'Don't look so glum, *khozyain* [landlord]!' he said, his eyes twinkling with good-natured mockery. 'There's nothing to apologize for. When I was a boy I couldn't stand bullying or killing. I thought I could do a tiny bit about it, at least in my secret garden. I trimmed and tied up my bushes in such a way that everything, big and small, got its proper share of light and moisture. I placed stones and bits of wood at the edge of the pool, so that butterflies and insects could come and drink in safety. I even climbed up trees to fasten little strings between branches where birds could build their nests safe from predators. I wanted those few square yards to be a haven of peace and harmony.

'One day a fledgling fell out of a nightingale's nest in the lilac bush, and before I could stop her, Byelka had caught it. I had to finish it off. I kicked the dog so hard that she cringed and whimpered, as she looked at me uncomprehendingly. Then I sat down and cried: I sobbed my heart out, Byelka nuzzling me diffidently. It was a turning point in my life, and I believe I left my childhood that day. I looked around and saw the garden in a new light. Suddenly I realized that everything that lives and grows does so at the expense of something else. If I wanted to set up even a square foot of real peace and harmony, first I would have to root out everything that lived and grew there, in fact turn it into a desert. The awful truth struck me that only in absolute death and non-existence can a sort of negative peace and harmony be attained. After that day I never set foot in my garden again. But I haven't hated anything either. Not even when I shoot at the Germans. I believe I'm a good, tough soldier.' He glanced down at the stripes of a sergeant-major.

'But isn't man supposed to have risen above nature?' I exclaimed. 'Judge for yourself. Anyway, if he ever does rise, let it be through nature and not above it. Nature is the source, the life-blood, and to cut oneself away from it is to shrivel and to fall as pathetically as Icarus.'

As I gazed towards the house, I thought of the looting soldiery, I felt the flicker of anger once again. Unconsciously I blurted out 'They even drank the water-glass!' When Petya frowned, I bit my lip, for the remark sounded particularly stupid and petty. 'Well, your comrades have been behaving like vandals.' I explained about the water-glass, and how a drunken sergeant had smashed a crucifix. 'Try to see farther than the end of your nose, khozyain!' Petya said. 'Poor devils, alive today, and quite likely dead tomorrow. And you expect them to have regard for such niceties? Besides, many of them come from the backwoods, where they never clapped eyes on such frippery, including your wretched water-glass. Take me. Drunk and on the front line, I too might have smashed your crucifix and drunk your water-glass, hoping it was alcoholic. What does that make me? My father was no better than an illiterate serf. I don't regard my existence as "good", for that's meaningless. The point is that life is better for me than it was for my father. I expect one day my grandsons will shudder at the thought of the slavery of their grandfather's times, and good luck to them! At least something progresses in this cruel world.'

Four days later I saw them get ready to leave. 'Got our marching orders, khozyain. We're off to the front line!' exclaimed Petya.

I watched him leave, driving a cart harnessed to a pair of horses. His legs apart, slightly crouched for better balance, he looked squatter than ever, his fair hair escaping from under his cap, the ends of his crumpled and stained tunic flapping in the wind. 'Stupoi s Bogom, drug!' ('Go with God, friend!') I shouted earnestly. 'Bud'te zdorovy, dorogoi vrag!' ('Farewell, dear enemy!') he cried back.

I looked after them, and when the dust settled made haste to Bronek's cottage. 'Here! Pass these on to our men,' I said gruffly, handing him a couple of magazines complete with ammo, for automatics. 'I managed to pinch them from one of the tents in the confusion.' 'Splendid, splendid!' cried Bronek. 'Maybe I should have told Petya.' Bronek eyed me narrowly, with a blend of concern and incredulity. 'Tell one of these Bolsheviks that you've swiped their arms? You must be off your rocker! You'll end up in Siberia!'

'No, I do believe he'd have thought it a huge joke!' I said lightly. Bronek's mouth dropped as he stared at me in complete stupefaction.

By this time, Resistance activity had become virtually as frequent and well-organized as under the Nazi occupation. People were bitter and desperate at finding themselves under another occupation, after almost a quarter of the population had died in the cause of liberty. We were goaded further by arrests, deportations to Siberia and the tragedy of the Warsaw uprising, where the Soviet armies stood inactive only a few miles away, while the Germans methodically turned the entire city into one vast tomb.

The aristocracy was high on the list of the Communist police. We duly received our 'visit' – a truckload of police surrounded the house. I was out in the woods at the time. When I saw them, I was terror-stricken; I not only had a stock of Resistance pamphlets in my room but, worse, a revolver. Fortunately, my governess knew about the revolver. As I crept towards the back entrance she threw it from an upstairs window. No sooner had I grabbed it than I heard the ominous click of a bolt being drawn. I looked around, straight into the barrel of a policeman's rifle.

They grilled and cursed and threatened me. They dragged me before their commanding officer, who interrogated me alone. But the charge was dropped 'mysteriously'. It turned out that the commanding officer was a Resistance man who had infiltrated the Communist police. No more was heard of my arrest, and life limped back to what passed for normality. Soviet troops continued to descend on us, but seldom stayed longer than a week before moving on westwards. The problem of looting remained but on a lesser scale, partly because there was little left to take. Hardly a day passed, however, without some sinister rumour reaching us concerning our future. There were variations of course, but the spectre of the Russian revolution loomed over us alarmingly. What would become of us? Our one comfort was the attitude of the villagers. Instead of rounding on us they moved to the other extreme. At considerable danger to themselves, they petitioned the Communists: 'We do not want their lands. We wish them to stay.' Little did we know at the time how much we would have to pay for this heart-warming loyalty. For anyone who enjoyed firm support among the people was marked.

Four weeks later, in October 1944, the police returned. Once again they searched the house thoroughly. This time they found nothing; we had taken plenty of precautions to ensure that they wouldn't. We watched them as they prepared to leave, without strong emotion. The officer in charge walked slowly up and down the line, then paused to light a cigarette. Suddenly he seemed to make up his mind, and marched briskly across to where my mother and I were standing.

'You are coming with us,' he announced brusquely. 'You have ten minutes.' Too shocked to protest, we stood rooted to the ground. The officer watched us for a full minute, his small sharp eyes narrowed into jeering slits, before he strode back towards the truck. When we had hastily packed a few essentials, my mother walked over to ask if we could say good-bye to our staff.

'That is not permitted.'

As we climbed into the truck, I couldn't help noticing that a handful of the local people had gathered to watch us leave. Tears were streaming down their faces and I too felt tears running down my cheeks. My mother, pale but self-possessed, squeezed my hand. 'Hold your head up in front of these gangsters.'

During the Nazi occupation I had often thought of the day of liberation. I had conjured up a happy picture of riding in a British or American truck with the victorious allies. By a cruel twist of fate, I now found myself in the back of an American truck, a Dodge provided on Lease-Lend, peering out over the heads of our police escort for a last glimpse of the white walls of Zaleze, as they swiftly faded into the distance. As those dear walls vanished I felt that a chapter had closed. The chill autumn wind tore the leaves from the linden trees, and I watched them pirouetting fitfully above the bleak fields and thought that the brown leaves, spinning desultorily at the whim of the wind, held a sinister message for us.

My spirits sank still further when the truck drew up outside the police headquarters in Rzeszow, used until three months previously for the interrogation and torture of Gestapo prisoners. I jumped out first and held out my arms to help my mother down. She stepped to the edge of the tailboard and paused, surveying the prison door and the street milling with our captors, her face calm and faintly imperious. Then she grasped my hands and jumped lightly down. As she did so, her little bundle dropped on the grimy cobblestones. One of the policemen, who had sat staring at her all the way with a sneer on his face bent down to retrieve it, the barrel of his automatic scraping the stones. 'Here you are, m'lady!' Suddenly I felt pride and confidence rush back into me. We had lost our freedom and the patrimony of generations and were now desperately vulnerable in the hands of our captors. Yet even so that inner heritage of assurance had remained, inbred beyond hatred's reach. I offered my mother my arm. We winked at each other and, arm in arm, stepped briskly inside.

CHAPTER 3

We escape

*

WHEN our procession halted in front of one of the cellars, an appalling smell of unwashed humanity hit our nostrils. As the door clanged shut behind us, a babble of voices greeted us from the semi-darkness. 'Welcome to the kipper factory!' 'Move over there. Room for two more!' 'Hey, guard! Why don't you pour in some olive oil? Then we'd be canned good and proper!' As the laughter died down, and our eyes became adjusted to the light, we saw that, to all intents, there was standing room only. Over a hundred people were already crammed into the cellar. Every inch was occupied, except for a small area in the far corner, where a horse carcass lay rotting.

For hours, days, we stood or squatted on the bare concrete. No food or water was given us, and I kept eyeing that putrid carcass in the corner, wondering to myself how long we could last before hunger drove us to tackle it. But if the Communists thought they had developed methods of breaking our morale, they were far from successful. A few of our fellow prisoners had been incarcerated for some weeks; but most were landowners like ourselves, who had only just been arrested. Many of them were known to us, and as often happens when danger and hardship are shared, everyone swapped stories and jokes. For example, when one rather portly man committed the gaffe of mentioning the word 'Siberia', his neighbour reacted quickly enough with 'Well, what are you grumbling about? You always wanted to slim, didn't you?'

But the grim thoughts and sometimes mutterings were never far away. 'What d'you think our chances are?' I whispered to my mother. 'We'll just have to trust ourselves to the Almighty. Perhaps we'll know more when they start questioning us. We must run through all the questions they could possibly ask, so that we don't contradict each other.'

On the third day, the heavy doors were opened and a guard

brought in food. It was just watery potato soup, but from the way we eyed the filthy bucket, it might have been the greatest delicacy. As we queued up to receive our share, I couldn't help remarking to my mother that it smelt better than the rotting horse. 'Better than starving, too,' she added quietly.

Another bucket of soup appeared the next day. But on the fifth day, when we had finished scraping the rusty bottom for the last scrap of potato, the police burst in. Solemnly they intoned a long list of names, and those called began to file out for questioning. When the ninety lucky or unlucky ones had left, the ten of us that remained reviewed our situation. There were no jokes now; we sat in silence, each filled with his or her private fears.

After two agonizing hours, they gradually began to return under escort and the cell started to hum with half-choked whispers. 'What did they say to you?' 'What are they going to do with us?' 'What did they ask?'

Most of them looked happy and relaxed. 'It seems they'll release me tomorrow!' said the fat man eagerly. 'Me too! They said so definitely,' interjected another; 'It appears they won't let us live within fifty miles of our former properties,' said a third.

The rest of us looked on enviously. 'Oh, God, I hope our turn comes!' I blurted out. By the evening there were only the ten of us left who had not been promised immediate release.

The next day we were moved to a much smaller cell. Space was no longer at such a premium, in that there were only nine others there when we arrived. At least there was some straw on the floor, or on that part of the floor that was not under water, and enough room to stretch out. A little daylight even filtered in from a tiny window, high up on the wall – too high for us to see out from. But the pane was broken, and the temperature dropped at night to below freezing.

The lavatory down the corridor was already blocked and overflowing, and since the guards refused to let us out for days at a stretch, we had no option but to add to the puddle on the floor. To cap it all, the straw contained just about every variety and sub-species of vermin: lice, bed bugs, fleas, cockroaches, the lot. Every night I would wake up with cockroaches crawling over my face.

But we became experts at making the best of it, whiling away the time with games and stories and even the cockroaches provided a diversion. Bitten beyond endurance, I would take off my shoe first thing in the morning, and start bashing away at any bug I could see. This often went on for hours, as our cell-mates delighted in finding fresh victims. 'Over here, quick!' cried a young peasant woman, scratching her bottom energetically. 'Coming, coming, Orzechowa,' I would reply, hurrying over to debug her straw. 'Well, well,' she said, as I was finishing the operation. 'I do believe the young Count has found himself a hunting reserve!'

Most of our cell-mates were women from fairly humble backgrounds. Orzechowa was my favourite, if only because of her unfailing good humour. Her husband had been an active member of the Resistance; when the police came to arrest him he had shot his way out, killing two men before making his escape. The police had arrested Orzechowa, and took it out on her without mercy, avenging their dead colleagues. Although she was several months pregnant, they called her out every day for interrogation, kicking her and beating her. An hour or so later, they would fling her back into the cell. 'And that's where you can rot, you and your rotten seed!' Orzechowa would cry for a while, sitting on the cold floor, or leaning against the wall. Then she would perk up, and her round, open face would broaden into a smile. 'We're all in the hands of God. We must trust in God,' she would say, as we gathered round to tend her cuts and bruises.

In time, both my mother and I were interrogated. Although neither of us was ever physically assaulted, the tone was menacing enough. The questioning was usually held in a first floor office, bare except for a rough, ink-stained desk. Behind the desk sat the interrogator, a mean, ginger-haired bully, with photographs of Stalin and the heads of the Russian-nominated 'Polish government' nailed to the wall above him. I felt my best defence lay in my youth. 'Give me the names of those Fascists and warmongers you've been connected with. Come on, their names!' he would rap out. His icy stare heightened the bitter cold of the room and I would stand facing him feeling numbed and terribly alone. 'I don't know any such people,' I repeated. 'I hate the Nazis. But I am only fourteen. I regretted being too young to fight them, but I never could or would work for them.' 'Ah, but it's the Polish Fascists I'm talking about. Those that take their orders from London!' I stared at the ink patches on the desk, trying to draw composure and inspiration from their desultory shapes. 'Nobody has told me of such Fascists. And London is far away.' Sticking to this line with childish earnestness, I believe I eventually managed to convey to him an impression of a rather retarded schoolboy.

Our prospects nevertheless remained desperately bleak. A million of our countrymen had been sent to Siberia by the Russians in the earlier part of the war. Plenty more were on their way to join them now. It seemed almost inevitable that we should join them. Then help came from an unexpected quarter. The prison cook was a simple soul, in her forties, who, like almost every self-respecting Pole, had played her part in the Resistance. When she heard that we were in the cellar, she lodged a complaint with the authorities, saying she could not carry on with her work in the kitchen without more helpers, and that furthermore, she was going to select them herself. As no one objected, we suddenly found ourselves summoned to the kitchen. Greeting us with a flow of unprintable abuse about the Communists, she set us to peeling potatoes. It was a moot point, at first, which of us was the slower. Mother had never peeled a potato in her life. Often I would cut the wretched potato in half, and my finger into the bargain. But our speeds increased with practice, and to this day I fancy myself as a champion spud-peeler.

Working in the kitchen was wonderful. It meant warmth, enough to eat, and above all, something better to do than squashing bugs all day. No wonder I dreaded the evening summons back to the depressing cold of our stinking cell. Once, as the hour of doom was approaching, the cook ladled an extra large helping on to our plates. 'You mark my words,' she said. 'I'll get you out of here. I don't know how,' she added mysteriously. 'But you leave it to me, I'll find a way.'

It turned out that the prison Commandant had revealed his Achilles heel. He had taken a fancy to the cook's daughter, and, to put it mildly, was getting nowhere fast. He was a thin, cold, sadistic bully and despite his threats she avoided him like the plague. Since she was a pretty girl, her mother was not slow to realize that this situation might be put to some good use. The following evening she confided in us that she had spoken to her daughter, and that the daughter would be glad to help. 'She's going to lead him on a bit, you know,' she said with a sly wink. 'Then say at the right moment that he has got to release both of you.'

The daughter must have chosen her moment well, because

within forty-eight hours we found ourselves in front of the Commandant. We were led in separately. When we had signed a statement that we would never discuss what we had seen or experienced in prison, he issued us with discharge slips. This tiny slip of paper represented the most wonderful news I had ever had, and I even felt a surge of friendliness towards our tormentor. I thanked him and moved back towards the door, feeling as if I was walking on air. Then I remembered something vital.

'Please, Comrade Commandant, may I have my Identity Card back?' I asked, rather nervously. He looked at me for a moment. 'I will keep your Identity Card,' he replied icily. 'You may go.'

Five weeks after we had been arrested, we walked out into the street again – free. The discharge slip stated that we were going home, but we found out soon enough that we were forbidden to return to Zaleze.

An order had been issued prohibiting landowners to live near their former estates and chaos had reigned at Zaleze since the Communists moved in after our arrest. In a final bout of pillage they had left nothing but the bare walls and empty stables, while the land was shared out to the villagers, irrespective of whether they wanted it or not. We learned this from Mr Parecki, who had a butcher's shop in Rzeszow and had bought cattle from us for many years. When he offered us hospitality in his house, we moved in gratefully, relaxing in the glorious sense of freedom. Admittedly we had lost everything and our future prospects looked grim, but the spectre of Siberia had been removed so, for the moment, it was enough that we were free again, in the sunlight, with clean beds and a lavatory, good food and, above all, friendly faces around us. After a long chat over a glass of vodka with our hosts, I got down to ridding myself of the lice, by soaking my hair repeatedly in petrol.

Our freedom was short-lived. Scarcely two weeks had passed before a message arrived from one of the Resistance men 'planted' inside the police, that we were to be re-arrested that evening. Within minutes we were packed and out of the house, heading for the small town of Przeworsk. Our hosts here were a young married couple, Jan and Helena, both brave members of the Resistance, who lived in a house well away from the main road. This suited our purpose ideally. Assuming the name of Wojtasinski, we remained with them for six weeks in self-imposed confinement, grateful for each day spent in relative freedom. We reasoned that the police had never intended releasing us in the first place. Obviously they had now discovered more about my mother's involvement in the Resistance; it was common knowledge that such people were being hunted down with a resolve equal to that of the Nazis, and so we took good care to lie low. In a sense, we had to hibernate, for neither of us had warm clothes and I only ventured outside to chop firewood. Soon there was more wood in the shed than Jan and Helena knew what to do with.

Jan worked in the local brewery, and used to come home at about six o'clock, when it was already dark. One evening the three of us were sitting around the table in the living-room, when we heard him opening the front door. We looked up to see him staring at us, as white as a sheet, his mouth twitching in an effort to speak.

'Jan, whatever's the matter?' Helena asked.

He wiped his forehead, and blurted out in a stifled voice:

'We're surrounded by police.'

We sat there, stunned. Then the implications came flooding over us, and I looked at my mother. We had both often talked of this moment, of how we would prefer to die rather than risk the consequences of capture. Rising, she came over and laid a hand on my shoulder.

'Come, Arthur,' she said quietly. 'I think we had better go to our room.' The room next door had whitewashed walls and was modestly furnished with two beds standing on the rough floor-boards, and a table in the centre, covered with a spotless white tablecloth. Reaching under her bed, she pulled out her small cloth-wrapped bundle. She unfolded it, without speaking, and took out ouremergency kit, two phials of cyanide and a hand grenade. Placing two glasses of Jan's vodka, the two phials and the bomb on the spotless tablecloth, we drew up our chairs and waited.

We waited for what seemed an eternity, without uttering a word. Nobody stirred, it was as though the silence of death had descended. I stared hypnotized at the five objects on the spotless tablecloth. What a shame, I thought, that when the bomb exploded, that beautiful cloth would be spoiled. Jan was so kind, so houseproud. But how absurd! When the whole room had been torn to pieces, and ourselves . . . The silence grew oppressive, and my thoughts began to wander again. I had been through some close shaves in the past, when the German patrol had shot at me, and in that prison. Whilst outwardly I watched with a sharp eye, ears strained to catch an approaching footstep, inwardly I felt deep down, that this time we had come to the end of the road.

After three hours, Jan came in. 'Well, I think it must have been a false alarm,' he said quietly. 'I'm going to have a look outside.' A couple of minutes later he returned, looking relieved, but perplexed.

'They must have gone. There's nobody there.'

The sense of relief was so overwhelming that I gulped down both glasses of vodka in quick succession. We slept fitfully that night, secretly afraid that the police might be playing cat and mouse. Just before dawn, Jan set out to investigate. He hadn't been dreaming. The next door house was shared by two girls, couriers for the Resistance. The house was now empty. While waiting to arrest them, the police had surrounded all the neighbours, in case the girls had been out visiting. It was dangerous for us to stay; it was clearly time to move on again.

This sudden departure ushered in a period of ten months on the run. For the rest of that winter we hid in various woodmen's cottages in a large forest. Our hosts had been members of the Resistance, and helped us as if we were part of one family. The warmth of their friendship richly made up for the hard conditions. Often we slept on floors of bare beaten earth or on straw in primitive huts. We were beginning to forget the feel of a pair of clean sheets; all our attention was concentrated on how to lie low and not get caught. The cold didn't worry us, for wood was plentiful, and the chimneyless huts often became almost suffocatingly hot. But food was a problem; luckily game was plentiful, and I helped out by trapping hares.

April 1945 found us in Cracow, still moving every few days to elude our pursuers. Although we needed money desperately, earning it was virtually impossible; not only were we constantly on the move but neither of us had been trained in any skill.

To add to our troubles, I contracted typhus. For three weeks I hovered between life and death. In addition to the typhus I had an abscess in my ear; racked by fever, and tortured by the pain in my ear, I was frequently delirious, and would rave and yell. This, in itself, made our situation all the more precarious, because we could hardly keep changing accommodation while my condition was so critical. We just had to stick it out, and hope for the best.

We were at our lowest ebb in Cracow. I couldn't eat, or keep down any solids, and became so weak that I couldn't even sit up without support. Bitten all over by the bed-bugs, I was too feeble to squash them, or even to scratch. As I lay in bed, I was dimly conscious only of my mother, hovering by my side, nursing me with the devotion of a saint. It was a miracle that she never caught the disease – all the more miraculous when I think that she was subsisting on a diet of dry bread and onions, which was all we could afford, and was exhausted by lack of sleep and nursing me through the long nights. Occasionally I had lucid moments, and asked her to gag me if I became delirious again.

But, according to her, I was as quiet as a mouse. 'Anyway, nobody knows about your illness,' she added. 'So don't worry.' It was hardly surprising that word of my illness leaked out. One day a deputation from the other tenants bore down on Hela, our landlady, insisting in no uncertain terms that we be thrown out. But they had not reckoned on Hela. She faced them at the door of her room downstairs, arms folded in defiance, and let rip. 'So you think he's got typhus, do you?' she roared, her eyes flashing in anger. 'Well, I've got news for you, you cowardly, ignorant bunch of bastards. All he's got is a nasty bout of the shits, and if any of you thinks he's got anything more, they can reckon with me here and now.'

According to my mother, who had been watching furtively from the top of the stairs, no one moved. No more was said of our eviction, and I passed the crisis.

A month or so later, things began to move at long last. The Germans had brought many Italians and Frenchmen to work for them in Poland; the Russians now decided that the time had come for these men, many of whom had lost their identity documents in the upheavals of war, to be repatriated. The Polish Resistance was not slow to seize this opportunity as cover for helping their more compromised members to escape to the West. In fact, many transports heading for Odessa in Russia or Prague in Czechoslovakia carried only a sprinkling of genuine repatriates; the majority were Poles with 'assumed' foreign names and 'arranged' documents.

I shall never forget the exhilaration we felt when we heard that we were to join one of the trains. Weeks followed of almost unbearable tension, as meetings were organized, plans drawn up, details settled. In the general confusion in these initial post-war months, the only department within the Communist organization to function efficiently was the police. Three times we heard at the last minute that spurious passengers had been discovered on the trains, and shot without further ado. Three times we were plunged into gloom, when all our carefully laid plans had to be scrapped.

Eventually we were woken one morning in November 1945 by a discreet tap on our door. It was Hela, to say that a messenger was waiting. I hurried downstairs to find a contact whom I had met only once before at the house of one of the organizers. 'Your train is leaving in an hour. You will meet Mrs Markiewicz and the others at the station. Hurry!' My heart raced with almost unbearable excitement, as I bounded upstairs.

'Oh, wonderful!' exclaimed my mother, when I told her the good news. 'That's one advantage in not having any possessions! At least the packing won't take long.'

Since there were no private telephones at the time, we couldn't say good-bye to anybody apart from Hela. 'Hela dear, if it hadn't been for you, we would've been on our way now to Siberia. How can we thank you?' Hela held me tight in a motherly embrace, wetting my lapel with her tears. 'God be with you and see you get safely to freedom . . . I'll pray for you.'

It was cold and blustery as we tramped towards the station, clutching a cloth bundle and a tatty old suitcase Hela had found for us, containing our meagre belongings. Still not daring to trust our luck, I dreaded some last minute hitch. But the train was there, its engine puffing expectantly. Mrs Markiewicz, our transport leader, an intrepid woman who had already piloted six transports to safety, met us on the platform where some sixty other people had already forgathered. 'Ah, vous voilà! En wagon, s'il vous plaît. Nous partons dans dix minutes!' As we clambered with the others into the waiting cattle-truck, the tension was such that nobody cared to speak. When the trucks were locked from the outside, the train lumbered off towards the Czech border, stopping frequently at small wayside stations and sidings. For hours we sat huddled on the floor of the truck, not daring to voice our feelings. It appeared that nobody knew as yet or cared about their final destinations; all the hopes and attention concentrated on the burning issue of how to get out in one piece. Once or twice we were let out to stretch our stiffened limbs and satisfy the call of nature. Darkness fell early and we huddled for warmth, trying to rest in anticipation of the trying days ahead.

The tension dispelled any thoughts of sleep. 'A few more miles and we'll be out of our fatherland; into exile, however self-imposed and unavoidable. . . .' an emotional voice rose out of the darkness. 'Yes, but we shall return,' another replied fervently. 'This is only an interlude.' 'When we come back Poland will be free, really free.' We all sighed our hopeful approval; no one doubted that.

In the early hours of the morning a rumour sprang up, apparently picked up at one of the stations, that the border guards had been alerted about a train-load of 'Fascists' masquerading as French and Italian repatriates, and that we were heading for trouble. It was one of those stupid rumours that so easily could have been true. Our nervous strain became all the more acute for the knowledge that we were sealed in the trucks. 'Shall we try to break out?' somebody whispered. 'No. We've already got through so much. Besides, where would you run to?'

We reached the frontier at 7 a.m., twenty hours after we had left Cracow. The train stopped and there was banging from the trucks ahead, presumably as the doors were being unbarred. When I stood up, I noticed I was wringing and clenching my hands with the tension. The bar was soon raised and the door began to slide unwillingly along its track. The unshaven face of a border guard peered in. 'Wysiadac! Form up a single file,' he muttered sleepily, in a language we feigned not to understand.

Since we were amongst the few who spoke French, we found ourselves pushed to the front of the line.

'I wish I were going where you are,' the guard said, as he frisked through my pockets.

'Pardon? Je ne comprends pas,' I replied dumbly, hardly daring to breathe.

'All right,' he said grumpily as he reached the end of the line. 'Get back in.'

After another week of exasperatingly slow progress, we crossed the border past Pilsen and entered the American Zone in Germany. Suddenly a flood of pent-up tension was released, and we went almost mad with excitement. Everyone danced, cried, sang and laughed. We were free at last, after more than six crazy years of crushing terror, free to walk, eat, sleep, free to live without the fear of hunted animals. With two of our friends from the truck, we raced to throw our arms around the first American GI we saw. The poor man must have thought he was being waylaid by lunatics. 'Hey! Lay off!' he cried, struggling to free himself. 'You think I'm in skirts or somp'n?'

We roared with laughter, and embraced him again.

*

Once across the West German border, our party soon dwindled away as various members headed for their respective destinations. Our destination was Meppen, on the Dutch border, which meant crossing war-scarred Germany. The journey took five days. Rail communications were erratic, trains grossly overcrowded. There were also persistent rumours that escapees without proper papers were being forcibly sent back as 'Fascists' at the bidding of Communist agencies in the West.

'Where do we go from Meppen?' I asked my mother, as we gazed at the devastation from the window. I knew the question had no sure answer. 'Perhaps to England or France,' she said. 'We've got friends in both. Or to Italy, where the Second Polish Corps is stationed. I don't really know. After existing for so long like a hunted animal and living for the moment, I have lost the luxury of making plans and being sure of anything.'

We reached Meppen in mid-December 1945, six weeks after leaving Cracow. There were a number of relatives and old family friends serving in the Polish forces there, whom we had not seen for six years or more, and we spent Christmas in Meppen, reminiscing for hours.

My elder brother Stanislas (Stas) arrived from England as soon as he learned of our escape. Together with my sister Sophie, Stas had left Poland before Hitler and Stalin had invaded, and they had gradually found their way to the Middle East and Egypt. Sophie remained in Cairo, working for the Red Cross, while Stas joined the army and served with distinction through the French campaign in 1940, then in North Africa and eventually Normandy with the returning Allied forces. An officer of a Commando Parachute unit, he headed a Polish detachment which after a stiff battle had thrust into Meppen.

Having looked forward to this reunion with such desperate eagerness, we felt confused when the moment arrived at long last.

'How is it on the other side?' he asked, thumping me on the back, trying to cover up emotion with brusqueness.

'Other side?' I stuttered. 'You should know. We've only just arrived!'

'Dope!' he roared. 'Here "the other side" means the Communist one.'

'Well, habits die hard,' I laughed. 'For six years "the other side" has meant the free West to us. The promised land of hope and liberty!' The initial embarrassment broken, we fell into each other's arms, talking and laughing all at once.

However, the joy of the reunion was marred two days later by the news of my father's death. Saddened and depressed by the loss of so many relatives and friends, and also of all his ancestral possessions, he had died of pneumonia in Cracow.

We decided to go to Italy. My mother was keen to get a job, perhaps in the Red Cross with the Polish Second Corps which formed part of the British Eighth Army. According to Stas, the Polish Army in Italy ran a college for boys like me. Besides, Italy was closer to Egypt, where my mother hoped to visit Sophie, and in mid-winter the Mediterranean sunshine was infinitely more appealing than the bitter cold and food-rationing of Northern Europe.

'I'll drive you to Ancona in central Italy,' said Stas. 'That's where the HQ of the Second Corps is located. Let's pick up my car in Brussels. We can go there by train.'

So we headed for Brussels. In Nice on the way we had a reunion with Madame Rolland.

'So you're safe, my children!' she cried. 'God be praised. And Stas! I thought I'd never see you again. You *are* a big boy now, mon cheri.' She stood on tip-toe to straighten his tie, Stas being over six feet tall.

Madame Rolland had stayed on in Zaleze after our arrest, having nowhere else to go. It must have been a dreadful ordeal. Alone, jeered at by the Communists who had moved in to take the building over, she had clung to her one room, vainly trying to protect the few of her belongings that remained. In her late sixties, frail in health, she had to witness the futile wanton destruction of a way of life of which she had become an intimate part over almost fifty years.

Yet even before such odds she never gave up. She had applied for repatriation to France; eventually she had managed to return, after months of waiting in Zaleze, followed by another two months of misery living in the shacks of a transit camp in burnt-out Warsaw, culminating in a fortnight's train journey in cattle trucks.

While still in Zaleze, she had earned a little money by giving French lessons in Rzeszow. Three times a week she had trudged the six miles to Rzeszow and back through the mud. Once she fell down, rupturing herself badly; but a few days later, bandaged up, she again made her way along that path. She had written to me in Cracow: 'I have earned a little money which I am sending over to you. Buy yourself some sweets or whatever you like.' I was moved to tears. I calculated that the sum involved must have involved fifteen of these trips to Rzeszow.

We were hungry at the time, and needed money desperately to buy food. But I couldn't bring myself to spend any of it in that way, or in any other way. I carried those notes around in my breast pocket like a holy relic, at a loss what to do with them. I never brought myself to spend one penny. Eventually it was all confiscated from me by drunken frontier guards soon after we had left Poland. I felt sad, but in a way relieved.

Her harrowing experiences had aged her alarmingly, and despite her gaiety she looked weary and ill. 'I was determined to make it this far to leave my bones in my native land. That, and to see you all alive and safe from all this ghastliness was my constant prayer. The Good Lord has granted both my wishes, so now I can rest.' It was awful to part with her again as we drove on across the border into Italy. Four months later, we learned the sad news of her death.

Driven by Stas, we reached Ancona in mid-January 1946. His leave was over, and he had to return to England.

My mother got an administrative job with the Polish Red Cross, as she had hoped, whilst I, after waiting three months for a vacancy, went to Trani, right down on the heel of Italy, to enter college. Both my mother and I now wore uniforms, and we cherished the new-found freedom of a settled life.

In the Trani college I found myself amongst men who, through the war, had lost even more schooling than I had. Many of them were in their twenties and knew much more about war and fighting than geography and algebra. We lived in a nearby barracks which had once housed an Italian regiment; every morning we marched a mile to the college, four abreast, singing lustily.

College life was a novel experience to me and I loved it despite the toughness. This was real enough, not so much because of the military discipline, but owing to the temperament of some of the students. Many were embittered by their brutalizing experiences in concentration camps, torture cells and front-line fighting, and would sometimes give vent to their spleen by thrashing the daylights out of the younger students. My own war experiences had left me at the time with some degree of pugnacity. I made a point of standing up to the bullies, even though I usually got the worst of it, ending with black eyes and sore ribs.

My stay in Trani was cut short by the impending evacuation of the Allied forces from Italy. In recognition of their outstanding service to the Allied cause, Great Britain had offered hospitality to the expatriate Polish forces and their dependants. Most of the Poles could not face returning to risk prison in Soviet-occupied Poland, after all the blood shed by their units for the goal of freedom.

In September 1946 I returned to Ancona, and my mother told me the happy news of her impending marriage to Captain Tadeusz Strugalski, whom we had known well in Poland. Tadeusz had been one of the most distinguished Resistance leaders in the south of Poland, before he escaped after the war, and eventually joined the Second Corps. The news delighted me as I was very fond of him.

We talked a lot about where we should eventually settle, but we had really made up our minds already. In October Tadeusz's regiment was due to entrain for England; Stas, my maternal aunt and some other relatives and friends, both Polish and English, were already there and Sophie was shortly leaving Egypt for London. By one of those sad ironies of fate, our escape from Poland had rendered us legally stateless; and our lack of nationality or passport restricted our choice of destination. So England was the natural choice of both sentiment and reason.

My mother told me the distressing news that she had to undergo

a major operation. 'I've consulted several doctors here,' she told
me. 'After carrying out some tests, they informed me that I have
cancer of the breast and chest in a very advanced stage. The
moment we reach London I must go to hospital.'

'But, but why did you leave it so late?' I stammered, the sense
of shock preventing straight thinking.

'I have suspected it ever since 1942, for I had a rather painful
lump in my breast. But what could I do during the war? So I
decided not to say anything about it.'

CHAPTER 4

London and the Travel Bug

*

TRAINS filled with troops and dependants were leaving daily for England; our turn came in December. Five days after leaving Ancona the transport reached its destination, a camp in Yorkshire. The corrugated-iron barrack huts, which the soldiers sardonically called 'barrels of laughter', were set in the dank gloom of a pine forest. In fact, we couldn't have come at a moment better designed to create an adverse impression. Arriving straight out of the Italian sunshine, we were greeted by the fog, sleet and drizzle of an English winter. Three times daily we tramped to the canteen, squelching through mud in the continual drizzle. Our feelings were summed up by Maria, an effusive Neapolitan girl married to a Polish serviceman. 'Mamma mia,' she cried, as she hung up her colourful washing inside our barrel of laughter, 'how shall I ever sing again without the sun?'

Though we vaguely felt that London might see the end to our Odyssey, what we would do and how we'd live still remained unclear. The moment my mother's discharge came through from the Red Cross, we left for London where she immediately applied for hospital admission. Tadeusz Strugalski joined us and they were married on the eve of the operation. The happiness of the occasion was clouded with apprehension, for the London doctors who had examined my mother looked grave and told Tadeusz that the cancer was so advanced that, provided she survived the surgery, she would have hardly more than three or four years before her.

When she left hospital at the end of March 1947, six weeks after admission, she appeared to our relief to be in remarkable form and spirits. This dispelled much of our anxiety, and we turned to the matter of our future. My mother had bought some shares long before the war; we didn't even know what had happened to that investment during the upheavals of war or indeed if the records could be traced. But enquiries showed we were in luck. We decided to sell the shares and to buy a house, which we all craved more than anything else. The possession of a home again suggested security, the pleasure of putting down roots, which we wanted desperately after living as hunted vagabonds.

Tadeusz noticed a house for sale at 35 Queensborough Terrace, W.2. It looked like just the thing we wanted; five storeyed, it was large enough to accommodate us and leave four floors for letting purposes. It was going cheap, for most of it was dilapidated as a result of German bombing. We liked the house, the street and the proximity of Kensington Gardens. So Tadeusz bought it and set to work, putting it back into shape. He worked hard; I helped him with the painting, paper-hanging and the like, while my mother cooked for us and did the household chores.

Once the house was back to a reasonable condition, I turned to the matter of my education, sorely neglected over the war years and its aftermath. I found that I had almost completely forgotten my English; so I joined first a good day school, attending an English class for foreign students, and later working full-time to prepare for matriculation.

Apart from that brief five months in Trani, this was the first time I had ever attended college with other boys. I was happy and carefree, as I threw myself into the pleasures and pursuits of college life – book work, sports, the thrills and disappointments of dating girls. To be involved in things like geography, history, Latin, algebra or football felt infinitely better than being on the run, trapping game in forests for subsistence. All the same I was both flattered and a little amused to find that these grim experiences acted on my classroom friends like a magnet.

'Gosh, I do envy you,' Georgie would sigh, looking up nostalgically from his well-thumbed copy of the Latin classics. 'To hunt and be hunted in a large wild forest like Tarzan, that's life!'

'It never quite felt that way at the time!' I laughed.

*

In 1952, I joined the Regent Street Polytechnic to read Economics. The student community was truly cosmopolitan; hardly a nationality was unrepresented, and in time I could claim without exaggeration to having friends drawn from the four corners of the globe. But it was the company of Asian students that attracted me most. The very word 'Asia' exerted a strange fascination. I couldn't explain to myself why this was so, but I felt I wanted to learn all I could about these countries and their people.

Indian students were particularly numerous at the Poly, and I soon got to know most of them. One of them Keshari Deb, son of the Rajah of Bamra, was related to several families of the Indian nobility whom my parents had known before the war. Moreover Keshari was a crack shot and a keen sportsman (Bamra lay in a remote jungly part of India, the habitat of numerous tigers, elephants, big game and primitive tribes); he loved and knew India particularly well, and never tired of answering my questions.

I remember the day he showed me his Upanayana thread, the string worn across the chest by all Hindus of the upper, so-called 'Twice Born' castes, that is the Brahmins or priestly class, the Kshatryas or warrior-rulers, and Vayshas or the commercial class. 'To us Hindus the Upanayana is most sacred, an intimate part of much of our history, religion and the place of each of us in society. The investiture usually takes place in childhood, and is somewhat like Baptism and Confirmation in Christianity; but to us the ceremony is even more meaningful. It ushers one officially into the age of studenthood, into one's caste and more subtly into the scheme of creation.' 'Tell me more,' I asked, fascinated. 'For instance, why is it woven of three strands? Has this any meaning?' 'Of course! Virtually everything is imbued with symbolism and ulterior significance in India. That's why many outsiders find it hard to understand us really well.' Keshari chuckled.

'Broadly speaking,' he said, 'these three strands stand for the triadic nature of creation and life's unfolding, at least as we believe it, the trinity underlying all existence. Only Brahmins may spin the Upanayana.' He went on to describe how the wise old *guru* (spiritual mentor and teacher) of his family had invested him with the thread when he was about eight. 'You should witness such a ceremony some day. Since you're interested in our culture, it would give you an insight more revealing than those monuments tourists flock to see.' 'I wish I could, but India is so far away.' I said dejectedly. Yet I felt that the people and culture of India and some other Asian countries attracted me more vitally than anything else.

Having graduated, I really didn't know what to do. The prospect of a safe, conventional career did not appeal to me. I could not visualize myself sitting behind an office desk, striving to earn a bigger salary to pay for newer gadgets. I hankered after a challenge, a tough assignment, preferably of humanitarian value, that would lend some purpose to my life.

To earn some money, which was badly needed, I did some interior decorating and toured offices on behalf of an employment agency, working on a commission basis. But these were dead-end jobs, that brought little money and even less satisfaction. It all seemed rather futile and the little I earned I spent on girls. Inwardly I craved for some mission that was imaginative and fulfilling, especially if it could be in the service of the needy in Asia to whom I felt myself strangely drawn. I seriously considered joining the Red Cross or some religious order engaged in work in the underdeveloped countries; but although the service aspect appealed greatly, I felt that I lacked the necessary vocation for this type of work.

For the time being I took refuge in the quiet pleasures of reading. Indeed some of my happiest memories of this period are of the long winter evenings at Queensborough Terrace, engrossed in some book by the fire. I had read avidly, if somewhat indiscriminately, since early childhood; Madame Rolland and Miss Peggy had fostered my taste for French and English literature. My mother's influence also had a great deal to do with it, for she had always read extensively and with a remarkable capacity for recollection. From the plays and novels by authors like Molière, Anatole France, Flaubert, Balzac, Dumas, Hugo, Shakespeare, Galsworthy, Kipling, Wilde, Shaw, etc., I moved onto many of the Russian, German and to a lesser extent Italian and Spanish authors in translation: Tolstoy, Pushkin, Dostoyevsky, Gogol and also Schiller, Mann, Brecht, Dante, Boccacio, d'Annunzio, Cervantes and Lorca. In my early twenties I turned to the arts and culture of Greece and Rome, and I read a number of the better known plays and classics as well as many current books about these civilizations. This was followed by two or three years when my reading became almost exclusively directed at philosophy, the arts and civilizations of antiquity, sociology and history.

But for two or three years now my interests veered increasingly towards Southern Asia, especially India and the Middle East. The cost of going there was high, while the prospects of finding a reasonable career out there were slender; but at least I could learn vicariously through books. I became a regular visitor to the Paddington and Kensington public libraries and read voraciously everything relevant from 'travel' to 'philosophy', from 'agriculture' to 'religions and sociology'. My involvement soon came to the notice of the library attendants, since many of the books I asked for had to be secured after some research through the interlibrary loan system. 'I've seldom seen anyone working on his thesis so assiduously,' said Miss Jones, one of the librarians, puzzled by my requests for ever rarer and more specialized volumes. 'It's not for a thesis,' I laughed, 'but nonetheless I feel that *something* positive will come out of it one day!'

I soon realized that what had begun as a strong interest was fast developing into a passion. I joined the libraries at the India Office and of the School of African and Oriental Studies. Between them they contained just about every book ever written about these countries, and in my spare time I happily immersed myself in their archaeology, history, arts, and, above all, in everything that touched on the life of the people.

One day, in April 1953, I was sitting on a bench in Kensington Gardens reading the Bhagavad Gita. It was one of those lazy Sunday afternoons; on the Round Pond the ducks splashed and quacked, chasing one another in the perennial rites of spring. The bright yellow patches of daffodil blooms were broken with the subtler hues of crocus. In the air there was the smell of new-mown grass, while from a gramophone under the chestnut-trees came the strains of a Greek melody.

I tried to concentrate but my mind kept returning to the previous evening, when Tadeusz had been describing some of his experiences in war-torn Poland. There was something indefinable, something that eluded me about his story. I was suddenly aware that an elderly man, well-dressed and bowler-hatted, had joined me on the park bench. He kept staring vacantly before him, his expression glazed. After a while he remarked that the daffodils were especially fine this year. I politely agreed, and picked up my book again. But the ice had been broken, and he began to talk.

He was a company director, who had struggled hard to make good. In fact, his was a classic success story, the humble origins, the hard climb from clerk to junior executive in an advertising agency. From then on, he had battled his way to the top. He had given his wife a comfortable home, his son an expensive Public

School education. Then he had pushed the boy into a business career in South Africa. 'Although he was earning a decent salary out there, he hit the bottle,' he remarked, wistfully. 'Committed suicide.'

There was an awkward pause, while he doodled on the ground with the tip of his cane. After a while, he continued telling of how he had tried to comfort his wife. But it was no good. After thirty years of married life, they found themselves total strangers underneath the outward trappings and comfort of life.

'It's ironic, you know. I'm an expert in packaging. I've made a fortune over the years for my clients. But I never took much interest in *what* I was packaging. I never used or tasted the products. Strange, isn't it?' He tapped his gold pocket watch and stood up. 'Time for me to go. I wish I were your age again! When I was a boy, all I ever wanted apparently was a set of toy trains, and my father couldn't afford them. Now I have quite a collection, laid out over two rooms in the attic!'

He chuckled to himself, but it was the self-indulgent chuckle of a sad and lonely old man. As I watched him climb into his Rolls, while his chauffeur held the door for him deferentially, I wondered if there was a moral somewhere.

My elderly friend returned to his toy trains: I returned to the Bhagavad Gita. I knew quite a lot about India, the Middle East and other parts of Southern Asia. But it was all *book* knowledge, or impressions that I had acquired vicariously from friends. What did I *really* know of life in these countries?

By the time I reached home I had made up my mind to go there in the summer. 'The Middle East? But how will you manage? It'll cost a bomb!' Tadeusz remarked when I mentioned this plan. 'No, it needn't. I'll hitch-hike, rough it and try living as the locals do. What better way?' When we had discussed it a little more, my mother gave me her blessing. 'You'll be following in the footsteps of your ancestor, the explorer Jan Potocki. We'll do all we can to help,' she said.

Early in July I stood on the ferry, with the white cliffs of Dover retreating into the distance behind me. As I fingered the fifty pounds' worth of traveller's cheques in my pocket, the sum total of my savings and budget for the trip ahead, I remembered the Polish saying: 'Charge the sun with a pick-axe!' I felt there was something vaguely apt in the proverb. I was on my way to the sun, towards the vast expanses of Asia, her countless millions and convulsive problems.

A fortnight later, rucksack on my back, I had hitch-hiked right across Europe and into central Turkey. A letter from home awaited me in the little town of Kayseri, the Caesarea of antiquity. I stopped there for a couple of days, putting up, by invitation of the headmaster, at the local college, empty for the summer vacation. There I struck up a friendship with Orhan, a student who still remained in the college waiting for his parents to come from Istanbul before joining them in their native village close by. 'Why don't you come along with me?' Orhan said, 'and see life in a Turkish village?'

It was from that village that I re-read Tadeusz's letter. 'What in hell draws you to these countries?' he wrote. 'Are you still as keen about it, or have the poverty and primitive conditions cooled you off a bit by now?' The evening light was failing, as I sat in the porch of my host's modest cottage, and I smiled to myself. The village square was deep in fine dust. Chickens scratched around in the animal droppings for food; a flock of ducks came wobbling across the square hustled home by a ten-year-old in baggy trousers with missing fly-buttons, his round chubby face in striking contrast to his oversized cap. He whistled sharply, raising his stick towards the laggards who were trying to dispute the droppings with the chicken, and shouted gaily 'burda, burda!' ('this way!').

Now a herd of cattle ambled to their sheds, trailing dust, lowing softly, the resonance of their bells mingling with long-drawn shepherd calls which the hushed clear air seemed to hold for ever, so that they lingered lazily like the dancing dust that tarried over the square. Last of all the bullock-carts lumbered in, ponderous on their spokeless wheels of solid wood, their axles whining and complaining with a note of ever-changing pitch.

Lost in thought, I didn't notice Orhan, who had brought a hurricane lamp and a dish of sour milk. 'There!' he smiled, 'you can't write home in the dark. The night falls fast here. Eat this soon, or it'll be swimming with gnats.' 'Tashakur!' ('thank you!'), I grinned back at him, 'I wish my Turkish were half as good as your English!'

'You ask me if I like it here,' I wrote. 'Oh yes, intensely, but how can I explain? It's a bit like meeting a girl, when everything clicks, and you fall in love. I feel gloriously alive and very much at home, almost as if I were regaining a homeland. But probing more deeply what can I say? You have to feel it and to live it. These lands suckled the earliest civilizations, nurtured the first roots of man's timid gropings towards the tree that we are now. Beneath the outward poverty, under the grime and the tatters, there is a culture as old as time itself, infinitely complex and wise. These weathered lands hold out the corrective to our brave new world, of the sobriety of age and experience, of diversity in life's options: especially to those seeking to apprehend the ultimates and the quiddity within the ebb and flow of appearance. To me this last is particularly appealing: the directness and immediacy between man and his natural environment.

'At the same time there is so much need here, so much wretchedness that *could* be remedied. The challenge is enormous. The poverty is crushing, perhaps less so here in Turkey than in other parts of Asia, a poverty often aggravated by the former exploitation by European colonial powers. I believe everybody in the West should be aware of this and its profound consequences for all of us. Help and alleviation of this wretchedness can come essentially from a better understanding of its causes, nature and extent, and in this every one of us can help, can contribute his humble little brick.

'I daresay this may not answer your questions very satisfactorily, for it is written in the heat of the moment, real no less than figurative – 96°F in the shade!'

When Orhan saw me off at the bus stop the following morning, he left me with a huge box of *lukum* (Turkish delight), 'You never know what and where you'll be able to eat on the way, Arthur!' I returned to Kayseri, posted my letter and then set out, bound for another country – Iraq.

Luckily I had a stomach of iron and the swill I downed never gave me trouble. Turkish cuisine can be exquisite, especially that served in well-to-do houses or the top restaurants. But the food of ordinary people is as rough and dull as anywhere. The mutton is prepared into a kebab or as a stew with a great deal of fat; sweets are usually nauseatingly syrupy. I don't care much for mutton, especially when I can see the carcasses hanging dust-blown, fly-flown and wasp-ridden in open butchers' shops; and so I contented myself with bread, sweet tea without milk served in waisted glasses, and during the summer, the commonest and cheapest of all dishes, *fasulia*, stringy runner beans in tomato sauce swimming in half an inch of tepid mutton fat. Fasulia became my staple diet, eaten at breakfast, lunch and dinner, except for the equally greasy tomato gruel-soup often served for breakfast in the villages.

Language proved much less of a problem than I had feared. When you arrive at even the remotest of villages, everybody knows that you need food, somewhere to wash and sleep, that you'd like to have a look around, and so on. With a bit of imagination and practice it is surprising what an expressive gesture and a little mimicry will achieve. But I took one precaution which proved extremely useful: I selected a hundred or so of the most practical and commonly used words and phrases, which I would persuade somebody to translate phonetically into the local language. Please, thank you, good morning, very good, I want to go to, how far is it to, cheap, clean, dirty, flea, bug, sheet, bed, hot, cold, etc. It all fitted on two sheets of paper which I always carried on me, and which I memorized within a few days. Considering that an average person's commonly used vocabulary seldom exceeds a thousand words, it is not surprising how far a hundred well-chosen phrases will take you, backed with suitably eloquent gestures.

Another thing that I quickly discovered was that hospitality, to most Asians, is not merely a matter of social nicety. The Arabic term for it is *karam*, which means hospitality, generosity, nobility all in one word. Karam is a sacred duty, an honour in the discharge of which the host takes immense pride, sharing everything with his guest down to the last morsel of food. This is accomplished so naturally that it leaves many an innocent Westerner unaware of the increased hardship which his host will have to endure for weeks afterwards.

I remember an instance of this, when I reached Iraq. I was hitch-hiking around some of the ancient sites of Mesopotamia, and was very anxious to visit Warka, the biblical Erech. But getting there was not so easy, for Warka lies some thirty miles across trackless desert from Samawa, a little town along the railway line to Baghdad.

When I reached Samawa, I found that no transport of any kind, let alone a public bus, went in the direction of Warka. Just as I was preparing to give Warka a miss, I decided as a last resort to try the police station.

'How nice of you to take the trouble to see our country,' the sergeant replied, when I mentioned the problem. 'Unfortunately there are marauding tribesmen in the area. But let me see if I can arrange something for you.'

I thanked him profusely, without daring to expect anything positive to come of it. Experience had already suggested that in the East the desire to please often outstrips what proves possible. But half an hour later I found myself in a police truck, lurching over the desert towards Warka. A sergeant sat beside me, and five constables at the back; a light machine-gun was fixed on top of the roof.

It was all rather reminiscent of that last ride out of Zaleze. But when I tried to tell them of that incident, my phrase list and evocative gestures weren't up to the task. They laughed heartily, slapped me on the back and offered me a cigarette. Any resemblance with that grim occasion was very superficial and I left it at that.

After two hours of this gut-shaking ride, we saw the rumpled mounds of Erech sprawled right ahead of us. The grey monotony of the ruins did not break the starkness of the desert, merely furrowed it with low walls and trenches, as if burrowed by some huge, prehistoric mole. The only sign of human habitation was a miserable shack, where Mohammed the guard lived with his wife and five children. As soon as we jumped out of the truck, he came over, insisting that we rest in his hut before proceeding to the site. As he fussed around us, preparing coffee, I noticed that apart from two worn reed mats, which we were sitting on, the hut was bare of furniture. Their only possessions seemed to be a box over in one corner, containing grain and other provisions, a bundle of rags and a large earthenware pot on a stand. The pot was filled with brackish water, and filtered, drip by drip, into a smaller pot underneath. I looked up at Mohammed's face, bony and gaunt like his hut. The effects of poverty and malnutrition were only too apparent.

I sipped the strong and bitter coffee, wondering how this luxury affected Mohammed's state of dismal penury. In case it involved the splurge I suspected, I thanked him more effusively than I would normally have done; to give him plenty of 'face', by which Bedouins set great store, I asked the sergeant to tell him in proper Arabic before the other men that it was an even better brew than I had ever tasted in Baghdad.

'That is all right,' the sergeant replied. 'After we visit the ruins, Mohammed invites us for lunch.'

My heart sank. Desperately I racked my brains for an excuse.

'It's very kind, but really I am not hungry,' I said, rather lamely.

'No, no, you must accept,' the sergeant replied. 'He would be very hurt and offended.'

Mohammed had already sent his son to kill the two chickens, which I had seen scratching in the dust outside. As we emerged from the hut, I caught a glimpse of his wife plucking feathers at the back.

Mohammed led us over the ruins, pointing out the fragmentary walls and entrances. Once they had been part of temples and palaces, but now, after a lapse of over four thousand years, it required a great effort of imagination to conjure up the splendour of those noble edifices out of the humble dust and crumbling mud-brick. 'Look, old decoration – perhaps even Moses see it,' Mohammed said, pointing to a wall set with blue and green topped cones to form a kind of a rudimentary mosaic, notable amidst the ashen drabness of the ruins. Jumping over walls and down the narrow streets, in places still discernible, we slowly made our way towards the Ziggurat, the most outstanding feature of Erech. 'This was cosmic mountain the people of Warka built. It was like pyramid, only built in big steps, each painted different colour,' Mohammed was saying in his scanty English. I tried hard to concentrate in the stifling heat, but my thoughts kept wandering back to the present and those two chickens. I knew they were his only ones. Now his children wouldn't even have eggs for protein. Thousands of years ago men had built these palaces to beseech the gods for a better life. Now children were starving in the shadow of their ruins, and would starve that bit more because I had come intent on glimpsing the dawn of Man's worldly aspiration for civilized existence.

By the time we had finished our tour, the meal was ready. Two large tin trays had been prepared by the unseen hands of Mohammed's wife; they were heaped high with steaming rice and chicken (*djaj ala timen*), some vegetables and the flat, unleavened bread of the Arabs. Sitting cross-legged around the trays, we helped ourselves with our fingers, while Mohammed sat crouched in a corner, playing his role as host with perfect karam watching keenly that everybody should have their fill and more. There was more food there than the six policemen and I could possibly eat. But custom ordained that we should consume as much as we possibly could; Mohammed and his family would have whatever was left. As I tried belching my appreciation, I asked the sergeant how much this feast would have cost, and how much Mohammed earned. When he quoted the figures, I made some calculations. I couldn't believe it.

'But that's a month's wages!' I said, feeling the sweat come out on my face.

'Yes, you are right,' the sergeant replied carelessly.

The food made me feel sick and helpless anger surged through me. Mohammed was now offering sweetmeats, visibly proud that we appreciated his hospitality. Looking up, I saw that the children had come in, and were giggling shyly, their eyes swooping on the food that remained. Stealthily, I pulled three dinar notes (about three pounds) from my money belt, and tucked them under the mat, in the hope that Mohammed would not find them until after we had left. But the sergeant spotted me. 'You should not have done that. Anyway, money cannot pay for most of the good things in life.'

Such sentiments are truly Arabic, and typical of these proud sons of the desert.

What with my phrase list and words I picked up from the people around me, I could hold a rudimentary conversation in Arabic after a couple of weeks. In the local tea-house at Samawa, I happened to sit next to a Bedouin Sheikh. We were soon exchanging stunted remarks, my smattering of Arabic no better than his few words of English. He was a warm-hearted, jovial man in his early forties, whose flowing robes not only made him look taller than he really was, but helped conceal his paunch (among Arabs, a sign of wealth and status). As we drank the hot sugary tea, he watched me with unconcealed curiosity, the gaze of his burning brown eyes steady and sharp.

'You come to my people,' Sheikh Ali exclaimed after a lull in the conversation, smacking his lips loudly over the scorching brew. 'You come see how we live yourself?'

The author's home
at Dukla
(south wing)

Zaleze under the
German occupation

The author's mother,
Countess Wanda
Tarnowska

Arthur, 5 years old

With Sheikh Ali
in Iraq

In Bali, a few
days before
contracting polio

Preparing a paddy field

A village market in Bali

Despite his peremptory tone, befitting someone more used to issuing orders than polite invitations, his manner was warm and affable. 'Thank you, I shall be honoured.' I said solemnly.

Two days later, after another gut-bashing ride, this time in a bus that looked as if it had been dug up from the very ruins of Babylon, I rode into camp, my host having sent an escort with a spare pony to the nearest village where there was a bus station. The camp was a depressing sight. The black, rough-spun tents were dotted around the flat, parched plain. Scraggy dogs barked angrily as we approached, while children in dirty rags gaped and giggled. As my escort showed me into one of the low-slung tents, which had evidently been set aside for my use, a strong smell of rancid sweat hit me. 'My God,' I thought to myself, 'What the hell did you come here for?'

Left alone, I looked around in vain for somewhere to wash. Every pore seemed clogged with dust, but it appeared you hardly ever washed here, water being so scarce. Thoroughly tired and grumpy, I sat cross-legged on a threadbare rug on the floor. Immediately the fleas went into the attack; within minutes I was scratching all over.

Suddenly there were voices outside, and Sheikh Ali appeared. My discomforts vanished quickly in the warmth of his embrace.

'Allah be praised,' he said, kissing me on both cheeks. 'Welcome. Welcome.'

Soon I was sitting down, at Sheikh Ali's right hand, in front of a large dish of *habeet*, mutton and rice with vegetables. About a dozen of the elders joined us, but sat rather stiffly, contributing little to the conversation, content to tear the mutton with their fingers and convey it to their mouths with loud smacking of lips, the fat glistening on their beards. In fact conversation was distinctly laboured. 'How much you brother, sister?' Sheikh Ali asked me.

'Two,' I replied, wondering where this might lead. 'And you?'

'Me eleven! Father very strong . . .' He flexed his muscles and roared with laughter.

The atmosphere grew more relaxed as the evening drew on, and formality evaporated altogether during the days that followed. My presence became accepted. The blank, gaping faces that craned at my arrival filled out into characters; the children no longer squirmed and sniggered, but pranced about merrily, as they showed me around the camp. One of my favourite characters was old Hassan with his shaggy, grizzly beard. Apart from the word 'yes' he spoke virtually no English, but I deduced that he had fought for the British in the First World War against the Turks in Mesopotamia. Still limping from the wound he had picked up forty years previously, he would charge across the hot sand, shouting 'Turki boom, boom!' in a mock bayonet attack. Having dealt with one imaginary victim, he slit the throat of another, snorting fearfully, before hobbling off towards the coffee-pot simmering on a fire of dried cow-pats. Nobody could make a better brew of coffee than old Hassan.

I felt free as never before. One evening, as Sheikh Ali conducted me back to my tent, I gazed up at the sky shining with a million stars. It was beautiful and awesome and I said so. 'Yes,' he replied enigmatically. 'This us. This is our life.' As I lay on my rug, having bade him good-night, I realized that here lay the great difference between us. The beauty in nature can be appreciated only too easily when one stands isolated and reasonably secure from the elements. But to the Sheikh and his people, the panoply of creation is like a womb. They are born and die on the earth, they eat and sleep on it, they prostrate themselves on it in prayer. In this lies the key to what they are.

Once I had become accepted, I ventured to share in some of their work. Accompanied by the children, who became my inseparable companions, and the young shepherds we would set out in a party to look after the flocks of sheep and goats. Jackals and other predators were a real menace to the animals, no less than the scorpions and particularly kraits to the shepherds. At noon, we would rest under improvised awnings while the sun poured lead from the heavens, turning the plain into an inferno. Twice, we rode to the nearest market in Samawa, loaded up with sheepskins, wool and rugs, and I watched while my friends bargained furiously, amidst the general hubbub, for a few essentials to buy for the camp.

During the two weeks that I spent in camp, I never spoke to a woman. The women stayed apart, doing the chores, and it would have been the height of tactlessness to try to speak to any of them. But we were constantly aware of their presence, if only from the occasional appearances of young Abdul, who had just taken another wife. Eyes bloodshot, hair tousled, he would occasionally dive into the communal tent for a quick coffee, before self-consciously disappearing, accompanied by howls of coarse laughter.

On the eve of my departure, we had a feast, for which an entire sheep was roasted on a spit. When I saw that animal rotating, my stomach tightened; the sheep seemed to be looking straight at me with its bulging, bleary eyeballs. I stared back, repeating to myself that I mustn't be sick, whatever happens, I mustn't be sick. When the moment of truth arrived, I watched with a sinking feeling as Sheikh Ali's hand reached out to the head, and deftly gouged the eyeball from its socket.

'Come, honoured friend,' he grinned, motioning me to open my mouth wide. I took a deep breath and closed my eyes. It felt like a burning ember on my cringing tongue.

'Good, good. Eat!' Sheikh Ali was encouraging me, and laughing at the same time. Thank goodness the others were laughing too, as I carefully manoeuvred the object under my tongue, and chewed away, my jaws moving up and down. Grinning like an idiot, I munched and swallowed for several minutes, relieved that no conversation was expected of me, desperately racking my brains for a way out. Luckily for me everybody's attention was diverted momentarily by the arrival of one of Sheikh Ali's numerous cousins. Seizing my opportunity, I quickly raised my hand to my mouth, spat the eyeball out into my palm, and hid it in my pocket. Later that night I buried the object furtively in the sand.

Some thirty of them rode off with me next morning, to accompany me back to Samawa. Although they were shouting and shooting their rifles in the air, I sensed that underneath we all felt sad, as if the parting were taking me away from my own family.

'You come back, brother,' Sheikh Ali said warmly as we embraced. 'You always with us.' 'I know. One day I will, Insh Allah.' 'Insh Allah, Insh Allah,' they echoed, firing their rifles into the air, their horses rearing.

As I got into the railway carriage and stood waving at them, I felt that I had learned more in two weeks than during a whole year at university. As the train puffed its way towards Baghdad, I sat staring into the open vistas of the desert. Suddenly I saw them again, galloping to keep up with the train, yelling ferociously.

A soberly dressed Baghdadi sitting opposite me in the compartment looked up anxiously from his book.

'They are Bedouins,' he informed me disparagingly. 'Very wild and uncivilized people. Can be very dangerous.' And with that pearl of wisdom he returned to his book.

In the next few years, I set off every summer with my rucksack on my back, with the barest minimum of money. This developed into a principle. It was not merely because I could not afford more comfortable travel. I discovered that by limiting my daily expenditure to around five shillings a day, I was able to make the kind of personal contact with the ordinary people in the back streets and villages which the more affluent travellers find elusive. There was a challenge in it, too, which taxed one's wits and one's hardiness. I lived amongst the people, learned at first hand about their conditions, attitudes and hopes, all in a completely natural atmosphere. In this way I escaped the constraints peculiar to those well-intentioned sorties from a comfortable hotel 'to find out how the natives live'. In time, I grew to feel more at home in an Asian village than in the drawing-rooms of London.

In my spare time I continued reading as avidly as before, but now the choice of books was often influenced by the places I had seen and wanted to know better. When I set out the following summer, almost half my rucksack was filled with books. One of the most satisfying places for reading about a subject, I concluded, was in its own setting. What better spot to read about the Pyramids than lounging in their shadow?

I remember vividly the joy in climbing Mount Parnassus clutching the *Idylls* of Theocritus. It was a stifling hot day, the air scented with thyme. Far below lay the ruins of Delphi and the temple of Apollo where the Pythia had uttered oracles; deeper yet the silvery-green olive-trees shimmered in the valley, so profusely overgrown that it had been poetically called 'The River of Olives'. The valley issued onto the Gulf of Corinth, glazed with sapphire of the deepest blue. Sweating profusely, at times half running, I clambered through the thorny scrub and sharp stones, to sprawl over some rock and read passages aloud. It was glorious.

On another occasion I lugged a gramophone into the desert outside Baghdad to play Beethoven's Fifth and Seventh Symphonies at full volume. The cascades of sound billowed across the solitude, impassive, enduring, as the dunes surged and rippled into the distance, into the expanses of grandeur. As if both were drawn from the Absolute, the sound and the stillness coalesced to conjure up moments of that rare ecstatic rapture, when one's spirit transcends time and identity to partake of the Divine.

I was in Bali, Indonesia, in 1958, staying in the village of Ubud. I had been roughing it in Asia for several months, well away from home comforts and the sight of Westerners. One day I went with a couple of Balinese friends to Denpasar, the capital, and we strolled past the Bali Hotel, the only modern hotel on the island. A party of Western tourists was lounging on the terrace, sipping their whisky and sodas; the spectacle seemed so strange that the three of us stopped and gaped for a few moments. Then one of my friends pulled me by the arm.

'Come on,' he said, 'this place is not for *us.*'

When we were out of sight of the hotel, I suddenly realized that quite spontaneously he had paid me the most wonderful compliment. Such experiences brought the problems of East and West sharply into focus for me; by travelling extensively in this way, I was beginning to realize just how wide the gulf is that yawns between the rich and the starving. Most of us in the West are at best only vaguely aware of these problems, much less of their dire consequences for the future of man. Ideological differences can hardly be as explosive as those separating full stomachs from empty ones.

I had noticed that many young people in the West had a genuine desire to travel in the East, and that many, particularly students, succeeded in doing so during their vacations. But I felt that many more were held back, fearing that the cost would be prohibitive, ignorant of the art of low cost travel. Gradually an idea began to take shape in my mind, a project which would not only permit me to travel myself, but at the same time make a contribution towards solving this problem. I decided to start a travel agency specializing in travel-on-a-shoe-string. From my own experience, such travel had proved infinitely more effective and worthwhile than whole libraries of learned books. Why not for others, too?

A guide book would be essential. I had already collected a mass of information, but a great deal of further research on the spot would be necessary before I could contemplate publishing it, and launching the agency.

When I set out for Southern Asia again, in the autumn of 1957, it was with a flurry of high expectations.

At last I had found something to get my teeth into, a vocation that was potentially useful and profitable, but also challenging and adventurous. 'Please write regularly,' was my mother's principal wish. 'We shall follow your adventures like instalments from *Pilgrim's Progress*.' 'Come to think of it, that's just what it might turn out to be!' Tadeusz added with a chuckle.

Hitch-hiking and riding in local buses, more often than not with goats, suckling babies, trussed up chickens squawking for dear life, sheep and spitting, munching and puking humanity, I reached India in October 1957. My notebooks were filling up fast: costs and schedules of local buses and trains, types of eating-places serving cheap but reasonably safe food, second-rate but clean and bug-free hotels. For instance I discovered that one could travel overland in about three weeks from London to India, by train as far as Turkey and thereafter by various local buses, for a total of just under forty pounds. 'A student can go for a three-month overland journey to India and back, everything paid, for less than an average British smoker spends on cigarettes in thirty months,' I wrote home. 'Tadeusz, from the amount you smoke, you could save it in a year!'

But costs were by no means the only item of information I was collecting. I intended that my guidebook should provide all the ancillary facts the prospective traveller would find useful: how to plan the trip, and budget for it; a bibliography for introductory reading; what organizations might be profitably joined or contacted; what to pack so as not to leave any essentials out, while not taking more than one can carry. Was it preferable to take a rucksack or a suitcase? What type of shirts, how many pairs of socks, rubber-soled or leather-soled shoes? What drugs and first-aid kit to carry; the safest way to carry money; precautions to take with drinking water and other liquids; tips about techniques of bargaining; how to rid oneself of touts and how to behave amidst riots or angry mobs. For language problems, I thought that my phrase list, which I had perfected with practice, would come in most useful. Suggestions concerning local etiquette would also be essential.

There was a great deal of such information to include, and when it came to the crunch, its accuracy and thoroughness would make all the difference between a successful, informative journey and one to be later recalled with distaste for its vexations.

I covered over 10,000 miles in India by all manner of transport, both common and exotic, from train to elephant, bicycle to bullock-cart. Then I proceeded to Ceylon, Malaya and Indonesia. By April 1958 I was in Singapore, on my way to Burma. The boat was due to sail for Rangoon that evening, and I had a hundred and one things to do that day. The previous night I had run a high temperature, with a pain in my back so intense that I had been reduced to chewing the sheet. I felt groggy and in a feverish daze, increasingly irritated that my legs felt so sluggish. With grim determination, I tramped on from place to place, collecting my visa, ticket, money. By the evening I was limping badly with the heavy rucksack on my back. But as I boarded that boat, I felt that whatever the trouble, at least it had not prevented me from making it to the ship and getting on with the job. As I inflated my pneumatic mattress on deck, I looked up at the million stars across the tropical sky; racked with mounting pain, I prayed for the strength to surmount whatever was sapping the power from my limbs.

The next morning, after another night of intense pain, I could hardly stand. Realizing that there was something seriously wrong, the other deck passengers, all of whom were Asians, came to keep me company. One brought some oil to rub my legs, another a bottle of country liquor, a third an inexhaustible repertoire of salacious jokes. But despite their touching sympathy and assistance, my condition was deteriorating fast. I decided it was time to see the ship's doctor. When I asked one of my friends to deliver a message, he returned with the startling news that the doctor never came down to see a deck passenger. So, supported by two helpers, I limped off to his cabin.

Without leaving his chair, he asked me to close my eyes and to stand still. I did as I was told, and my friends caught me as I was falling.

'Nothing serious,' he said brusquely. 'Probably a hangover.'

When the ship docked next day off Penang, I was taken off, dazed with fever, strapped to a stretcher. The ambulance took its time, and the stretcher-bearers put me down on the side-walk in front of the dock gates. Whenever anything unusual happens in Asia, people assemble – and this was no exception. As the crowd stood around in a circle, watching and waiting, I felt strangely embarrassed, as if I were some dangerous maniac who had to be strapped down.

Eventually the ambulance arrived. We drove through streets lined with trees in gorgeous red blossom, my legs inert, my arms lying tanned against the clinical whiteness of the sheet. An ominous apprehension crept over me, as if I were travelling in a padded coffin; I longed to break free, back to the sun, back to life. I wondered what lay ahead, and felt afraid.

CHAPTER 5

Polio

*

I WOKE up the next morning in a large, third-class ward of Penang General Hospital. The fever had dropped, and my first sensation was one of relief, as if I had woken up from a nightmare. Slowly I looked around me at the neat row of beds. There were about thirty of them in all. Then I stared at my legs and tried to jerk them. The blanket seemed to move even less than it had the previous day. 'Good God,' I murmured, 'this *is* a nightmare.'

Two doctors, a Chinese and an Indian, stopped by my bed on their morning rounds. When they asked me to contract my calf muscles, I failed miserably, although I tried desperately hard. 'Well, try and sit up.' As I strained to lift myself, I felt that my body was sulking, that if I tried a little harder I might shake off the paralysis that seemed to be creeping slowly up my body.

But it was useless, and I lay back panting from the effort, while the two doctors consulted in an undertone. When I asked them for their verdict, the Chinese doctor tried to pacify me, telling me not to worry, that I would be all right. But to me this felt glib and unsatisfactory and I asked them to tell me the truth. They exchanged a quick glance, and nodded.

'We suspect it's polio. Though there should be some recovery within three to six months, your chances frankly depend on how thorough the paralysis will be and on how far up your body it will go. If it stops at your waist, which it seems to have reached already, probably you may eventually be able to walk, with artificial aids, or failing that, get around in a wheelchair.

'But if it reaches your chest, you'll have to go in one of those.' Two nurses were wheeling an iron lung towards my bed. I gazed at the monster as it approached, wondering if it would swallow me up within its steely bowels. 'And after that?' I asked. Instead of replying, he smiled wanly, and drew his forefinger gently across his throat. But I knew that the Chinese often smile when they tell you the worst; the doctor was not being callous or unsympathetic, but realistic and honest.

I was seven thousand miles from home, in a strange town where I did not know a soul. I was stranded, in fact, with funds barely sufficient for living rough, let alone for coping with an emergency such as this. As I lay there, trying to take stock, the nurses wheeled my bed with the iron lung alongside up to the top of the ward, near the table where the duty nurse sat. I gazed at that living coffin poised beside my bed. As the hours passed, I kept feeling my muscles, only to realize that the stillness was creeping inexorably higher.

'Just let me know if you have any difficulty in breathing,' the staff nurse said. 'Yes, of course,' I replied, breathing self-consciously in and out. Never before had I breathed so hard, so consciously, in and out, in, out. Was I dying piecemeal, muscle by muscle, joint by joint? I put myself in the hands of God and hoped for the best.

One thing was quite clear. The paralysis was gradually creeping up, and had already wiped out the remaining flickers of movement in my legs. My abdominal and lower back muscles were already hardly even twitching, and I had increasing difficulty in moving my left arm. Despite pain-killing drugs, I developed an acute pain each night in my back, which kept me awake and sweating. In the dim light from the nurse's desk, I listened to the soft pad of her feet, fascinated by their tread. Within my narrow line of vision, I could see her take five steps. To move seemed such a natural thing; every time she walked across in front of my bed, I took those five steps with her. I had never thought that walking could be so wonderful.

After nine days, the progress of the paralysis seemed to have spent itself, and I was free of pain. By some act of Providence the virulence had stopped, and the nurses came to push the iron lung away. It had been a close shave; but the victory was Pyrrhic, for all that remained mobile in my body was my chest, arms, toes and head, and even so my left arm, chest muscles on the left side and neck were all much weakened. Would I ever be able to walk again, however inadequately? I desperately clung to this chance, clutching at anything that offered a crumb of hope. The alternative was a wheelchair; the very idea was almost as sickening as that of the iron lung.

Now that the crisis was over, I felt the time had come to write home. It was a task which I could hardly bring myself to face, realizing the anguish it was bound to cause. I decided it was essential to write the letter myself rather than to dictate it, but this was easier said than done. I couldn't sit up unaided, as this involved the most painful cramps; lying on my side proved equally ineffective. Eventually the nurses pushed an adjustable sliding table some ten inches above my head and pinned a sheet to its underside, on which I managed to scribble something painstakingly, providing I gave my arm a rest every few minutes. I addressed it to Tadeusz: 'If you've opened this in Mummy's presence, please tell her that you must quickly go to the loo and then read it.' I described as casually as I could what had happened, stressing that I felt all right now, and that I could move my toes. 'If motion remains in the legs' extremities, there's a good likelihood that it will return higher up my limbs.' This seemed to make good logic, and I half believed it myself. Then I went on to describe what I had done and seen in the last three weeks before my illness and since my last letter. In my awkward position, lying flat on my back, it took me two days to fill as many pages. Six days later I had a telegram: they sent their love, and told me not to worry. 'Toe movement excellent sign. Letter follows.' This scrap of news was exceedingly welcome, and I kept re-reading it over and over again, my throat tight with emotion.

Many people had started to keep me company by this stage; I no longer felt totally alone. Goodness knows there were plenty of patients in that ward who were far worse off than I was, suffering, dying, crying out in pain; why such solicitude was lavished on me I shall never understand. When most of the staff hurried home in the evening for a well-deserved rest, one of the doctors, Victor Roseverne, used to stay behind for a chat. Often these sessions lasted several hours, since Victor was Polish and we also shared a passion for things Oriental. Victor would bring a huge bag of fruit and chocolate with him, so that the night table groaned under the weight. By profession he was a radiologist, but he was also an excellent psychiatrist.

We discussed my fears and problems frankly, so that their terrors began to dissolve like morning mists. His main argument was that even the most complicated situations could usually be broken up into simple component parts; that I should tackle my predicament in this way. 'It requires ingenuity, but if you have an agile mind, this process can be quite stimulating. Besides, all disasters have some of the proverbial silver lining, you know! Let's see for instance how to get out of bed onto a chair.' Availing himself of the next bed, empty at the time, he tied his legs together with his belt, and slid two small boards inside his trousers to stop himself using his lower trunk muscles. Then he proceeded to try various ways of heaving himself off the bed in this awkward position, while most of the ward patients watched intently, throwing out suggestions. 'Grab your legs and move them closer to the edge first!' 'Put your left arm under you – a little lower – that's it! Try now!' Thanks to Victor, I discovered that the process of finding the best way to get out of bed with a handicap could be both interesting and exciting.

Other visitors included members of the local British community, journalists, French Jesuit fathers and members of the Penang Buddhist Association. I remember especially the Venerable Sumangalo, a high-ranking Buddhist monk – formerly Robert Clifton, an American convert to Buddhism.

'As you probably know, Arthur,' he said one day, 'critics have often claimed Buddhism to be an ethic of despair and worldly nihilism. But I feel this to be false. Above all, we find our beliefs to be those of unblinking realism. Be of the world and play your part to the hilt; but draw the line at involvement in the flux of existence. Our way is the Middle Path that eschews extremes. We consider that all truths and perceptions are relative, unfolding along the way to Enlightenment on to ever wider and deeper insights, like the horizons of a mountain climber.' 'It is curious, Father,' I said reflectively, 'I have read and thought a great deal in the past about Buddhist precepts. But now that this has happened to me, I see them in a new light, almost a new dimension. I don't think I'll ever become a Buddhist; but it's true that some of these precepts have been of great help to me in re-establishing an inner balance and perspective.'

Despite his many duties and activities (he was engaged in teaching at the local Buddhist schools and helping to spread the gospel, and indeed he was so busy that he hardly had time to sleep), Sumangalo told me that he always found time for medi-tation. 'It confers equanimity and a sense of perspective, out of which ultimate detachment arises. It's like the surface of a lake

when absolutely still and clear, reflecting all things both profound
and superficial. Though I never consciously try doing this, I feel
I glimpse the future in my meditations. Call it vision or prescience,
but it usually comes true, all right. Last night, for example, I saw
you coming back to Penang after a number of years. You were moving slowly and painstakingly in pursuit of some worthy mission.'

I looked at him blankly: such a trip seemed beyond the range of
possibility. Yet . . . I had a strange feeling that his prediction
might come true one day.

The nurses were all grossly overworked, but many of them
found the time to stop for a chat when they were going off duty,
or when the doctor or duty sister was not looking. We used to joke
and gossip and it was wonderful to feel that in their eyes I was still
a man, despite what had happened to me, not merely a patient to
be humoured. One of them was a particularly lovely girl, called
Li. She had the grace of a doe, especially when she wore a
cheong-sam off-duty. I found the way she lisped the final 'r' in my
name, as the Chinese usually do, particularly endearing; I used
to tease her about this, as we flirted mildly after lights out.

After the onset of polio I was badly constipated; in fact, despite
enemas, injections and laxatives, nothing happened for fifteen
days. The record was over a hundred days, or so I was told, but I
found little comfort in that. Eventually the enema was successful,
but every other day I had to endure this procedure: the moment
that it had been administered, I would be lifted up, the bed-pan
slid under me, while I sat there with two nurses supporting me on
either side, and a third keeping my cramped legs in a bent
position.

One morning Nurse Li was on duty, and was ordered to start
this off. I raised hell. Anyone else, I screamed, but not Nurse Li.
The matron bustled in, and reprimanded me for getting hysterical.
For the next twenty minutes I sat on that pan, with Nurse Li
holding me on one side, pressing my fists into my eyes to stop the
tears rolling down my cheeks. I felt I had sunk down to the very
pit of degradation and wished I were dead. Afterwards, I pre-
tended to be asleep whenever she came into the ward, and hoped
that I would never have to speak to her again. The next day, to
my surprise and delight, she sent me a love letter.

Another regular visitor was an illiterate Tamil from Southern
India called Das, who came to mop up the wards and sweep with

his short broom made of coconut palm-leaf stems. He spoke virtually no English and I no Tamil, so communication was not easy. But every morning he came up to my bed with an expression of enquiring concern on his weathered face, a posy of flowers in his hand. I would smile to signify that I was feeling all right, whereupon he would put the flowers in a jar by my bed, removing the bunch that he had brought the previous day. These were not expensive flowers from a florist, but simple country flowers that he had picked by the side of the path on his way to work. He went barefoot, his clothes tattered and torn, and was the perfect example of the Asian at whom most Westerners usually shout, while thanking the Almighty that they were not born Asian. Yet his was the gift that I treasured most of all.

One day, when this little ritual was over, I reached for my wallet, without stopping to think, and pulled out a ten Malay dollar note. Such a sum must have represented many weeks' wages. But when I motioned to him to take it, tears welled in his eyes. 'No, no, Sahib,' he kept repeating, and I quickly stuffed the note back into my wallet, feeling like a heel. When he returned the following morning, he looked unsure of himself. A large bunch of orchids stood by my bed, brought by a visitor the previous evening. I winked at him; he beamed at me, whipped the dignified orchids away, put in their stead his motley bunch of marigolds, hibiscus, and frangipani and went on his way, mopping and sweeping up the ward, humming to himself.

I stayed in Penang hospital for nearly three months. In fact, they could have discharged me after a month, for the disease had come and gone. What I had to cope with now were the after-effects, and to learn to readjust to my new circumstances. This I knew would require not only time, but the facilities of a specialist rehabilitation department, which a general hospital like that in Penang did not possess.

Meantime, others were busy behind the scenes; every two or three days I had letters from home, with news of enquiries that they had been making. 'We've found that the Royal Orthopaedic hospital at Stanmore would be one of the best to go to after your return. It's on the outskirts of London so we'll be able to come and see you regularly. The difficulty is to get you back here, as obviously you are in no position to travel by regular ship or plane. But don't worry, we're trying to get you taken back in a military plane or troopship, equipped with a casualty ward. Everybody is being so helpful and understanding, which is heartwarming! So all is in good hands,' my mother wrote.

As all this was obviously going to take time, the doctors felt I should be transferred to Singapore. 'It's important that you should start as soon as possible on the physiotherapy treatment,' Victor said. 'There are facilities for this in Singapore, which is also the place to be when military ambulance-planes and troopships are leaving for England. Penang is an out of the way place with few facilities in this respect.' Sad as I was to part with all those friends, so remarkably good and trusty, I agreed and the arrangements for my transfer were duly made. When I was told one evening that I was to leave next day in an ordinary passenger plane seat, I was excited – and frightened. Half my body was paralysed; how was I going to cope? I was going to have to readjust from scratch – to learn all over again how to walk, how to feed and dress myself, how to use the lavatory, all the hundred and one things of daily life which normally one takes for granted. When a male attendant dressed me, I noticed with dismay that my trousers were much too large around the middle, owing to my wasted muscles. As I was lifted onto the stretcher, I clutched grimly at the waist band. The cage was still around me, firmer and more permanent than ever; but at least I was leaving alive.

Six of the nurses, including Li, came along in the ambulance to see me off. 'You must come back to Penang some day,' somebody was saying, a trifle self-consciously. 'It's got so much, beautiful beaches, scenery, restaurants. They say the snake-temple is unique!' I looked up at Nurse Li, who was trying hard to smile. 'Where I'm concerned you forget the most important attraction,' I said. I felt my throat tighten as I kept glancing furtively at her. 'The human kindness, love and generosity that you've all shown me. Yes, God willing, I'll be back some day. But it won't be because of the beaches or even the snake-temple!'

I realized, as I watched the trees flit past the window, that I had passed the most significant crossroads of my life, a crossroads that related not only to my body, but more subtly and significantly to my mind, deeply affecting my attitude towards other human beings. What I had experienced in Penang had brought a new dimension to the meaning of love and brotherhood of man.

When we arrived at the airport, the bustle left no time for

more than a quick handshake, but one of the nurses managed to throw a garland of orchids over my neck, while another pressed a box of chocolates on the stretcher beside me. 'Take care . . . I'll be thinking of you,' murmured Nurse Li as she gave me a quick kiss on the cheek. We weaved our way quickly through the throng of passengers checking in, and on to the tarmac where the Dakota was waiting. I felt acutely self-conscious, as if everyone was staring at me out of pity or curiosity. My nervousness was increased by the glamorous stewardess. 'Would you like some magazines?' she asked, smiling a little too intensely.

'Thank you,' I replied, feeling that I might collapse like a pack of cards at any moment.

'Can I fetch you a drink?' No doubt she had noticed that I was sweating profusely.

'No. No, thank you.' I replied, rather hastily. The thought of having to ask such a pretty girl for the urine bottle made me shudder.

As the other passengers climbed aboard, I hid my self-consciousness behind the magazine. When the call sounded to fasten seat belts, I slid as far down the seat as I could, to prevent myself jack-knifing forward and hitting my head on the seat in front. As the plane roared down the runway, I half-sat, half-lay in my seat, with the seat-belt over my ribs, quietly thinking to myself that life was now fraught with strange little problems. No amount of prior theorizing was of much use. They just had to be coped with or adapted to as they arose.

'So far, so good,' I thought, watching the lushness of Malaya below. But then disaster struck. My magazine slid down, off my lap, until it lay, tantalizingly out of reach, at my neighbour's feet.

'Is this your paper?' he asked, rather coldly.

'Yes, ah, well, yes, it is,' I replied. 'But I wonder if you could pick it up for me?'

He frowned. Evidently he was not used to being asked to pick up magazines. Fortunately the stewardess appeared at that moment, and rescued us from this impasse. When she explained that I was an invalid, I blushed furiously, and he stammered his apologies.

'Oh, I do beg your pardon. Please forgive me. I, ah, didn't realize.'

Having handed me back the magazine, he enquired politely if

I would have a drink with him. I thought once more of the urine bottle. But I would have to jump this fence sometime, and sometime might as well be now. I accepted gratefully.

*

After a long drive through Singapore in the dusk, I was carried into a drab cubicle at the General Hospital. My spirits sank when I saw the cramped room, the high bare walls with their peeling paint and the small window that faced a brick wall, like the prison cell in Rzeszow. A nurse on the point of going off duty, bustled me into a pair of tatty striped hospital pyjamas, bade me a curt goodnight and left. The other two beds in the cubicle were empty. Suddenly, after all the excitement, I felt lonely and depressed.

Since I could not prop myself up in bed without help, I could not reach either the light switch or the bell. I was not only tired but hungry into the bargain; evidently I must have missed the hospital dinner, as no one came with food or a cup of tea. As the last of the daylight faded away, I realized that on top of everything else the room was infested with some sort of tropical earwigs, which were crawling all over me. They did not bite, but I lacked the means to shake them off. Flustered and miserable, I began to shout for help.

Eventually a nurse appeared, and I poured out the list of my miseries. Of course it was not her fault, but I am afraid that I complained bitterly. She fetched me a detective story, and left the light on. The next morning an angry British surgeon steamed in and told me off in no uncertain terms for having upset the staff. He was partly right, of course, but I couldn't help wondering if he had ever been on the receiving end, as helpless as I was.

To my relief, I was moved after a couple of days, to the Middleton Hospital, an isolation hospital with a specialized physiotherapy unit. The wards consisted of separate lightweight prefab buildings, their blinds and shutters opening directly onto pleasant lawns and trees. The atmosphere was friendly and relaxed; soon after I arrived, a nurse brought me a large cup of tea, and sat by my bed chatting, while I sipped it gratefully.

Three days after I was admitted I started on my exercises, which were far from relaxing. At first I had to stay in bed, trying to lift my head and shoulders, or to move my legs over a board smoothed down with talcum powder to offer the minimum of resistance. The exercises were supervised by Joan, a pretty twenty-four-year-old physiotherapist, who would concentrate on the exercises almost as hard as I, bending over the board, sweeping her golden hair impatiently from her tanned face.

'Come on Arthur,' she would call out, as I struggled, panting and sweating. 'Push a bit harder. Come on now, push. Push harder. NOW HOLD IT!' Dear Joan, of whom I grew very fond, was one of several British physiotherapists in Singapore who came in voluntarily almost every day to help. I would push away until I was red in the face, putting every ounce of concentration and effort into it, my eyes tightly closed, willing some flicker of movement to return. Every day Joan and I watched for this desperately; I believe that it was almost as important to her as it was to me.

In a case of paralysis such as mine, the essential object of physiotherapy is to develop the maximum power in the affected limbs. The secret of success lies in hard work, persevering with the exercises until blue in the face and pouring with sweat. Where one set of muscles has been knocked out, another set had to be encouraged to take its place. In a sense the exercises resemble those undertaken by the body-building fraternity, except that I was more concerned with primary movement than impressing the girls with my beautiful muscular physique. In cases like mine, where the physiotherapist had to deal with muscles that are entirely powerless or at best very weak, the most the patient can hope for is partial recovery, to build up in some muscles a degree of motion that might be of practical use in conjunction with crutches or other appliances.

The polio paralysis itself is caused by highly contagious viruses, which find their way into the spinal cord through the digestive system and blood stream and attack the so-called 'anterior horn cells'. These cells are essential for any body movement. Whenever a given bodily function is 'ordered' by the brain, these cells act as the transmitters, passing the message from the brain to the relevant muscles. Thus the extent and severity of polio-induced paralysis depends on the havoc wrought by the virus amongst the horn cells. Depending on the proportion destroyed, the paralysis may vary from something so negligible that the person concerned may never be aware that he has had polio, to complete loss of power and motion in all limbs. Thus when a limb becomes paralysed, it does not follow that the cause lies within. The situation is not unlike a man fumbling around in the dark after an electric light bulb has failed. He fits a new bulb, without success; when he tries the lights elsewhere, he finds the current is still on; it is not until he checks the power flex, the transmission, that he finds the cause of the trouble. But a new electric cable is easy to fit; unfortunately, the horn cells cannot be replaced. Once they are destroyed, that is that; unlike other types of cells they do not regenerate.

Unlike a broken back, another frequent cause of paralysis, polio leaves the individual concerned with sensation in the affected limbs. At times this can be unpleasant, for a limb over which control is lacking tends to get bashed about more often, as the bruises and scratches on my legs testified. Moreover, polio leaves the victim neither incontinent, a particularly unpleasant result of a broken back, nor impotent. I wish that I had known this when I was first admitted to hospital in Penang. Fearing the worst, I spent many dark hours of anguish, wondering if I had been made impotent, unable to pluck up courage to ask.

Although I sweated by the bucketful, the loss of muscle power in my legs and lower trunk was almost total. Days passed without so much as a twitch in my legs, and it seemed probable that they were going to stay that way, which was depressing.

Every few days the muscle charts were drawn up in the ward. This was a time of great anguish and excitement, more so than at any school examination. The power was graded from zero to five, with pluses and minuses, and each muscle or set of muscles was awarded its mark. Discreetly Joan never entered my leg muscles in front of me on the chart; but with the middle and upper part of my trunk, only partially affected, I would strain and heave until I was blue in the face, while she put her hand on the muscle to see how it tensed, pencil at the ready. 'Two plus for the biceps in your left arm.'

'No, Joan, please. At least a three.'

'All right. Try again.'

As I returned to my grunting, she would mark me down for a three minus, knowing how vital it was for my morale. A better mark on the muscles chart made my day, and Joan knew it. It felt like so much power regained, even if the power was only in the mind.

Three weeks after admission I 'graduated' to the small physio-

therapy department at the far end of the ward. Here were the
special beds, 'Guthrie Smiths', which look rather like four posters
with various cross-pieces on top with strings and pulleys attached.
The gadgets are designed so that any part of the body can be
exercised; any muscle power generated by the patient is offset by
a spring, which can be adjusted to give greater or lesser resistance
according to the strength of the muscle. This department was run
by Bah-chi, a jovial, somewhat plump Chinese physiotherapist.
His assistant was Nurse Rosario, an even fatter Christian Indian
in her late thirties, who combined an inexhaustible cheerfulness
with an impressive repertoire of mildly dirty jokes. Every Sunday
Nurse Rosario would hurry off to confession, so that on Mondays
she would be full of good resolutions. But by Wednesday she
would have shed them, and the ward would be echoing with her
squeals of laughter. The atmosphere achieved no less than the
physical therapy.

One day, a sleek Jaguar pulled up outside the ward. I watched
with interest as the chauffeur pulled a folded wheelchair out of
the boot. In a moment, a lanky Englishman with neatly trimmed
moustache, with the unmistakeable air of a British officer, came
wheeling himself into the ward, interrupting one of Nurse
Rosario's more enlightening stories. 'Legs' Seagroatt was a
regular outpatient; having completed his exercises, he stopped by
my bed for a chat. Since Legs was the first disabled person I came
to know after my own attack, I regarded him with a mixture of
curiosity and fellow-feeling. In his early forties, he had contracted
polio about six months before I had, and had lain in the bed I
now occupied. He had obviously been a great *bon viveur* and a keen
sportsman; he had taken the blow very hard, particularly as the
paralysis left him initially with little movement in his legs. I
welcomed his visits; he taught me a lot, passing on useful hints
about life in the hospital, as well as describing in detail the habits
of the two golden orioles outside the window. Every morning they
came very early and settled on the Durian tree, whose ripening
fruit pervaded the ward with a nauseating stench of putrefaction.
(Despite its atrocious smell, the Durian is a much appreciated
delicacy. As Bah-chi described it to me: 'Mr Talnowski, eating
Dulian is like eating delicious ice cleam in a stinking lavatoly.')

Legs represented a pointer, a practical example of what disability entailed and how I might have to cope with it. But this was

only valid up to a point, for Legs had not been so badly paralysed, and a lot of movement had returned to his legs in the first few weeks. All the same, the extent of his recuperation was encouraging, and I envied his range of movements. He could move virtually every muscle, even if he could not stand up unaided. To him this was a cause of much depression, while to me, it gave rise to envy. How deliriously happy I would be if I could move as he did! I remembered how, when I was in Djakarta only four months previously, an iron girder had fallen, missing my foot by inches. How relieved I had been at the time; a few inches to the left, and I would have lost a foot! I had shuddered at the thought. Now I lay in bed, envying a man who couldn't even stand.

But I shall always remember Legs for one invaluable piece of advice. Sitting in his wheelchair, he turned to me one day and said: 'Arthur, never be ashamed, when you feel particularly bitter, to have a good cry. It does help, you know.'

It was largely through Legs' example that I eventually plucked up courage to try my hand at a wheelchair. He made it look simple. I waited until after dinner, when there was least chance for my efforts to be observed, asked a nurse to help me into one of the chairs, and pushed off.

It was awful. It was unwieldy and cumbersome. I hated the beastly thing, not only because it seemed to set the final irrevocable seal on my infirmity, but because it was so infernally difficult to steer. Although I tried hard to master the various manoeuvres, wheeling myself between beds, around corners, reversing, braking, I just could not control the brute.

Eventually, as I was beginning to get the hang of it, the wheelchair struck a bed, one of its legs having got caught up between the folding footplates. I leaned forwards to push myself backwards, but my weakened back-muscles failed to hold me; I lost my balance and nose-dived onto the corner of the bed.

'Nurse,' I shouted in a panic, with little regard for those who were trying to sleep. 'Nurse, quickly. Please get me out of this.'

Back in bed, utterly depressed, I still had the feeling of being trapped. That night I slept fitfully, dreaming that the wheelchair had turned into an octopus that was dragging me slowly with tentacles of steel down into a dark abyss.

But the depression soon lifted. As in Penang, people began to drop in. One of the hospital doctors used to appear regularly with an armful of detective novels. I had never been too keen in the past on this kind of book, but now I read avidly and with pleasure. Another regular called was a French Jesuit missionary, who had spent many years in the remoter parts of China, until the Communists threw him out.

There was Caroline, too, whom I had known several years previously in England. Now Caroline suddenly turned up in Singapore, with books, and flowers, and above all, her charming company. But deep down I was torn between the pleasure of seeing her again, and resentment at my condition; in fact, I was scared lest she be motivated by pity. Feeling grotesque in bed, utterly vulnerable before this soft girl whom I used to know so well, I sought in vain for some scrap of condescension. I think that she sensed this; but she was always so delightfully and provocatively feminine that I could not help but feel a man again. In a sense, Caroline helped me far more than she can possibly have known. After all, rehabilitation embraces far more than equipment in a physiotherapy gymnasium; its real concern is with the subtleties of re-making the man. Largely as a result of the human warmth and support, from Caroline and from others, I have never grown to consider myself disabled. Just inconvenienced.

Douglas Seward was another of my 'regulars'. 'One of the nurses told me that you didn't have too many friends in these parts, so I came running!' Bowled over by the impetuous warmth of his manner, I mumbled my thanks, but he cut me short. 'Nonsense, my dear chap, nonsense!' he cried, slapping the bed, 'aren't we in this world to help one another? Here! Brought something to cheer you up!' He thrust a hand into his bag, pulling out three bottles of wine.

'This bed has lots of painful associations for me,' he continued more quietly. 'Before you, Legs, and before him, my own wife Vera. On top of everything she was pregnant at the time . . . ' Then his voice boomed again. 'We've got a beautiful son now!'

Douglas was a dynamo of effervescent faith and enthusiasm. When I got to know him better, I found out that he had endured some harrowing experiences in a Japanese prisoner of war camp. He was a director of a large firm of wine merchants in Malaya, and was happily married to the pretty and gentle Vera. Tragedy struck when Vera contracted polio, which left her paralysed roughly to the same extent as I. A lesser man might have succumbed: but not Douglas. Whenever I felt depressed by the extent of my own paralysis, by my abortive attempts in the wheelchair, or more generally at the mountainous problems that loomed over literally every step of my future life, I would lean on Douglas. Having faced similar problems with Vera, he knew the ropes. He would speak with such verve and conviction that he restored my spirits as if by magic.

Suspecting that what I really needed was a glimpse of the outside world again, Douglas suggested one day that the three of us might go out to dinner.

'But that's marvellous,' I replied. 'But I can't really manage a wheelchair yet. Anyway, I haven't got one.'

'Well, why don't we ask Legs if you can borrow his for the evening?'

Legs willingly agreed, and Douglas arrived punctually at seven o'clock to pick me up.

'Hello, Arthur,' he boomed, his voice echoing down the ward, 'all ready for the fray?'

Without waiting for a reply, he picked me up as if he were lifting a bride over the threshold, and carried me bodily to the car. Vera was already in the back, and was grinning mischievously at my worried expression.

'Don't worry,' she said, as he placed me gingerly in the front seat, 'he won't drop you.'

As we drove off through the busy streets of Singapore, my worries began to fade. Here I was, dressed in my own clothes, heading for a delicious meal at Johore, fifteen miles away. Things were beginning to look up, at last.

Parking as near the restaurant as possible, Douglas unfolded both wheelchairs from the boot, and brought them round to the side of the car. By the time he was ready to lift me out, a crowd of onlookers had assembled, staring dumbly at the spectacle. As in Penang they were there just to watch an unusual scene. Where so many people had come from, in a matter of seconds, I could not imagine. As an able-bodied man I had never given this familiar phenomenon a moment's thought.

But now I felt distressingly self-conscious, like an animal in the zoo. Douglas was still busy extricating Vera from the back of the car: there was only one thing for it, to get the hell out myself, under my own steam. 'Mind your legs please,' I shouted, charging at full speed ahead towards the restaurant entrance. By some miracle, I reached safety without colliding with anyone, and was inside with a silly grin on my face when the others caught up.

Fortunately Douglas had reserved a table, as the restaurant was pretty full. He steered each of us expertly in turn around the other diners, before sitting down himself. 'Here we come,' he cried, rubbing his hands in glee, as the waiter brought the two Peking Ducks, roasted whole, the flesh cut but still left on the bone. With a bottle of Chinese wine to wash it down, the prospect was out of this world. For the first time I was eating at a table again like anyone else. The only trouble came when I leaned forward to pop a forkful into my mouth; owing to the muscle wastage, my whole body fell forward, and I had to reach out with both hands to stop my nose from banging the plate. Which left me no hands free for knife and fork. Realizing my predicament, Douglas passed me a large napkin, suggesting that I tuck it under my chin, and sit well back in the chair. This worked fine, even if it meant cutting everything up at a distance. Otherwise, we had no trouble; no one took any notice of us, and it was wonderful to feel 'one of the crowd' again. Normality seems so trite until you are deprived of it in some way.

Shortly after this memorable evening, a heart-warming letter arrived from my mother. So long as the fare was paid, the army were willing to bring me back home aboard a troopship. I was to wait for my sailing date to be confirmed. Thanks to a recent experience at the Middleton Hospital, I was keen to be on my way. A new Chinese doctor had joined the hospital staff, hotfoot from taking his final exams in England. From the moment he saw me, I sensed that he disliked me intensely, for no better reason than the fact that I was European. In itself, this neither surprised nor worried me; I knew from my Asian friends in London that most Asians find our Western way of life hypocritical, grasping and unsociable; often their initial friendliness turns to rancour as a result of the snooty and frequently insolent manner in which they are treated because of their race or colour. But I was taken aback when, towards the end of his rounds one evening, this doctor returned to my bed. 'It's high time you were discharged,' he said, without preamble. 'Medicine has done all it can for you. You are not sick any more.'

I stared at him speechlessly as he turned on his heel and walked out of the ward. I had done nothing to provoke such an outburst, except to ask the nurse for the inevitable, humiliating enema. But of course he was absolutely right, even if I had never thought of it that way. I was as helpless as a babe in arms, but I was not sick any more.

Mercifully the message came shortly afterwards, that I would be sailing in a week. When the ambulance arrived to take me to the troopship *Nevassa*, I could not help feeling a twinge of sadness. So much warmth and kindness had been lavished on me, both in Penang and Singapore; now I was lucky enough to be going home, not only to a family who would welcome me back with a warmth that only families can offer, but to further specialist treatment in English hospitals. As I drove for the last time through Singapore, I couldn't help noticing the beggars and cripples in the streets. Most Westerners who travel in Asia are appalled when they confront them for the first time. But after a while they become hardened to the outstretched palm, to the bundles of human wretchedness shuffling along the sidewalk, often with hideous deformities crying out for surgery or specialist treatment. I confess that before I contracted polio myself, I had developed a degree of philosophical resignation. The misery appeared so widespread, so utterly hopeless, that gradually I began to defer to it, trying not to think too hard of something that seemed irremediable.

Now everything had changed. When I thought of what lay ahead for me, I couldn't but help thinking of what would happen to them, still shuffling along the same street, mute, defenceless, hopeless and unloved. How do *they* feel when the doctor comes along and says that medicine has done all it can for them, and that they must go? Come to that, what proportion ever see a doctor at all? It seemed almost unfair that just because I was born in a different country, I should be spared.

When the ship docked at Colombo, I propped myself up in my bunk to see the palm trees out of the porthole. As I lay there, with the bustle and pungent odour of an Asian street wafting in, I wondered wistfully if I would ever set eyes on a palm tree again. It seemed unlikely, and the thought depressed me. Yet I was going home, which in itself implied a debt to humanity, and my fellow-sufferers in particular. Sometime, somehow I would do something about that debt, and the thought raised my spirits again.

I had never taken a bath, in an ordinary tub, since I caught polio. Whenever the nurses gave me a 'blanket bath' in bed, I longed to be back in a full-size tub, for a long, hot soak. As the ship neared Portsmouth, the corporal physiotherapist in the sick bay, who had been giving me exercises every day, decided that the time had come for me to try the tub again. Lifting me bodily from my bunk, he carried me to the bathroom, and eased me into the steam. While I rejoiced in the sensation of the hot water again, I held on grimly to the sides of the bath so as not to slip under. 'You O.K.?' he asked. 'Mmm.' 'Fine. I'll just go and get a towel. Won't be a sec!' But the ship rolled again, and I lost my grip on the wet enamel, sliding helplessly beneath the waves.

'Help, Corporal, help!' I gurgled, fighting for air.

Fortunately he had not gone far, and came leaping to the rescue.

'Don't worry, old son,' he said, 'you'll learn in time.'

We reached Portsmouth late that evening, nearly three weeks after leaving Singapore. I was lying in my bunk, clean and scrubbed, watching a bit of jetty I could see through the port-hole, when one of the ship's officers came in with a grim face.

'Sorry, but no one can go ashore until Customs have cleared us in the morning.'

I was bitterly disappointed, especially since my mother had written to say that they would meet the ship. But just as I was dozing off, at about ten o'clock, the officer returned once more and tapped me on the shoulder.

'Your parents are here,' he said, smiling broadly. 'But don't be too long, or we'll be in trouble with the Customs!'

CHAPTER 6

A Goal in Life

*

THAT evening, the family reunion aboard the *Nevassa* turned out to be a bitter-sweet affair. Naturally we were delighted to be together again, but after they had left me that evening, I couldn't help sensing that it had been a sad shock for them to see me so helpless, however bravely they had tried to disguise their feelings.

Next morning, I thanked and said good-bye to all those I had got to know aboard the *Nevassa*; it was still early when Tadeusz picked me up off my stretcher on the pier and placed me on the rear seat of the car, beside my mother. 'Back in Queensborough Terrace in time for lunch,' he said. But we soon realized that the drive was going to take much longer than he expected, for anything but the gentlest of braking made me lunge forward. Realizing how disconcerting such effects of paralysis must be, particularly to parents, I felt ill at ease and kept wondering to myself whether they would not have been saved much anguish had I gone directly to hospital.

When Tadeusz carried me up the stairs to their drawing-room on the first floor, I felt a rush of sadness at being carried up these stairs I must have run up and down thousands of times with such natural ease. He had some difficulty in squeezing through the narrow door with me in his arms, afraid to hurt my legs dangling in the way. While my mother held my legs, he managed it slowly and placed me as gingerly as an egg into the waiting armchair. After that the tension, which we were all desperately trying to hide under a smokescreen of happy banter, relaxed a little and we talked for hours.

My mother had prepared *borsch*, of which she knew I was very fond, and some other favourite dishes. I was only too delighted to get away for a change from the routine of hospital life, with its clockwork events of temperature-taking, washing, meals, and doctors' rounds. Yet I looked forward, in a sense, to my return to hospital the following day, since problems continued to crop up, and I could see that these distressed my mother. Sitting in an armchair, I couldn't lean forward more than an inch for fear of nose-diving into the borsch; Tadeusz resolved this by placing a board across the armchair. He had already thought of buying a urine-bottle which solved another likely difficulty, but then he asked me whether I wanted to go to the lavatory: 'No problem, I'll carry you down.' 'No, no, I don't need to,' I said quickly. Whereupon my mother whispered something, and Tadeusz said he was popping out to get some cigarettes. He soon returned with a bed-pan, having guessed that I was unable to sit on a lavatory seat without high arm-rests to steady myself. I bit my lip, blushing furiously. 'Oh, thank you, Tadeusz, but really, I don't need it for the moment.' Fortunately this was true. Later, when he carried me from the armchair to bed, I found that I couldn't move or turn in bed without a 'bed-cradle' to take the weight of the bed-covers off my legs. Resourceful as ever, he soon improvised one with cushions and the back of a chair.

I was taken first to a hospital in Neasden, in North London, where a rather awe-inspiring physiotherapist called Miss Atkins gave me exercises every day. Miss Atkins was an efficient physiotherapist, and I felt that life was looking up. The hospital was within easy distance of home, so my parents were able to visit me regularly.

I still hoped for a measure of recovery in my legs. While I had been travelling on the *Nevassa*, I had felt an almost imperceptible movement of a tendon under my right knee and had yelled for the corporal. The poor man had come running at the double, fearing the worst. 'Look! I've got a flicker, a real flicker!' Puzzled faces looked in while the corporal bent over to scrutinize my knee. 'Well, I don't know,' he said slowly, 'You've certainly come up in goose flesh with the excitement!'

At Neasden another flicker developed, this time in my left foot. Once again I screamed for joy. 'Miss Atkins,' I cried, 'if that flicker grows any stronger, I'll kiss you on both cheeks.' 'I wouldn't if I were you,' she replied primly. 'Let's just concentrate on the exercises and see how it develops.'

I had not been at Neasden for more than two weeks before a bed became available at the Royal Orthopaedic Hospital, Stanmore. This was sooner than we had dared hope, since Stanmore is acknowledged to be one of the best orthopaedic hospitals in the world, and so there is always a waiting list for admission. When we arrived on a wet and blustery October morning, I found that, like the Middleton in Singapore, it was situated in open country, with single-storied wards separated from each other by neat lawns. My own ward was about four hundred yards from the physiotherapy unit, connected to it by a tarmac path. Every morning and afternoon, we would proceed in convoy down this path for our exercises, returning to the ward for meals. For the first week or so, one of the male nurses pushed my wheelchair; but my arms quickly became strong enough to propel myself.

Initially much of the physiotherapy I had, was on the familiar Guthrie Smith beds, suspended on slings and springs. But I graduated in time to the specially equipped swimming pool. With splints bandaged to the back of my legs, I would be helped into the water, which was heated to blood temperature. Then, holding on for dear life to the parallel bars which stretched the full length of the pool, I would walk very, very slowly up and down, helped by the buoyancy of the water, thankful to be in a vertical position once more.

When I had progressed a little in the pool, I was fitted with long braces, so that I could try 'ambulating' between parallel bars in the gym. By this time, I topped ten stone on the scale, and so two physiotherapists had to heave me up from my wheelchair, one pulling from the front, the other pushing from the rear. As I stood on dry land for the first time in eight months, I realized that I had grown accustomed to viewing life from wheelchair level. I felt lost with the floor miles away below me.

'Tell us if you feel giddy.' But I just smiled. To be standing again had reduced me to silence.

When I had managed two trips up and down the bars, I was all in favour of trying crutches, even though I was still panting with the exertion and dripping with sweat. It took me three weeks of hard practice between the bars before they would allow me to try crutches. When the time came, I set off across the forty or so feet of the gym, and reached the far side in ten minutes flat, at an average speed of four feet a minute, which almost equalled the dizzy speed of a garden snail. This, admittedly, was counting half a dozen stumbles; there would have been many more had I not been firmly gripped around the waist by the charming Miss Rice, walking Arab-fashion behind me. 'I hope I'll see the day when you'll be walking by my side,' I teased her and she had the grace to blush.

With practice, I even managed to walk a little on the asphalt paths outside. But the four hundred yards back to the ward took me forty minutes flat. Despite the grim determination with which I did the prescribed exercises, the two twitches that I had experienced never developed into useful movements. Naturally I was disappointed, since the paralysis in the lower part of my trunk, buttocks, abdominal muscles and lower back remained to all intents total. If you are paralysed in the legs, but still have use of these muscles higher up, you can work up a fair gait on crutches by hitching up one leg after another, and balance yourself into the bargain. But without them, as I was, walking on crutches is an extremely precarious procedure, 'like a card balancing on its edge,' as I described it at the time. Any obstacle, a step, a slight bump in the ground, a stone, a closed door, let alone getting up from a chair or trying to carry something when the hands are fully engaged in gripping the crutches, poses a problem that is often insuperable without help. After a full year of trying this, and goodness knows how many tumbles, I resigned myself to the prospect of relying entirely on the wheelchair in future. Parallel bars are now reserved for exercise purposes, to limber up occasionally, and to counter heart disease, kidney trouble and other health hazards to which the wheelchair bound are prone.

Since we spent most of our day in a department swarming with physiotherapists and doctors, we soon became experts at the technical names and functions of every muscle in the human body. Much of our talk was peppered with these terms. 'Ah, you should have seen my right quod today,' one of my fellow patients would say, fondly caressing his thigh. 'Lucky you,' I would sigh, 'I haven't even got a flicker in my gluts.' But the most revealing comment about these buttock muscles, which are essential for walking and balancing, came from Sarah, a peroxide blonde in her late thirties. Sarah was a former lady of easy virtue; her confinement to a wheelchair had certainly not robbed her of her loud and robust sense of humour. 'Arf me life I worked wiv me arse, luv,' she confided to me one day, 'but I never realized all its uses!'

Since there was always a long queue for admission to Stanmore, no patient was kept for longer than about three months, if possible. So I found myself celebrating the New Year of 1959 with another move, this time to a hospital at Hendon. No notable improvement had occurred in my affected muscles, and I was realistic enough by this stage to have given up hope that it ever would; but I had nevertheless made considerable improvement in other directions. I could now dress myself, use the lavatory, eat at a table without undue difficulty, get in and out of the bed or the bathtub by myself, and wheel myself for virtually any distance. Also, after eight months of continual humiliation, my digestion was functioning properly once more.

The atmosphere at Hendon was no less efficient, but rather more subdued. The polio patients were housed in a large ward divided by an entrance hall into male and female sections. This more intimate arrangement enabled patients to get to know one another more easily. Up till now, virtually all the fellow-sufferers with whom I had come into contact had been paralysed to a lesser extent than I, which left me with a wistful sensation of being at the end of the line. Now I met three or four who were far worse off, and saw the situation from the other side. Often I felt that they were secretly nursing that familiar feeling of envy that I had experienced so often.

Michael Prestige lay in the bed opposite mine. The previous summer, Michael had used his vacation from Oxford to hitch-hike to Turkey, where he had contracted polio. It had affected him from the waist upwards, almost exactly the reverse to my own case. His arms hung limp and useless by his stooped body, which was reduced to little more than skin and bone. For months he had been confined to an iron lung; though he was free of it now, he could only breathe with difficulty, and gulped air like a stranded fish. Often, out of the corner of my eye, I watched him staring into space in utter despair.

Another whom I got to know well was Joan, a pretty twenty-four-year-old, who was married, and had two children. She had been affected by polio to more or less the same extent as I had been, and was confined to a wheelchair. One day, when we were resting in the gym, she told me about her husband, who worked in a factory, and their deteriorating relationship. It seemed that he had come to see her regularly at first. But after a time it had started to 'get him down,' as he had put it and the frequency of the visits dropped off. 'When he realized that I may never walk again, he walked out on me,' she said, her voice trailing. I waited in silence for the sequel which came soon enough. 'He's living with another woman now.'

To cheer her up, I asked about the children. They were in an institution, but occasionally she took them home at weekends. The neighbours were kind and helpful. 'But it's awfully difficult to look after children when you're in a wheelchair,' she said. 'I pulled a pan of boiling water off the stove the last time I tried cooking, and scalded myself pretty badly.'

Despite all these trials, Joan managed to put a brave face on things. Often we used to 'fight' each other from wheelchairs in the gym, to the amusement of staff and other patients. Yet, deep down, Joan was insecure and afraid, as well she might be. 'You know, Arthur,' she said one day, 'we are really a race apart.' I shall never forget the poignancy on her face.

The most severely crippled patient was Alan, whose bed stood next to mine. A year previously, having just completed a technical course, he had been on the point of emigrating to Australia with his wife and two young children, when he was struck down with polio. He was left paralysed from toe to head; even his neck was affected, so that his head would slump onto his chest if he moved it too far forward. He could just about breathe without help; otherwise he was completely dependent – he had to be fed, washed, helped with all bodily needs, even to shift his position in bed. I remember thinking to myself that if I were in Alan's position, I would take steps to do away with myself. With a sudden shock, I realized that even if Alan was thinking along these lines, there was nothing he could do about it.

Alan was particularly vulnerable when it came to visiting hour. We would all watch the glass doors from the entrance hall as the witching hour approached; it was vitally important that a visitor should be on time, a matter out of all proportion to the few minutes involved. Somehow it demonstrated they cared. On the dot of 7.30 in the evening, the glass doors would be opened by a nurse, and a horde of grinning Goths would stream in, bearing their booty in the form of flowers, chocolates, books, fruit and other goodies.

Day after day, Alan's eyes would stay riveted on those wretched doors, long after the rest had streamed in. Five, ten, even fifteen minutes would pass, with the hubbub of chatter bubbling around

him, his face growing sadder with each minute, tears welling in
his eyes. I remember once when his wife appeared about twenty
minutes late, how desperately he tried to wipe the tears against
his pillow, but couldn't quite make it.

Maybe because so much was stacked against him, Alan's
courage had a deep and lasting effect on me. Propped up on his
pillows, with an electric typewriter strapped to a table across his
lap, he spent a good part of the day with a long rubber-tipped rod
clamped between his teeth, teaching himself to type.

At first Miss Perry, the occupational therapist, would sit by his
side, both of them frowning in concentration as Alan tried to
master the awkward technique. But in time, with patience and
determination, he worked up a fair speed.

One evening, after Miss Perry had gone home, Alan asked the
staff-nurse for his typewriter and stick. 'I'm going to write a
letter. To Miss Perry. My first letter,' he confided to me. The
typewriter tapped surprisingly fast. 'Come and see how it reads,'
he eventually asked me. 'Dear Miss Perry,' I read, 'Writing this
letter is the first positive thing I've been able to do in the nineteen
months since I got polio. Up till now it has just been exercises of
whatever there is left in me to exercise. Now this letter is going to
be dropped in a post-box, stamped and addressed, to join the
thousands of other normal letters. I feel that by this token I too
in some small way shall join the ranks of normal people; this
letter opens before me the prospect of leading a life not entirely
that of a vegetable, even of being able to work and help support
my family. Dear Miss Perry, I owe this to you.'

I was finally discharged from Hendon in May 1959, a little
over a year after I contracted polio. I left with mixed emotions.

The National Health Service has often been criticized in the
press and among sections of the public, for poor care, little
personal attention, slapdash methods, the soullessness of an unwieldy processing machinery, and such like. Such criticisms
anger me, for I find them carping or exaggerated. In the first
place, I was extremely glad and relieved to have been on the
National Health Scheme, like any other member of the British
public and to have contributed my weekly stamp. I owe a great
deal to this splendid and humane scheme – neither family
resources nor any standard insurance policy would have met the
costs of such a protracted period of hospitalization.

Secondly, if prolonged stay, and the intimate experiences of several hospitals and of literally hundreds of doctors, administrative staff, physiotherapists, nurses, attendants, etc., qualifies me to express an opinion, then I hasten to say that I met only with kindliness, care, and helpfulness beyond the call of duty, in varying degrees perhaps, but amongst all those with whom I came into contact.

Indeed I had made many friends, both amongst staff and patients. But the inevitable hothouse atmosphere of infirmity was beginning to get me down; when everything revolves around disability, every conversation, all the toings and froings in a busy ward for twenty-four hours of the day, the infirmity is liable to invade the subconscious to the exclusion of everything else. If I may digress for a moment, I believe that this question of how a patient can retain his ego unwarped by his physical affliction is something of which hospitals should be more aware. Precious little time was devoted, when I passed through the rehabilitation wards, to the psychological impact of disability.

I am glad to hear nowadays that the practice of herding the disabled together for special outings or in clubs has been markedly reduced. This had always struck me as unhealthy, as a common disability is a poor link to bring people together, coming a bad second to shared interests and activities. Of course there are exceptions, such as with the elderly disabled who sometimes prefer to find a kind of security among those similarly afflicted; or with those so severely crippled and permanently hospitalized, where outings can only be organized in practice on a group basis; or again for purposes of sport, a growing outlet, in which great strides have been made recently, particularly in Britain, where a similar handicap, brings both interest and equality to the game. But otherwise I felt this should be avoided.

I might mention in passing another habit which I used to find distressing, which I understand is still current. I refer to the way in which hospital staff sometimes refer to patients, not by name, but by their illness. I remember how one of the porters at Hendon always referred to me as 'The Polio'. It so happened that he had a nasty wart on his neck, so one day I retaliated by calling him 'The Wart', which made him very angry indeed. 'But it's fair enough,' I said. 'Anyway, polio is more serious than warts, isn't it?' That stopped him in his tracks. 'I'd never thought of it that way,' he replied lamely. However, I would like to stress that these were minor irritants or pinpricks, which in no way detracted from the sympathy, help and devotion which was lavished on us by the entire staffs, from surgeons down to attendants. Confronted by such personal disasters we felt acutely insecure and vulnerable, and appreciated such support and encouragement all the more gratefully.

Although technically discharged, I had not quite finished with hospitals. The doctors felt that there was still some scope for improvement, and so I became an outpatient, first at the Orthopaedic Hospital in Great Portland Street, and then, in August, at the Camden Road Rehabilitation Centre. Every morning, rain or shine, I waited by the door of my home in Queensborough Terrace for the ambulance 'bus', which would come lumbering down the street. Harry, the driver, would lift me on board from my wheelchair and we'd rumble off.

When I arrived on my first morning, I was immediately struck by the brisk, efficient atmosphere. Prominent in the large gym was the rear half of a London double-decker bus, complete with stairs and seats, with patients practising on crutches how to get in and out. 'We discharge you from here in one of two ways,' the physiotherapist said as he showed me around. 'Either as fit as you're ever likely to be, or on a stretcher.' This was not a threat so much as a warning – don't expect any mollycoddling. Most of the staff were male, many of them ex-Royal Air Force sergeants, which accounted for the parade ground atmosphere.

We were issued with standard kit of blue shorts, singlet and blue windcheater, and started the day with half an hour of gymnastics done to music. As the loudspeakers blared tunes like the 'Blue Danube', 'Roaming in the Gloaming', 'Rock around the Clock', Paul, one of the physiotherapists, stood facing us, bursting with health and vitality, and would bawl: 'In, out, in, out, up, down, up, down, stretch and stretch,' as he performed various jerks with feline ease to the rhythm of the music, while forty odd patients puffed and groaned, striving to follow suit.

Those of us who could not stand were not excused, and we drilled sitting in chairs or from our wheelchairs. After this, we were each assigned, according to our condition, to different classes, which lasted for three quarters of an hour each, and were mostly group exercises done against the clock: mat exercises, crutch walking, weight lifting, getting up steps with the help of crutch and banister, and so on.

They were great believers in the 'Second Wind' theory. According to this, you had to perform a given exercise until you were absolutely exhausted; you then had to pick yourself up and do it again, because the real benefit was derived from the 'extra'. I shall never forget those extras. With felt pads fixed to my hands and knees, I had to crawl round and round the gym, 'polishing the floor'. This not only brought into play just about every muscle that I had left, but was excellent for the balance. To begin with, I could only manage about two rounds before collapsing with exhaustion; then, after resting awhile, I could just manage a third. But after a fortnight, I could manage five rounds before I collapsed, and by the time I left Camden Road, was quite capable of forty or even fifty non-stop. After about thirty, I could hardly see where I was going, but kept going round and round, doggedly following the trail of my own sweat, oblivious to everything and everybody except my aching muscles that screamed for mercy and the glistening, endless trail in front of me.

To propel a wheelchair for any distance (or to use crutches) requires considerable strength in the arms and in the upper part of the body. To help develop this, I used to perform a cycle of press-ups, weight-lifting and spring-pulling, six different exercises in all repeated ten times over, all against the clock. At first, I just managed two cycles at a session, averaging ten minutes each. But towards the end of my time there, I achieved twelve, at four minutes a cycle, in spite of the number of springs and dumb-bells being increased. In addition to giving me the necessary muscle power, these exercises had the effect of broadening my shoulders so that all my jackets began to split at the seams. No effort was spared to help restore confidence and self-reliance. To maximize our chances of mobility, all wheelchair patients were given regular driving lessons in the little blue invalid carriages, or invacars, provided to those who can't do without such aid by the Ministry of Health.

Much progress has been made in developing these cars since the days of the manually-propelled contraptions, open to all weathers, which invalids had to use in pre-war times. Nowadays these cars are entirely covered and take a folded wheelchair. The two-stroke engine at the back is capable of speeds of up to forty-eight mph.

The controls are entirely manual: a kind of joy-stick for the left hand, which you pull towards you to turn left, away for the other direction, and down to brake; the throttle is in the grip, and is twisted in motor cycle fashion, with the clutch lever next to it. This leaves the right hand free for the gears, four forward, one backward, and the handbrake.

When my invacar had been delivered ex-factory, shining brightly and smelling faintly of paint and newness, my first reaction was of alarm mixed with a sense of exhilaration. For eighteen months I had been reduced to virtual immobility, or at best to pottering about in a wheelchair. Now I was to drive a car on open roads, and master an entirely novel system of controls without an instructor sitting by my side.

Paul showed me the controls. 'Have you driven before?' 'Yes, ordinary cars.' 'Fine! You'll soon get the hang of it. Don't exceed five mph and leave her in the first gear to begin with.'

I found it was the steering and braking that were most awkward to master at first. Several times I bumped the kerb, but without damage thanks to the low speed. Some ten lessons later I was using all four gears and driving along busy streets, though still restricting myself to twenty-five mph. A few days before leaving Camden Road, I felt confident enough to drive home along a wide open street at top speed. The needle touched forty-seven mph before I stopped at traffic lights. To my horror a policeman walked up to me: 'You've been speeding!' I looked at him with feigned innocence. 'In one of these things, Constable? It's probably all the noise it makes that gave you that impression!' 'All right,' he grinned, 'but remember this is London, not Brands Hatch.'

The great day dawned on the 28th of October 1959, when I said good-bye at last to hospitals and official rehabilitation. It took me over an hour to take leave of all the patients I had got to know and particularly to the staff, thanking them wholeheartedly. 'Never lose your sergeant-major's touch, Paul,' I said squeezing his hand so hard that he winced. 'I wouldn't have got anywhere near to my present degree of mobility without it!' When I got into my new invacar, I folded my wheelchair and lifted it in after me as easily as if it were a toy; despite my useless legs, I felt fit as never before. I could swing myself on my arms in and out of the car as readily as any monkey up in the trees. With a smile I recalled the time I slid under in the bathtub on the *Nevassa* when the corporal had left me for a minute. 'You'll learn one day', he had said; in my despair I had almost doubted him.

But as I weaved in and out of the London traffic, bursting with my new-found confidence, I reflected that when all was said and done, Camden Road had benefited me more than any of the others. The atmosphere of thrusting activity had been a tonic, like a bucketful of cold water, dispelling the cobwebs of the sickroom, spring-cleaning my whole attitude until it shone once more with a healthy aggression. I felt confident that I could lick anything now that the disability might put in my path.

As I settled back into the routine at home, I found that with ingenuity I could do a surprising number of the odd jobs about the house, taking care of correspondence, accounts, small electrical repairs and so on. But we all knew that this kind of thing would not serve as a permanent outlet for my time and energy. While I busied myself over the ledger, my mind was back in Asia, amongst the disabled there, most of them living in conditions that would make the imagination boggle.

When I made my way to the various libraries, I discovered with some surprise that this subject had never been investigated properly. Missionaries and doctors, who had spent their whole working lives amongst the needy, had described their own experiences, and the area that they had known, in depth; virtually none of the Western visitors who had taken an interest had penetrated beyond the larger cities, with their showpiece hospitals. Admittedly this should not have come as too much of a surprise, considering that an accurate census of the disabled has yet to be carried out in Great Britain, and their conditions have not been investigated thoroughly in most European countries. But from my experience, I knew that such reports about conditions in the East were unlikely to reflect prevailing conditions in the area as a whole, since four Asians out of five live in villages, and many have never even heard of the nearest town, let alone visited the hospital there if they were sick.

One evening I was sitting by the gas-fire in my room, reading one of those innumerable travel books on India. The author described the rows of crippled beggars squatting on the steps leading to the holy river Ganges in Benares – I had seen them myself when I visited that city. He went on to refer to the per-vasiveness of the problem of physical disability and begging in most countries of Southern Asia, and wound up by quoting an official estimate putting the total of disabled in Asia at over fifty million. 'Fifty million!' I said aloud; 'but that's the total population of Great Britain!'

At the back of my mind there flashed the picture of a disabled leper I had once seen in front of a small town railway station in Northern India. His nose and upper lip had literally rotted away, his bulging eyes were almost blinded with bloodshot scales. His fingerless arms and legs were twisted and contracted so that he could only shuffle along in a permanently half-crouched, half-prostrated position; his trunk was deformed, a patchwork of tattered clothes and suppurating, fly-ridden sores. People gave him a wide berth, occasionally throwing him scraps of food which he munched hungrily. I had never imagined such wretchedness to be possible. Admittedly this was a particularly ghastly case. But when I thought of such misery being compounded fifty million times over, my mind boggled at the sheer horror of it.

'I'm determined to return to the East. To work for the handicapped.' My mother gazed at me with dismay. 'But how? . . . in your . . . ?' she stammered.

'Yes, I know. My wheelchair, the conditions out there, and so on.'

'How on earth would you manage yourself, let alone help others?' said Tadeusz.

'I believe I might be of use, precisely *because* of my disability and not despite it.'

'But you can't consider such a thing,' said my mother despairingly. 'After you got polio in Malaya, there were moments I feared I'd never see you again. Now you propose to return, and in this condition!'

The pause that followed was broken by Tadeusz.

'Arthur,' he said with a smile, 'I don't know whether to admire your courage or to scoff at the foolhardiness of the idea. You remind me of the moth which falls down on the table singed by the candle-light; the moment it picks itself up, it flies straight back into the flame.'

We all laughed, the tension was broken. 'Look!' I said, 'what I want to do will not be anything new, but a continuation of what I always wanted to do, what I went out there last time for – to contribute my own little bit, however humble, to the creation of a better understanding between East and West. My disability has merely given this a new twist, a change of gear on the same road. Perhaps it was God's way of giving me the means to realize my ambition better.' From their expressions I knew that their initial reaction was softening. I developed my ideas about a survey of the *real* conditions, mentioning the statistics and describing the lepers in Benares. 'When you see someone drowning, you don't stop to calculate how cold the water is. You just jump in.'

Secretly, without admitting it to my parents, I knew that maybe somewhere along this line there lay the answer to another of my problems: how to do something in return for all the kindness and help received during those long months of my own illness. Admittedly I had no professional qualifications for working amongst the disabled. I had no medical knowledge, other than having experienced rehabilitation at the receiving end; I wasn't a sociologist and lacked experience in survey work. Although I was now highly adept in getting around in my wheelchair and invacar, this hardly qualified me to take a trip into the Home Counties of England, let alone to brave the rough conditions of Asia.

To be sure, the cards were stacked pretty high against me. But on the other hand I possessed one priceless asset, which I kept coming back to: my own disability. I was in the same boat, which was bound to make contact work with doctors and patients that much easier.

'What would you use for money?' my stepfather asked.

'Well, I don't know,' I spluttered, 'I'll raise it somehow.'

'Well, you can always count on our support. But I still shudder at the thought of where all this might lead to,' my mother added, sighing.

By the time we went to bed that evening, the expedition had been born. Over the next few days, I began to shape the idea into a viable scheme. To have a sporting chance of success, the trip must be bold, imaginative and thoroughly planned. An overland expedition seemed to be the answer, taking in all the principal countries in Southern Asia, from Turkey to Japan. The more I thought about it, the more convinced I became that to make the survey realistic, I would have to cover the ground right across this vast and varied continent. Apart from anything else, it would be vital to find out how the three great religions of Islam, Buddhism and Hinduism affect the position of the handicapped within these societies. On the personal front, I would need a personal assistant, despite all that the hospitals had done for me, a Jack-of-all-trades, above all a good companion. I should have to travel with a driver and with any luck I might find someone prepared to rough it, who would also look after the vehicle. Some sort of tough, all-purpose car would be necessary. Of course my head began to buzz with ideas, the project literally swallowed me up so that I had no time or inclination to talk or think of anything else.

Fortunately, my family and most of my friends stood by me, cheering. Some, I guessed, did so because they didn't have the heart to disabuse me over something that mattered so intensely to me, rather than because they shared my conviction that the scheme would come up to scratch.

My first problem was to find a striking name for the expedition. After tossing any number of ideas around, I rejected 'Through Asia in a Wheelchair' in favour of 'The Unbeaten Track Expedition'. This seemed altogether more appropriate; as I sat in my room at home writing 'The Unbeaten Track Expedition' carefully on each of my new notebooks, I wondered how I should phrase my 'aims' for my prospectus. After burning a good deal of midnight oil, I eventually settled on the following:

1. (a) To assess in Southern Asia the plight of the disabled and then endeavour to bring further to the attention of the Western public the circumstances and needs of the infirm in Asia. (b) To provide a *vivid demonstration* to the widest possible range of handicapped and able-bodied people alike that a physical disability need not be an insurmountable obstacle to an active and useful life. (c) To raise funds for organizations active in the field of the disabled in Asia.
2. The low cost travel in Southern Asia. To compile and submit in book form information on the opportunities for travel on a low budget in Southern Asia in the conviction that such travel is an excellent medium for the promotion of cross-cultural education and goodwill. Also that it develops the young traveller's capacities and moral fibre.

Before I could publish my prospectus, and start trying to raise funds, I had an immense amount of detailed work and planning to do. Fortunately I was free to do this at home. I lived in a large bed-sit on the ground floor of the house. It had a wash-basin and gas ring, which made it self-contained and myself virtually self-sufficient. I immersed myself completely in my work. I seldom went out, except to buy food and on errands connected with the project. In their enthusiasm about the scheme, my parents helped me with money for basic needs.

Bearing in mind that I was hoping to cover some sixty thousand miles overland in the car alone, I estimated that we would be away for between eighteen months and two years. I read avidly about each country that we planned to visit, sallying forth every week or so in my car to visit the libraries at the India Office or the School of Oriental Studies, returning each time with another armful of specialized works. I studied social problems, agricultural conditions, anthropology, customs, volumes written by the 'Old Asia Hands' from the Empire days. Experience had taught me that people's attitudes and life in Asia was in a sense too organic and interrelated to lend itself to an exclusive, narrowly specialized study. I felt my contribution would be all the more valid if I continued, as before, to take an interest in other aspects of Asia; by taking a broader view of the scene, I would be better placed to find out how the matter of disability fitted into the general social framework.

The question of equipment was another subject that I had to study with the greatest of care. A fair amount of technical research was needed, as we could not afford to omit anything that might prove to be of real use, although this had to be balanced constantly against the problem of overall weight and bulk. In every case, it was not only a question of how many but which was the most suitable type or brand. What should a car repair kit include? Should spare springs be taken, despite their weight? We would encounter a wide variety of climatic conditions which meant that in addition I had to bear in mind toughness, ease of handling, insect protection and a host of other factors. In view of the constant shaking on Asian roads, I had to think of packing, how to minimize chafing, and the effects of dust and heat. I checked all available reports about road conditions, petrol stations and the distances between them, repair facilities (if any), and customs regulations.

The medical kit could well prove a matter of life or death. I discussed this with several doctors and also sallied forth to the Hospital for Tropical Diseases. They all lent themselves to my badgering with good grace and often showed great interest; eventually a list of sixty-four items was compiled, and in the process I learnt about what to prescribe for hook-worm, how to disinfect and dress wounds, how to diagnose typhus, or distinguish amoebic from bacillary dysentery.

Gradually all the information from manufacturers' brochures, books, answers to my postal queries, suggestions of friends and old Asia hands with relevant experience, the whole mass of information was all sifted and boiled down to items in my notebooks. Once I made absolutely sure of the suitability of any given item, I'd tick it off. By the time my brochure was ready, I had studied 458 books in connexion with the expedition; made a list of 628 different items of equipment to be taken; and calculated that, allowing for daily outgoings on food, lodging, petrol, oil, repairs, insurance, and contingencies, the Unbeaten Track Expedition needed £8,657.

'Impossible!' I cried, feverishly checking my arithmetic to see if I had made some appalling error. But the second, third and fourth tries all added up to the same figure. It seemed an awesome sum of money.

I soon discovered in my quest for backers that the number of British companies with an annual turnover of over ten million pounds ran into hundreds, probably thousands, that there were about eighty thousand charitable trusts in Britain alone. I simply could not approach them all. Obviously I had to be selective, to find out what sort of enterprise was likely to appeal to a given philanthropist, what types of activity the foundations and trusts were limited to sponsoring. Since I was keen to raise support from Europe and America as well as England, to give the expedition an international flavour, I studied the American Foundation Directory, which lists about a hundred thousand addresses, with the details of scope in each case. Having made my selection of trusts and foundations, I moved on to industry and commerce, only to find, of course, that there was no single reference work suitable for my purposes, let alone a book with the addresses of cheque-happy millionaires. But after ploughing for fifteen weeks through *Who's Who*, the American *Thomas Registrar of*

Manufacturers, various UN publications down to the classified telephone directories, I counted eleven thousand names and addresses in my file, from twelve countries. These were the hopefuls; if I failed to obtain the minimum backing from amongst this lot, my expedition would never get off the ground.

It was tantalizingly slow and vexing. I knew from the start that what I really needed was a prominent backer, or the promise of material support, to start the ball rolling. After all, it is only human, when receiving a letter soliciting funds, to wonder who is behind the appeal, who has agreed to sponsor the scheme, if anyone has already put money into it. But I had no backer, no sponsor and no funds, except a small sum in personal savings. I wrote to about thirty addresses at a time, enclosing the brochure, a map, and a personal letter in most cases, subtly slanted (or so I hoped) to catch the eye of the individual or firm concerned. Anxiously I awaited the replies to one batch before sending the next. Every morning I wheeled myself out to the top of the steps outside, to wait for the postman. He got to know me pretty well, as I sat hunched in my chair, biting my nails. 'Sorry, nothing today,' he would say. Or 'Three for you. And the best of luck!' I would spin round and hurry inside, hoping against hope that amongst the three envelopes my cherished backer would appear.

My constant friend and companion at this time was a grey squirrel called Scooby Doo. He had been caught by my sister Sophie on Putney Heath, on the outskirts of London, with one paw broken; we never discovered why. Sophie gave him to me when she was going for a holiday abroad. She found it hard to look after him, for Scooby would create havoc in her kitchen the moment her back was turned. After a while, Scooby became very tame, and his injury did not prevent him from scampering all over the furniture and running up and down the curtains. He was scrupulously clean, using his cage for lavatory purposes, and I well remember the day when he decided for the first time that he should sleep with me. Pointing his nose disdainfully at the armchair, he leaped into my bed as I was turning off the light; from that moment he always slept beside me, rolled up in a pyjama top.

His tastes were impeccable. He loved marrons glacé, pecan nuts, avocado pears, a small portion of caviar (on the one occasion he was offered it); best of all, on high days and holidays, he liked a drop of liqueur. He also loved salads, and the way our relationship developed can be gauged accurately from the question of who was allowed to eat which part of the lettuce. At first, there was no nonsense. I ate the heart, while he had the outside leaves. After a while he began to turn his head and look at me reproachfully. 'Fair shares for all!' his eyes flashed, and I took to passing him his share of the heart. I have never quite figured out how we reached the third stage, all I remember is that for a long, long time I seldom tasted the succulent heart of a lettuce. The moment I returned from shopping, I would tear off the outer leaves for myself, leaving the heart for Scooby, who would run off with it to the top of the wardrobe to munch loudly as he held the crunchy morsel between his good paw and the stump of the other one. Often if he thought I was too slow off the mark, he would tear the paper bag into strips, before attacking the contents. Two beady eyes would appear from the top of the wardrobe while the tiny jaws demolished the lettuce, then jumping down on to my shoulder, he would insist on feeding the choicest bits directly into my mouth, as a kind of peace offering.

Scooby always preferred to inspect whatever I was eating, to make sure that it measured up to his standards. If he decided that he didn't like it, he would go to great lengths to prevent me from eating it. I remember the lunch for which I fried myself a pork chop. As I tried eating it, Scooby sat put on my shoulder, sniffing each forkful and then sneezing, shaking his head in utter disgust. My appetite waned before this resolute show of revulsion.

He also insisted on vetting any prospective girl friend. I never quite discovered his criteria, but if he failed to approve, he would scratch and bite. Exit girl friend smartly – the end of a prospect of another beautiful friendship.

He would only touch my papers if I had neglected him for too long. Then he would hop on to my desk, and sweep them with his stump one by one, until they were littered all over the floor. I couldn't blame him for this, since almost inevitably the papers were negative replies to my fund-raising letters. Scooby was a great personality with a fine sense of judgement.

Many of the letters that Scooby crumpled were couched in warm, complimentary terms—even if the hard cash was not forthcoming. But after seven months of nail-biting, I had my first lucky break. A book about the experiences and findings of the projected Expedition was commissioned. I felt immensely grateful and encouraged. To be sure, this was no more than a beginning. But although I now stressed in every letter that a book had been commissioned, it failed to achieve its magical effect. Surely, I felt, I was now respectable as I had someone to publish one of the books I planned; but the percentage of positive replies remained minimal. One or two foundations came up with small grants, which boosted my morale and kept the torch of hope burning. But it became obvious, as the weeks drew into months, that as things were going it would take me just over ten years to reach my target. What's more, I was getting through addresses at a brisk rate, and their number was strictly finite.

As I look back now on one of the most agonizing periods of my life, I tend to think that several factors were responsible for this shortfall. To begin with, 'expedition' had become almost a dirty word with foundations and industrial concerns. Since the mid-fifties, there had been a glut of expedition-raisers amongst young people, particularly undergraduates. Literally hundreds had been planned every summer, many of them thinly-disguised pleasure trips at little or no cost to the participants. Firms were badgered almost daily to support an expedition 'to seek out the Blue Lotus of the Amazon', or to follow in the footsteps of some obscure nineteenth-century explorer and rescue him from creeping oblivion. Many of them never got off the ground, while others collapsed en route, or returned empty-handed, with nothing to return to their sponsors. In consequence firms had grown wary of backing expeditions however glittering the prospects of success before departure, however substantial the publicity value for the product on their return – if they were heard of upon return. A representative of one company that had backed several expeditions put it to me bluntly: 'We like to support a spirit of adventure and enterprise among young people, especially if there is some worthy object to it; but we are in business and have to look at these things from the standpoint of returns as well. In this respect hardly any of these jaunts have justified so much as a penny of the outlay.'

I would be the last to blame go-ahead young people for wishing to get up and see the world before settling down to their careers. But such goings-on had spoiled the market, and I had reason to believe that many firms and foundations had become so exasper-ated with the flood of appeal letters from prospective expeditions that many of them were hardly glanced at before being thrown into the waste-paper basket.

Again, from many of the replies that I received, I gathered that many of my correspondents doubted that the project could be realized. They were doubtful not only on account of my disability, but also on the grounds that roughing it in the Asian outback was hazardous. Thus my undertaking was deemed 'medically unwise' by one board of trustees, of which various eminent physicians were members; they went on to remark that 'the bacteriological hazards in some Asian villages are considerable'. An even more withering comment arrived from three American pundits on Asia. In their opinion, nothing seemed to make sense about my project. 'The Count's catalog of camping equipment would need some drastic revision.' Evidently my costs were way out too, by their standards. 'Travel is enormously expensive now. By the time you add staff, which you *must* hire, to the cost of living, you might as well go to the tourist hotel in the first place.' Even better was to follow. 'There are some pretty unpleasant beliefs and customs connected with the matter of physical disability in these countries, and this has worsened since the departure of the colonial powers. A man with a glass eye used to be a marvel; now he is a menace, and in grave danger of starting an anti-white riot. In most of these countries there is just no law and order off the beaten track.'

Of course I had enough confidence in the people of Asia, from my own experiences, not to believe such statements; I only quote them now because such opinions were sadly common. What worried me much more were the doubts cast on my ability to go through with the Expedition physically. I felt as fit as a fiddle within myself, and asked a couple of doctors that I knew at home for their frank opinion. One of them replied that if I took extreme care, and had plenty of luck, I might just about get away with it. The other was frank all right. 'If you really want my honest opinion, I think you're crazy. In all probability someone will have to fly you back on a stretcher, probably from no farther than Istanbul.'

I felt that I had hit rock bottom. Scooby did his best to cheer me up by a display of acrobatics from the curtain rail. Sensing that I needed the full treatment, he fetched a choice nut, cracked it between his teeth, and popped it into my mouth. But I continued to sit huddled beside my wretched gas fire, which barely warmed my toes, let alone the rest of my room. I had slogged away for three years, but had only raised a third of the money needed. I had written over three thousand letters. I daydreamed of the wide open spaces of Asia, hot with the palm trees and the stinging dust of the desert. Fleetingly I saw once more the eyes of despair in the disabled. Was I chasing a will-o'-the-wisp? Was it all so impractical and unattainable? With a determination born of despair, I reached for my typewriter. 'Dear Sirs, I am writing in the hope of enlisting your support for the following project . . .'

CHAPTER 7

The Expedition sets out: Turkey and Persia

*

PERSEVERANCE finally paid off. Soon after I received this depressing medical report, I succeeded in enlisting the help of several influential personalities, who formed themselves together into a sponsoring committee. There was nothing passive about this committee. Although it seldom met in the formal sense, individual members – Sir Robert and Lady Jackson in particular – rallied actively and energetically to help with all the problems that arose. Decisions were made, action was taken. Things began to move fast.

One of the first things they did was to put me in touch with the World Rehabilitation Fund, the most prominent American agency in the field of the disabled, with headquarters in New York. Dr Howard A. Rusk, President of the World Rehabilitation Fund, wrote me a charming letter, from which I could see that he was impressed by what I was endeavouring to achieve. Letters began to whizz to and fro across the Atlantic, concerning the Expedition's programme and finances. Eventually, he decided that it would be much easier if I came across to New York.

The six weeks I spent at Dr Rusk's Institute of Physical Medicine and Rehabilitation passed in a flash. The days were packed with intensive discussions, approaching trusts and foundations, taking time off only for strenuous exercises in the superbly equipped physiotherapy department. Hitherto I had worked on the project alone, developing its purpose and details by myself within the four walls of my room, with Scooby for company. Now there was the Committee, Dr Rusk and many others interested and involved. I felt that with the help of such expert guidance everything had now fallen into sharper focus. Though there still was an enormous amount to be done, money to be raised and equipment to secure, for the first time I felt that the Expedition was sure to materialize.

The Committee had been far from idle whilst I was away. I

returned to London in September 1963, full of exhilaration, to find various journalists anxious to write about my project in the press, that Asian governments were now pleased to offer support and facilities. At last the Expedition was being taken seriously, not merely as an excuse for a joy-ride. I reached for my typewriter now with gusto, bombarding the committee with requests for help with this, that or the other. I prepared the ground work in each case, saying that we required such and such, that the product of this company seemed the most suitable. Throwing in the name of the chairman and the address of the company offices, I would enquire whether they could send a letter.

It hardly ever failed: within a few days I would receive a letter from the company concerned, expressing great interest in a 'remarkable' expedition. 'Could one of our representatives call on you to discuss matters?' The extent and generosity of this support was magnificent. Even the sea passages that we required east of India, and the personal insurance which, in my own case, had previously seemed quite unobtainable at any premium, were now offered at a fraction of their normal cost.

One of my larger headaches was resolved when the then British Motor Corporation, of Longbridge, Birmingham, offered to lend us one of their tough, four-wheel drive Austin Gypsies. Like the Jeep or Land-Rover, the Gypsy is designed to cope with any type of terrain that a cross-country vehicle can possibly tackle. To ensure that this particular Gypsy was especially tough and reliable, BMC took special pride and care with it from the moment it started life on the production line. At an early stage, Mr Roy Ammonds, representing BMC's export sales, wrote inviting me to come up to the factory, to discuss various details of construction and special features that the experts would like to include. Unfortunately the British motorways are out of bounds to invalid carriages, and so it took me the best part of five hours to putt-putt the hundred and twenty odd miles to Birmingham on the ordinary roads. I wondered if I would be bewildered by the mass of technical detail down for discussion; but they all took such an enthusiastic interest in the problems that I had no time to feel uneasy. 'By the time we have finished with this Gypsy,' Mr Ammonds said as I was leaving, 'You'll be able to drive it up the ruddy Himalayas!'

Frequent letters were exchanged as the Gypsy was being fitted out on the assembly line. Six months later, in April 1964, Mr Ammonds wrote saying that it was ready. 'Would you like to come and try it out?' So I was soon putt-putting up to Birmingham again. 'Now let's see how you like her!' It was a thrilling moment. The Gypsy looked even larger than I had imagined. Over fifteen feet long, it was painted grey and cream, with 'The Unbeaten Track Expedition' proudly emblazoned on each side. The automatic winch in front was bristling with yards of steel cable; the roof had a double skin for extra insulation against extreme heat; an outside roof rack had been fitted, and a powerful spot-light for operating by hand inside the car. I noticed that there was even a shovel in the back, in case we had to dig ourselves out, in addition to the extra jerry cans for water and petrol.

'Come and sit inside,' Mr Ammonds suggested, opening the door. 'See how she feels.' But as I wheeled myself to the side of the door, I saw his face fall. 'Oh dear, we never thought of that one.'

I saw what he meant. The car seats were at least two feet higher than the wheelchair, which would mean that I would have to struggle to get inside. 'Don't worry, I'm sure I can manage,' I said rather too loudly, hoping to sound more confident than I felt. Manoeuvring myself as close to the car as I could, I grabbed the car seat with one hand, and the wheelchair armrest with the other, and heaved with all my strength. I just made it, and we all breathed again. 'Paul, you did a great job at Camden Road,' I murmured.

The empty Gypsy seemed very roomy inside. One of the three seats in front had been built up with extra layers of foam rubber, to make it more comfortable for my emaciated bottom; special armrests had also been fitted to allow me to take some of the weight off my elbows when we travelled on especially bad roads. At my suggestion, the seats had also been upholstered with canvas, which breathes and absorbs sweat more readily than leatherette. All the gadgets that we had discussed were now in place; the special anti-burglar catch for locking the windows; a front windscreen that opened and closed in a second with a flick of the wrist (essential if we were to enjoy fresh air but shut out the dust of a passing car); an electric point on the dashboard, as a plug-in for an electric shaver, or to charge cine-camera batteries. A bunk had been fitted behind the front seat, folding up against the side when not in use; the extra strong light above the bunk, as well as the dashboard light, would enable me to work at night inside the car.

The controls were dual of course, that is both normal and hand-operated. When Mr Ammonds suggested that I take the Gypsy for a spin around the grounds, I was a bit doubtful, if only because I was used to the joystick on the invacar, and a wheel felt strange. After some persuasion, I took her in bottom gear around the sheds, with Mr Ammonds ready to lean over and grab the wheel. After narrowly missing a gatepost, I pulled hard on my handbrake. 'She feels like a tank!' 'Well, that's how we try to make them,' he replied with a grin. 'You see that ramp over there? That's where we test them,' 'You must be joking,' I said. 'It's practically vertical.' 'Not quite, just forty-five degrees.' 'Well, I think I will give it a miss now, if you don't mind. Save it for the Himalayas!'

Equipment started to arrive at home by the crateful. Stacked in great mountainous piles, it took up every inch of floorspace in my room and in the passage outside. As more crates arrived, we had to use the stairs and the basement, so that the house began to resemble a junkshop. The excitement mounted to fever pitch when we finally fixed our departure date. I still had a bulky file, in which I had noted a hundred and one jobs that remained to be done, items that had to be bought, letters that needed writing. As fast as I ticked off the items seen to, new ones kept replacing them. Should we take ordinary mosquito nets, or the tight meshed ones which keep out the sandfly, but are hotter to sleep under? To purify the drinking water, should we rely entirely on sterilizing pills, or take a water distiller as well, which was bulky and likely to get thrown around in the car?

We discussed the question of Customs clearance for hours on end, as to whether for example it would be wiser to approach the government of Nepal for clearance on our stock of film in London or on the spot. Our bankers wrote to ask for details of the countries on our itinerary, so that they could arrange emergency credit facilities in some of the major towns en route.

Luckily, I was no longer grappling with all this single-handed. Just at the point when I was getting desperate about finding a companion-cum-driver, one of the committee members had introduced me to Jocelyn Cadbury. The youngest son of the well-known family of chocolate manufacturers, Jocelyn had just left Eton at eighteen, and wanted something interesting to do before going up to Cambridge University. The challenge and adventure of our expedition appealed to him immensely, and we clinched the deal. Although he was willing to turn his hand to anything, his main job was of course to be that of mechanic; with his inimitable cheerfulness, he applied himself without delay to the mechanical problems that he was likely to encounter. BMC lent a hand, giving him a training course at the Gypsy factory. As D-Day approached, he moved down from Birmingham to his parents' London flat, armed to the teeth with impressive knowledge of crankshafts, big-ends, sparking plugs, petrol-feed systems, etc., and bearing a number of tough plywood cases that he had organized through the family firm for our camera equipment, medicines, tools and food rations.

Jocelyn could only stay for a year, but my luck held, in that I found a replacement for him in twenty-one-year-old Julian Ingram, whose father was connected with the firm of insurance-brokers backing the expedition. I had met Julian first over a year previously, when he was working near London. He was now on his way to Egypt for a year; when he heard about Jocelyn, he immediately agreed to step in for the remaining year, joining us in India.

Thanks to these two, I had few worries on the personnel side. Although Jocelyn was helping to manhandle and check all the equipment, the last few days passed in a whirlwind of activity. We had a number of outside engagements; BMC, for example, held a press conference for us; at home the telephone seldom stopped ringing. We carried out several 'dummy runs', loading the Gypsy up with all our kit, to find out the most practical arrangement. New entries kept adding themselves in my file, and I was kept busy checking that nothing had been forgotten.

As the great day approached, I began to feel a twinge of anxiety again as to how I would stand up to the rigours of expedition life. Qualified opinion on the subject was still far from reassuring; so much work and international support now depended on my being able to withstand whatever Asia might have in store. My life at home had necessarily been rather sedentary in recent months, and I had been hoping to take a refresher course at Camden Road before we set off; but the pressure of work did not leave me the time. Scooby was uneasy too, sensing my imminent departure in the inimitable way that animals have. Refusing to play, he would sit for long periods on top of the wardrobe, just looking at me, his head turned quizzically to one side. Although I was confident that he would get used to living upstairs with my mother and stepfather, and would receive a great deal of love and attention from them, I confess that his eyes made me feel sad and guilty. He trusted me implicitly; I felt that I was betraying him.

Somehow, despite any number of last-minute crises, we made it. We climbed aboard early in the morning on the 7th of July 1964, on schedule. My parents came to see us off at Dover, but press interviews and customs formalities had left little time for extended good-byes. Once over the English Channel, we sped on our way through France and Germany, with the object of reaching Turkey as fast as possible.

Apart from a few rattles, and the inevitable worries about what been forgotten, my major concern was for my mother. Her cancer had recurred some four years previously, and was spreading rapidly. Although she was in severe pain, she still led a perfectly active life, bearing her affliction with good humour as if it were a trifling inconvenience. Her fortitude confounded those who were aware of her true condition, particularly the doctors. Shortly before leaving London, I had phoned the Royal Marsden Hospital, which she attended for the scanty treatment that medicine could offer, to ask the doctor there for his candid opinion. 'It's hard to say,' he told me, 'the crisis might come at any moment. She's virtually making medical history now, by being alive still. On the other hand, she's got exceptional resilience and will power, and so may go on for months yet.'

I had pondered this for hours in the night, debating as to whether I should postpone our departure. But the more I thought about it, the more convinced I became that postponement would wreck the Expedition's chances. She herself would have been strongly against it; too many people were now involved, what with press interviews and the rest. Reluctantly, I had decided that we must leave as planned, although it meant deserting her in the hour of her greatest need. But she was so proud and happy to see my ambition being realized. 'I know you worry about me, darling,' she had said at Dover, 'but you must never let this nuisance of mine affect what you are doing. I shall share every moment of your endeavour in my heart.' I tried to console myself with the thought that Tadeusz would remain by her side, as the wonderful companion and help he had always been.

After years cooped up in a bed-sitter with typewriter, Scooby and the telephone for company, it felt exhilarating to be on the move again. It was wonderful too, to find that apart from my feet which began to swell rather alarmingly as we drove through Austria, I was suffering no ill effects from the travelling. Jocelyn sang and hummed merrily as he was driving, and I was inwardly thankful for his incurable optimism. A minor disagreement took place in Yugoslavia, when he insisted on leering with unconcealed disdain at the first Communist soldiers he saw. I had experienced enough trouble from those types to last me a lifetime, without inviting more; so I rebuked him in a tone hotter and sterner than I had intended, which took Jocelyn aback and produced a sharp retort.

I was thankful when we left Bulgaria. The red stars on the soldiers' caps brought back unpleasant memories; even some of the tombstones had little red stars stuck on the top. When the barrier dropped behind us I breathed more easily, especially when a smiling Turkish official came up to the window. 'Ah, the Unbeaten Track Expedition,' he said, 'we were expecting you. Welcome to Turkey.' Pressing rapidly ahead, we reached Istanbul the following evening. As we drove towards the city centre, a taxi came up behind us, hooting impatiently.

'Good God, they drive like maniacs here!' Jocelyn muttered, pulling in to let him pass. To our astonishment, however, the cab drew level, whereupon the driver began shouting my name. 'Mr Tarnowski, please stop, please stop.' Wondering how on earth he recognized me, I asked Jocelyn to stop, whereupon the driver jumped out and rattled off in a mixture of English and Turkish how pleased he was to have spotted the Expedition car. 'I read about you in paper today,' he added, his unshaven face wreathed in smiles. 'My little daughter have polio, like you. Please I bring her please to see you.'

I was delighted and we fixed to meet the next day. They arrived at 8 a.m. the following morning at our doss-house in a narrow side-street. Jocelyn was only too glad to leave most of the talking to me, and sat on his bed watching curiously, as the cabby introduced us to his eight-year-old daughter, Fatima. She walked across the uneven creaky floorboards laboriously on crutches, with her legs in braces. 'Thank you to see me,' she murmured shyly, using her one English phrase that she had learned especially for this occasion. While I held her hand and tried to help her overcome her shyness, her father looked on lovingly, explaining that she had contracted polio three years previously, and that the local hospital had made the brace and fitted the special shoe. But evidently the hospital did not measure up to his expectations. 'Iron not very good. She in America, she in England, she all right by now,' he said, looking earnestly at me. 'How can I send her there to make her good? I am poor man.'

Although I had spent many hours theorizing to myself on how I should react, rehearsing what I should say when confronted by the disabled face to face in the East, I confess that I felt nonplussed. I desperately wanted to get through to the father and make him understand that the best course lay in exercise, not miracle cures beyond the seas. I examined her braces and shoes. Perhaps they were not up to the best standards in workmanship, but they were perfectly serviceable. This gave me my lead; I began to explain to Fatima and her father that in fact there was no special medicine or treatment for polio, that there really was precious little that anybody in the West could do for Fatima over and above what had already been done in the local hospital. His disbelief was total. 'You joking,' he said quietly. 'No, I am not joking,' I said. 'The only treatment for polio is exercise. Very hard exercise.'

From the expression on his face, I realized that his faith in the Golden West was boundless, matching his total scepticism in the local facilities. So I asked Fatima to take off her braces; leaving my wheelchair, I got down on the floor, and tried to teach her the 'floor-polish', as I was taught at Camden Road. 'You must make her do that a lot every day. Make her stronger.'

The father continued to grin sheepishly. Obviously I was now playing some game. Crawling was much too primitive a medicine for the West, the fountain head of all modern wisdom and knowledge. As I scrambled back into my chair, he turned to me seriously. Games over and back to business. 'If she go to America, they make her better.'

The following day, we drove on to the Bosphorus ferry boat; half an hour later, we were in Asia. As the countryside opened on to stark vistas of parched emptiness, I sat reviewing my notes in the car, wondering how I could put across the truth to better effect. The problem seemed even tougher than I had thought, and I had no idea at all of the answer. The only solution in Fatima's case seemed to offer a packet of placebo pills, to be administered only after some twenty minutes' worth of hard crawling.

Past Ankara we veered northwards, following the Black Sea coast. We aimed to cover about two hundred miles a day, but soon realized that this was going to take an increasing amount of time over the worsening roads. Conditions generally became more primitive with each day's driving. The food now available from the small wayside towns consisted mainly of green beans floating in mutton fat, or grisly mutton stews, and pancake bread. When Jocelyn pulled a face, I pointed out that the villagers of eastern Turkey often eat gruel soup with globs of fat floating on top for breakfast.

'So what? I still say that I'd throw up if I touched it.'

'But it's the calories that matter,' I persisted. 'Anyway, it all gets mixed up in the stomach.' Sheer hunger resolved that argument.

Even in the larger towns, choosing a suitable dish was far from easy; when we occasionally stumbled across a somewhat better restaurant, the menu would be in Turkish. Once or twice we lunched in restaurants that proudly put English menu cards before us, only to find that we had to choose from 'Hen Water Soup', 'Forest Roast', 'Paper Roast', 'Sawdust Roast', 'Dervish Roast', 'Hungarian Lamp (sic) Roasting', or even 'Ladies Thigh'. The choice of desserts included 'Ladies Navels' with a note appended explaining: 'The Imam, the Turkish priest, liked it so much that he fainted.'

Finding accommodation was also a ticklish matter. In the open country of course, we camped. But it usually took the best part of an hour to unload and inflate the tent, stow away all the other gear again, and so on. This was frankly a bore after a hard day; it also involved the business of cooking dinner, and, more often than not, going to sleep unwashed – streams were rare, and to camp too close to them invited the risk of malaria, or being assailed by insects. On the other hand, we were beset by a different list of vexations when we stayed in the small town hotels. I remember one particularly wretched night in Unye, a small Black Sea

U.T.   I town, when two strong and helpful Turks lugged me on their backs up the rickety hotel stairs, and then down a long, dark, cavernous passage. Arriving at our bedroom, we discovered that the beds were hard and creaky; worse, that the room was stiflingly hot. It was hot and humid enough outside, but nothing in comparison to this. I threw open the window, which let in a little air. Aha, I thought to myself, now for the door; the two will create some draught between them. But when I opened the door, a withering bouquet from an open latrine about two feet away made me close it again hastily. 'Do you know what Asian roads and Asian loos have in common?' I asked Jocelyn. He looked suitably nonplussed. 'When you hit the first, you'd swear it must be the worst in the world. But when you hit the next, that somehow manages to be worse still.'

We both got badly flea-bitten during the night. At daybreak, the Muezzin bellowed his prayer call through the loudspeakers from the minaret that stood next to the window. Wrenched from sleep, Jocelyn leapt out of bed to shut the window. But the sight of a beautiful day dawning over the leaden sea made him change his mind. 'Come on you bug-bitten Infidel,' he shouted at me above the noise of the Muezzin, 'time to hit the road!'

The track was now little more than a bed of stones and potholes following the coastline, hugging spurs and ravines of the steeply descending mountains, thick with hazel bushes. 'I had recently been reading Xenophon's *Anabasis*, and remarked that the author and his ten thousand Greek warriors had retreated from Mesopotamia along this very route. 'The scenery can't have changed much since then,' Jocelyn said, changing down to negotiate a particularly stony and winding gradient. 'Ah, but the people have,' I replied, stretching over the back of my seat to rummage in the crate that served as the Expedition's library. I flicked through the pages to find the place where Xenophon describes the *Mossynoici* who lived in these parts. 'The wealthy among them kept boys who had been specially fatted up by being fed on boiled chestnuts. Their flesh was soft and pale, and they were practically as broad as they were tall. Front and back were brightly coloured all over, tattooed with designs of flowers!' The outraged Xenophon then goes on: 'They wanted to make love in public to the mistresses the Greeks brought with them as this was the usual practice in their country.'

Excellent news was waiting for us when we reached Erzorum, a major town in eastern Turkey. I had mentioned to an official at the Ministry of the Interior back in Ankara that one of the things we would like to see best in Turkey was a game of Jirit, the old traditional Turkish game played by two teams of horsemen. I knew that it was commonly played by cavalry units during the period of Ottoman ascendancy, as it provided an excellent means of keeping the army proficient in throwing the javelin and fit for battle. For the purpose of the game, short sturdy poles are used instead of javelins; even so, I gathered that it was a hazardous affair, as thrilling to watch as it was dangerous to play. Since it was falling into disuse, I was especially thrilled when the mayor left us a message that he had received the message from Ankara, and that the two teams would be ready in two days' time.

Led by a jeep with four local officials we drove to a hamlet about twenty miles outside Erzorum, at the outskirts of which the village headman and elders received us with traditional Turkish hospitality. Having served us yoghurt and handed round a variety of sweetmeats, he took us on a conducted tour of the village. He was especially keen to show us the school, and I was pleased to see how this relatively remote part of Turkey had progressed since 1953 when I stayed with Orhan in his village near Kayseri. When our host entertained us to a meal at the conclusion of our tour, I noticed that he had tap water in his house, in addition to the sumptuous carpets that would have been the pride of any European or American drawing-room.

Suitably refreshed in preparation for the afternoon's sport, we were escorted to a large common outside the village, where the two teams were facing each other at opposite ends of the meadow, about a mile in length. Each team consisted of twelve jirit-wielding horsemen, mounted on the small but remarkably swift and high-spirited ponies of Central Asia. At the signal from one of the officials the leading rider from one team galloped forward, hurled the jirit at his opposite number, who tried to evade the javelin, turned sharply, and made off at speed, hotly pursued by the most experienced man from the other side, to the safety of his home team. The moment he returned to his base line, both teams charged. 'Ya Allaaah,' they screamed the chill traditional Turkish war cry, before which half medieval Europe used to tremble. 'Ya Allaaah,' they cried, tearing down the field towards each other in full cry and throwing the jirits at one another in a furious mêlée.

The initial jousts followed the pattern of medieval battles and tournaments, when the most brave and skilful knight from one army would challenge his opposite number to single combat before the two sides joined in battle. After three or four of these, the horsemen charged either all at once or in groups, till the 'battle' raged all over the vast field. Points were scored according to the number of direct hits; but jirit being a martial sport, the winning team is also judged on horsemanship, agility, the ability to 'fight' as a team and to outwit the opponents. As the battle raged, we could see only too clearly that the jirits were thrown in earnest, and with deadly accuracy. Often a man would grunt in pain when receiving a direct hit. Sometimes a rider, while tearing at full tilt, would suddenly flatten himself against his pony's flank, and hurl his jirit from under the horse's belly.

'What incredible horsemanship,' Jocelyn exclaimed.

'Yes, but look out,' I gasped. 'They're coming right at us!'

The riders continued to come, screaming their war-cry, oblivious to everything save scoring a hit. I looked nervously over my shoulder, but escape was out of the question through the ranks of villagers behind us. I held my breath as they surged past us about six feet to our right. 'That was a near one all right!' I said to Jocelyn as the dust began to settle. 'You all right?' From the flood of unprintable abuse that followed, I gathered that Jocelyn had been kicked by one of the ponies in the mêlée and, to add insult to injury, hit by a stray jirit. 'Boy, oh boy,' he groaned, rubbing his sore back, 'these lads certainly mean business.'

After a couple of hours the game ended with the horses lathered in sweat and several of the riders limping with cuts and bruises. As it was time to leave, we thanked warmly the players and our host. As we drove away from the village, I kept hearing 'Ya Allaaah', echoing murderously around the mountains that ringed the valley. How often my ancestors must have heard this battle-cry when fighting the Turks! When I mentioned this to one of the officials who joined us in the Gypsy, adding that our family crest features a star and crescent, he looked at me straight in the eye with a smile. 'We've always liked you Poles,' he said. 'We have a saying in Turkish that those who like each other, fight each other.'

'By a strange coincidence we have the same proverb in Polish.' I grinned back.

The following day we entered Persia, within sight of Mount Ararat of Noah's Ark fame. Road conditions now changed from the pitted and uneven surface of the Turkish Black Sea coast road, to a washboard track strewn with loose shingle. This type of surface, corrugated by the wheels of heavy trucks into wavy little ridges and depressions, offers the driver the choice between the devil and the deep blue sea. Slow driving involves the car and its unfortunate occupants in a murderous, incessant shaking which plays havoc with every joint and muscle, every screw and bolt. If you accelerate, to try and 'ride' the ripples, you are more than likely to slip on the shingle, and plunge down off the road into a ditch. To cap it all, I have always maintained that Persian dust is the most pervasive in the whole world, guaranteed to work its way into anything, however tightly sealed. I calculated that each of us swallowed at least a quarter of a pound of it every day.

One day we found ourselves behind a truck that was hogging the centre of the road at a steady twenty miles per hour. The dust billowing in its wake was so dense that I could hardly see the afternoon sun, or the fields on either side. I flicked the windshield shut, but this still did not keep all the dust out, but merely sent the temperature inside the driving cab soaring to about 110°F. At this crawling speed, the shaking from the road surface was appalling. After both of us had choked and spluttered for a few minutes, Jocelyn began to curse helplessly at the truck driver ahead. 'We'll suffocate if I don't overtake the swine. Hold on, Arthur.' With his hand placed firmly over the horn button, and his foot hard down on the accelerator, he pulled out. Suddenly I felt the whole car lurch through the air. As we came to a crashing halt, I banged my head hard on the windscreen.

As the dust began to settle, I sat up. Jocelyn was slumped behind the wheel. 'You all right?' I asked. He grunted. Neither of us, it seemed, had sustained any serious injury. Apart from shock, the worst we had suffered were bruises, and a small gash on my forearm that was bleeding. But the impact had dislodged the roof rack, which was now lying forlornly in front of the car. 'Hell, do you think we've broken the springs?' I said mournfully. 'Can you get out and have a look?' The nearest shanty town was Mianeh, about twelve miles away; the prospect of being stranded without springs was hardly a cheerful one. But a volley of abuse from underneath the car put my mind at ease. The springs were fine, to their great credit. It seemed that when pulling out to overtake, we had run directly into an unmarked open culvert or drainage ditch, which a road repair gang had dug into the road. Jocelyn walked back up the road and reported that this was five feet long, at a right angle to the road, over two feet wide, and about three feet deep. When we had driven into it, the impact and our momentum had somehow combined to throw us out again. As he moved around, refixing the roof rack, Jocelyn began to vent his spleen on the road gang. The shock was now beginning to wear off, and he moved on to the Persian highway authorities not to mention truck drivers who overload their trucks with water-melons. By the time he reached the subject of the Expedition, he had worked up a fair head of steam. 'I knew I should never have come on this bloody trip. The whole thing's bloody impossible.'

I knew that he did not really mean it. Anyway, the accident was hardly his fault. 'Chalk it up to experience,' I said. 'Expeditions are great to look forward to or to look back on, but hardly ever when you're actually on the road.' He calmed down in time; since it was now late in the afternoon, I suggested that we stop at the next small town to get some food, and call it a day. He immediately perked up at the thought of food; having patched up my arm from the first-aid box, we drove on to Mianeh. Stopping in front of a seedy-looking eating house, Jocelyn grabbed the mess tins, jumped the open sewer and dived inside. As I sat waiting, I watched the burly, unshaven peasants sitting outside, smoking their hookahs and spitting loudly on the ground as they consumed endless cups of tea, served by a dirty, down-at-heel youth from a large samovar.

I didn't have to wait long. Emerging at the double, he thrust a steaming concoction under my nose. 'Old Billy. Smells quite revolting, but at least it's hot.'

'How much is he asking?'

'Seventy rials. You had better start bargaining.'

In most of Southern Asia, bargaining is regarded as a king of sport, a battle of wits; to pay what is demanded without argument, especially at a dive like this one, means that you are being taken for a sucker. 'Thirty rials,' I offered when the ancient owner, evidently the youth's father, came up to the car window, wiping his greasy hands on an even greasier smock. 'Sixty-five,' he countered, throwing up his hands in a gesture of disdain, shaking his head crossly from side to side. The other customers of the *Chai Khaneh* or tea house watched impassively as the two prices converged, occasionally passing laconic remarks as they sat cross-legged on the carpeted bench, picking their noses, ears or toes. Eventually we both smiled broadly and shook hands.

A couple of miles out of town, we sheered off the road in a reasonably secluded field. The stew turned out to be *chelao pilav*, or mutton with rice, with some beans on top swimming in fat; but we were so ravenous that we ate the lot, without bothering to get out of the car. 'I wonder what they would say at Eton if they saw me polishing off this swill,' Jocelyn said, busily scooping the last few grains of rice out of his tin with his finger. Grabbing a large hunk of water-melon to take the taste away, he busied himself with the tent, while I brought my diary up to date, and worked out the next day's itinerary from the map.

The day after the ditch incident we reached the town of Qazvin. Fortunately the car appeared to be none the worse for its rude shock, except that the starter seemed rather temperamental. Jocelyn managed to locate the trouble without difficulty, but reported that he would need regular garage facilities to fix it. We decided that it was not worth bothering about, that repairs could wait until we reached Tehran; in the meantime, we would manage somehow.

Having surveyed Qazvin, I decided to sleep in the car, while Jocelyn retired to the sleazy Grand Hotel. We often argued who had the better deal of this. But the arrangement was a practical one in the towns, since it was hardly prudent to leave a vehicle full of expensive gear unguarded in the street, and hardly fair to expect Jocelyn to lug me up several flights of rickety stairs after a hard day at the wheel. But the arrangement also meant that for essentially personal reasons we had to make a hurried get-away in the morning. When I had first suggested to Jocelyn, earlier on in the Expedition, that Asian public lavatories were better avoided, he had pooh-poohed the idea. But after his first encounter with an Eastern public loo, he had emerged with a look of unmistakable horror. 'Point well taken. From now on, I'll stick to the bushes.'

I had virtually no choice in the matter, and so we took to

stopping by the first secluded tree out of town, so that I could perform from the open car. On this particular morning, we breakfasted off water-melon, washed down with several cups of tea, and were thus in an even greater hurry to be off. Pulling up on the first deserted stretch of road, I threw my legs out of the open door with a sigh of relief. To my horror I suddenly noticed a small girl standing by the car door, watching me with a mixture of surprise and curiosity. 'Imshi, yalla!' I screamed, ignorant of the Persian for 'scram', hoping for the Arabic to have the required effect. She stuck out her tongue, holding her ground. 'Jocelyn,' I shouted, 'for goodness sake get this confounded brat away from here before I burst!' But the sight of Jocelyn waving his arms and shouting 'shoo' was too much. In a piercingly high voice she screamed 'Aga! Aga! Aga!' In our hurry, we had over-looked *aga*, or father, working stolidly in the fields a few hundred yards away. Hearing his daughter's cry, he came running, pickaxe at the ready. The situation could hardly have looked more com-promising, with two strange men and one small girl, one chasing her round and round the car, while the other sat in the cab with his flies unzipped. Aga was only about fifty yards away, yelling blue murder, when Jocelyn jumped in. 'Let's get the hell out of here. I don't fancy being castrated by that pickaxe.' But he had forgotten about the starter; at the first and second attempts, it remained as dead as the dodo. Anxious looks. At the third attempt she fired. We shot away, narrowly missing both the girl and the pickaxe.

In Tehran, we were cordially received by Ministry of Health representatives, who told me in detail of their plans and problems regarding the work of rehabilitation, and showed me around a couple of hospitals where some of the disabled lay. As yet there were no rehabilitation facilities in existence outside Tehran; even within the city boundary, there was no physiotherapy unit as such, which meant that most of the disabled could not be given proper exercises. But at least the authorities were conscious of this and were hoping to remedy the situation in the near future.

In Tehran I was also introduced to Dr Vassai, who had become wheelchair-bound as a result of a car-crash. He told me of an association which some of the more enterprising amongst the disabled had organized amongst themselves. This group met fortnightly in the premises of the Persian Automobile Club; I was

Trying to raise funds

People gathered wherever we stopped

A game of 'Jirit' in Eastern Turkey

Step-ladder, Nuristan style

Grape harvest in
Afghanistan

Wearing a 'Pusteen' coat
in Ghazni

delighted when Dr Vassai invited me to attend one of their meetings.

From the start, I was deeply impressed by their enthusiasm and enterprise. When a disabled woman shuffled in, I noticed that she was still clutching her book of lottery tickets that she had been selling on the streets. The president was a barrister who had been so badly crippled with polio that he was a quadraplegic and could only move one hand. 'Our chief problem,' he told me as the rest of the members were gathering, 'lies in drawing attention to the fact that when given the chance, we can become useful members of the community again.

'Although my own disability is severe, in a sense I'm lucky, in that I have been educated, I can read – the majority in this country are still illiterate – and I can enjoy a variety of interests. I'm not wealthy, but I have a small income from private means, and I haven't altogether abandoned my practice.' He sighed as he watched the scene through the open verandah doors, as another member pushed himself along the street on his bottom, the trouser seat reinforced with a coarse leather patch, then struggled to heave himself up the entrance steps. 'The worst off are those who have depended on their hands and muscles for their livelihood. If disaster deprives them of their physical ability to work, it's often curtains for them. Their misfortune becomes compounded by the prejudices and apathy of the public, till the disability invades their minds and spirits too. This is the worst tragedy of it.' The twenty-odd members that had gathered were listening in hushed silence, even though most couldn't understand English. 'In fact I would say that our task is more a question of rehabilitating the able-bodied community in their attitudes towards the disabled. If only we could achieve that, we ourselves would have won more than half the battle.'

Dr Vassai sat beside me throughout the meeting. When it was over, I asked him about the poorer infirm. In the course of conversation, he mentioned the *Ordu Khas*, literally Workhouse, where I could see for myself. Would he take me there? Yes, he would, but I sensed that he was slightly reluctant to do so. I understood why, when we entered the tangle of gloomy, crumbling brick barracks.

The Ordu Khas, now mercifully closed I am told, was like a glimpse of the darkest pages of Dickens. Sited in the slums of

southern Tehran, at a comfortable distance from modern developments, it consisted of various blocks, separated by bare cobbled
courtyards, housing the old, the beggars, the sick, the morons and
the lunatics. Some of the latter were supposed to be dangerous,
and so there were uniformed guards strutting around by the gate,
flicking short whips.

We pushed ourselves in our wheelchairs into the barrack
nearest the entrance, which was for men. The moment I wheeled
myself inside this building I was almost overcome by the fetid
smell. As my eyes grew accustomed to the murky atmosphere, I
saw that there were tight rows of bunks lining the walls, with
rusting chamber pots beneath. There was hardly any room left
between each set of bunks; even so, evidently there were not
enough beds for all, to judge from the pallets on the concrete
floor. The inmates appeared to be a mixture of the old, the
paralysed, the deformed and the dumb. I remember one young
man especially: according to Dr Vassai who was translating, he
was all of seventeen years old, although his face looked ageless.
He was sitting on his bunk, his deeply set eyes looking straight
ahead without any expression in them. When I wheeled myself
over to talk to him, he never moved a muscle. Puzzled by this, I
touched him lightly on his emaciated forearm, hoping to make
some sort of contact. Still no reaction. Defeated, I asked about his
history; it transpired that his father was really quite well off, but
his mother had died when he was ten, whereupon his father had
simply consigned him to the Workhouse. Owing to his mongolism
and some congenital complaint such as rickets he could not have
measured more than three feet when standing, that is if he had
power in his twisted, lifeless legs to stand; he just sat there, day
in, day out, shrivelled and thin, staring into eternity. And would
go on staring, presumably until carried off by a merciful death.

As I was moving towards the door, I noticed an old man
groaning quietly to himself, his slobbering mouth pressed to the
floor. My first impulse was to get out of this hell. But when I called
out a greeting, he sat up. He was obviously dumb, as his toothless
mouth was gaping silently. Then he hitched up his ragged shirt
to show me the ulcerated stump of a leg and pointed at it, his
hand quivering convulsively, his open mouth shaping a mute
query. There was nothing I could do, nothing I could say;
desperate to find some word or gesture of consolation, I looked up

for inspiration. To my surprise, the wall above his bed was covered with a portrait gallery of Hollywood film stars with over-developed breasts. Other posters showed sumptuous palaces, with beautifully tended, ornate gardens. The dreamworld of escape was in poignant contrast with the misery it looked down upon. 'Paradise Lost peering on to Inferno . . . ' I murmured to Dr Vassai. The man's eyes followed my gaze and for an instant a pathetic smile flickered on his drivelling mouth.

In the courtyard outside I saw between sixty and eighty beggars, evidently collected from the streets in police sweeps, all lying around on dirty cotton coverlets, talking, gesticulating, some trying to catch some sleep. Although this yard was open to the four winds, the stench was still overpowering. I propelled myself over the cobbles, trying to avoid the excrement, through another block, into the courtyard occupied by the lunatics, where I was greeted by a mixture of jeers, catcalls and raucous laughter. Wheeling through this throng, trying to avoid those who were just sitting, staring silently at the ground, we found ourselves in the women's section. A thickset, youngish woman, with one arm missing, took one look, cracked an obscene joke at my expense, and slapped her neighbour on the buttocks, laughing uproariously. Somehow she reminded me of the female guards in the German concentration camps of the Second World War. When I tried to speak to some of them through Dr Vassai, most reacted with giggles or blank stares. Nearby another woman sat on the ground, her legs crossed underneath her, suckling her child. Her breast was generously encrusted with dirt, and I could see lighter streaks where the baby had slobbered. The flies crawled all over the nipple and the child's mouth, evidently enjoying their share. Close by, a group of five paralysed children aged between six and seven lay amongst the excrement on the cobbles. They just lay there, too sickly and emaciated to take notice of their surroundings, let alone show interest in strangers, while the wind swirled the dust and swarms of flies scuttled in and out of their open mouths to feed on their saliva. I watched, mesmerized, as a some-what older, able-bodied child appeared on the scene, to drag them out of the burning sun. As he dragged each one, gripping them under the arms, their thin, paralysed legs bounced cruelly on the cobbles. Only one of them managed to raise a soft whimper.

Our final point of call was the cavernous female dormitory. I felt a bit strange in this all-female barrack, and felt more grateful than ever for the doctor's company. It was depressingly similar to the men's barrack, except that the stench was perhaps even more sickening. Strung up on lines between the beds were the *chaddhurs* – the dark or spotted head-to-foot garment that women wear in Iran – poorly washed in cold water without soap. I felt as if I were floundering through a nightmare. Just as we were leaving, a crippled old woman hobbled up with tears in her eyes. She caught hold of my hand, and began to speak quickly, urgently, as if some dam of pent-up feelings had suddenly broken. At first I thought, rather unkindly, that she might be begging. When the doctor asked her to pause a moment so that he could translate, I realized my mistake. 'She is saying that we are all brothers in God, and that God will recompense you and give you happiness. She says that she was once a mother, and that she wants you to be all right again, and walking.'

When Jocelyn returned to collect us, I sat silently in the car for a long time, while Dr Vassai tactfully kept his thoughts to himself. When Jocelyn asked why my normal flow of conversation had dried up, I described briefly the appalling scenes we had witnessed. 'Yes, this is the pit,' the doctor commented. 'But before you let indignation run away with you, try to see this in its own perspective. In the West, such conditions would indicate unforgivable callousness on the part of those in charge. But here poverty still remains abysmal and generalized. For most of them existence in their own houses and hovels was hardly less grim. Here at least they are sure of getting some food and a place to sleep. Only a starving man will know what it means to have enough to eat.'

Yet the sense of numb, helpless anguish still weighed on me like a shroud of lead. 'It's not the conditions that dismay me most, doctor. I come and go as a mere spectator, when every nerve in me cries out to help, to change all this. But how can one start grappling with something so big?' 'I know what you mean,' he replied wearily. 'These things will take time, lots of time. It will take decades of hard work. What we must ensure now is that the cause of the disabled is brought to the front in terms of national priorities, rather than remaining at the tail end. Please bear in mind that this has been going on around here for thousands of years. But at least these things are now being recognized as problems.' 'You're right, doctor,' I sighed, 'the same conditions were the rule in Europe right into the nineteenth century. But in the meantime how many lives are doomed to languish in such hell?'

We left Tehran a couple of days later, along an excellent tarmac road that led over the Elburz mountains to the Caspian seashore. As we hummed along at a steady fifty-five mph, I could hardly help reflecting that any illusions I might still have had about the plight of the handicapped in Asia had been well and truly dispelled. But what could I *do* about it? What could I say to people like those cripples of the Ordu Khas?

The last stretch of road was singularly impressive, leading through a landscape shorn of all vegetation, climbing over interminable loops that overhung yawning bluffs. Once we had reached the top pass, close to Mount Damavand, the highest peak in Iran, the scenery changed dramatically. We found ourselves driving down through dense jungle among trees festooned with creepers. This austere region had been the haunt of the Assassins in the early Middle Ages, a fanatical sect whose members were inspired by their leader Hassani Baba, 'the Old Man of the Mountain', aided and abetted by generous consumption of hashish, to slay and plunder over half the Middle East. Eventually the Assassins were annihilated by the Mongol hordes under Hulagu Khan; but they lived on in our word 'assassin'. Their eerie citadels can still be seen, brooding on top of the mountain crags. According to the legend, some of these citadels and neighbouring caves contain buried treasure of great value. Lured by such prospects, several parties of adventurous climbers have scaled these inhospitable peaks and castles. But it seems the Assassins were as clever in hiding their loot as they were merciless in its acquisition.

Just as we were skirting a precipice, the brakes failed. Jocelyn grabbed the handbrake and brought her to a stop just in time to prevent us dropping several hundred feet. He soon located a leak of brake-fluid as the source of the trouble. He fixed it soon enough, while my grateful thoughts went out to BMC for having trained him so well. But the wretched starter continued troubling us, despite the repairs carried out in Tehran.

We were driving now into the bleak steppes of Central Asia, close to the Soviet border. The distances on the road proved longer than those indicated on the map, so that we had to take good care to fill up with petrol whenever possible. Driving for mile upon mile, across desolate country bare of human habitation, with no sign of a tree or a green field, we would occasionally catch a glimpse, in the far distance, of a strange structure by the side of the road. As we drew nearer, it seemed to be a roofless sentry box, thrown together with rough stones that blended into the dun wilderness of the plain. In a moment we would see a solitary figure standing by the roadside outside the hut, with hand outstretched towards the car in the frozen gesture of begging.

Some countries, such as Turkey, have outlawed beggars which may drive the problem out of sight but doesn't cure its causes. We often dropped a coin into the pleading hand, but to do so every time would have been impossible. Besides, one can seldom be sure if their infirmities are real or assumed; in some towns beggars are organized into mafia-type syndicates, a large proportion of the 'takings' going to line the pockets of vultures who often grow rich on this vile exploitation. But these blind beggars of the roadside wilderness in Persia were usually genuine enough, and there was a haunting dignity about them. Somehow they all looked the same; unseeing eyes drawn with scaly blinds, their faces lined like furrowed leather. They were a constant reminder of how ancient these countries are, how deeply patient and inured to pain are their people.

East of the Caspian Sea, we were in Turkoman country. The Turkomans are mainly a pastoral people of the steppe, but are also ferocious warriors markedly mongoloid, with high cheekbones; the men usually wear sheepskin coats and hats, often the same colour as their droopy, wispy moustaches. We happened to arrive at Pahlevi Diz on a Thursday, which was a happy coincidence, because on Thursdays the square turns into one of the most colourful markets in Central Asia. We wandered around between the stalls, together with sundry flocks of sheep, herds of camels and horses, examining the colourful displays of household wares, rugs, sheepskin coats and caps, bright red bales of cloth and the rest.

Jocelyn soon discovered a bald and burly Turkoman at work in his forge. For some reason they got along famously together, despite the fact that Jocelyn's grasp of Farsi (Persian), let alone Turkoman, was minimal. Before I knew what was happening, the blacksmith was brewing tea over a charcoal fire by the furnace.

We then found ourselves drinking a strong brew from little glasses that stood in perforated metal holders. Meanwhile our host hovered around, arms folded, like a blood-curdling mongol warlord straight out of some Hollywood epic.

Our next tribal encounter was rather more harrowing. We were driving over barren open country in the southern part of Afghanistan, shortly before the Jeshan celebrations which mark the main Afghan national holiday, when we suddenly spied a group of tents some 200 yards off the track. Drawing nearer, we heard drums and tambourines, and saw two groups of men and women dancing in separate circles. Having seen little besides the desolation of mountains and desert for the best part of a thousand miles, Jocelyn pulled up, grabbed his camera, and shot off towards the dancers. I lowered my window as quickly as I could. 'Look out!' I shouted after his retreating figure. 'These fellows can be dangerous!' 'Don't fret so much, Arthur,' he shouted back, without turning round.

As the dust was settling, I saw that the dancers were Pathans, who are amongst the most ferocious and quick-tempered tribes in the world. Pathans are quite capable of taking human life as cheerfully and nonchalantly as if they were picking daisies. To a mounting crescendo of the drums, they were dancing the Attan, the Pathan tribal dance, brandishing their *jezails* or muzzle-loaders. I sat hunched up in my seat, muttering my prayers, as Jocelyn rushed up and started photographing.

Normally, of course, there is never any real danger in approaching most tribes, providing that you obey the rules. In Islamic countries, you approach modestly, with empty hands, and greet them in the name of God, with words of peace. Then you wait for the traditional cup of coffee or whatever, to establish you as a sacred guest. At all costs you should never take any initiative, or make any reference to their womenfolk. To my horror, Jocelyn was now only a few feet away, snapping the men dancing. Shifting a few feet to his right, he began to take the men with the women in the background.

The dancing suddenly stopped. I saw a group of young Pathans milling around Jocelyn, shouting blue murder. Realizing his mistake, he doubled back to the car, hotly pursued by a group of about forty angry tribesmen, all brandishing rifles. 'Give them some money. They want some money,' he said, his face a deathly shade of white. The situation was ugly, especially as the tribesmen were now thudding the Gypsy with their rifles. I knew instinctively that to give them money would be fatal, literally fatal; money would merely whet their appetites to loot and kill. Several had now climbed on to the roof of the car, and were busy trying to rip open our tarpaulin; I knew that we had one course open, and only one. 'Jocelyn,' I said firmly. 'Just get in and start the car. Just start it and drive off.' Hands were now reaching out behind me into the equipment piled up in the back, roughly snatching at our gear. Remembering that Pathans despise fear as much as they respect a cool head, I forced myself to smile, as I tried to retrieve our possessions. Tempers were rising by the minute, and I realized with a shock, as they began to handle me more roughly, that if they succeeded in pulling me out of the car, we would have had our lot.

Fortunately Jocelyn managed his way back to the driver's seat. I watched in agony as he turned the ignition key. Would that wretched starter function? By a happy miracle, she fired first time. We shot away in a cloud of dust, changing through the gears with frightening speed, causing the Pathans to scatter.

We were too shaken to speak. After nine or ten miles Jocelyn had recovered sufficiently to enquire about our losses. I rummaged around, to find that we were missing one water container.

'Not too bad, considering, don't you think?' He commented with a completely straight face. I breathed a sigh of relief. 'Good old British stiff upper lip!'

CHAPTER 8

In remote Nuristan

*

FROM the travelling point of view, Afghanistan proved even tougher in many respects than Persia. Most of the country remains virtually untouched which makes it a fascinating place to visit, providing that you are willing to face up to the rugged conditions. The stoutly-built *caravanserais*, for example, look positively medieval; in Farsi *serai* means palace or mansion, but these inns fall miserably short of such standards. In Afghanistan these long-standing havens of steppe and desert are called *robats*. They usually form a quadrangle with no windows or openings on the outside except for a stout gateway or portcullis; there is a large courtyard inside, which invariably forms the centre of a robat's life and activity. Pack donkeys and the slobbering, supercilious camels grunt and ruckle as they are being loaded or unburdened. Sheep and goats are penned in a corner, while bales of merchandise, wool, cotton, pelts, rugs lie scattered amidst the animal droppings. When daylight fades, the rough, burly men, thankful for such haven of rest and company after long and gruelling trails, squat around tall samovars gossiping as noisily as they drink their scalding tea. Others squat preparing food, usually mutton stews, rice, bread, and, if lucky, some vegetables. As the large, smoke-blackened pots simmer over open fires on the dusty courtyard, flies by the million swarm hungrily, attracted by the smell of food, the poorly cured pelts and the rancid sweat of man and beast.

A night's lodging, usually without cots and certainly with no blankets provided, can be secured in the robats for a mere five to ten pence a night. But we avoided them, as being definitely below what we called 'the bug-line'. They have a reputation for being infested with all kinds of blood-lusting insects; to that prospect should be added the withering stench of the caravan-wallahs, who often have neither opportunity nor desire to wash for months on end. Back in 1957, when on my way out East, I stayed in a robat in Farah, in south-west Afghanistan; despite the fascinating medieval atmosphere, I regretted the choice. As the sleepless night dragged on, I kept vainly rubbing myself with DDT, listening wistfully to the night-watchman who stomped the narrow earthen alleyways outside, crying the hour in a high-pitched voice to assure the inhabitants that all was well, answered each time by a rabid chorus of pariah-dogs. But nothing disturbed the cameleers snoring loudly around me. Robats are very much a man's world, for as a rule women do not accompany caravans on their trading runs, while the nomads, who travel with their entire families on their annual treks to the high pastures, tend to avoid them, preferring to camp along the bridle-paths.

If life remains tough and primitive for the local population, it was not exactly a holiday for us either. Many of the desolate mountain and desert trails consisted of little more than vague earth tracks, rutted and littered with stones. The incessant bone-rattling, often in temperatures well above the hundred mark, in the all-pervading, swirling dust, was thirsty work; but drinking water posed quite a problem. In Persia, we had often played safe by stocking up with Coca-Cola or whatever soft drinks we could get; but it seemed that the long arm of Coca-Cola had never reached into the wildernesses of Afghanistan. The local water-melons were delicious of course, and very thirst-quenching; but past experience had taught me to be wary here of a dubious practice that I had first observed when visiting the country in 1957. This was, and still is, for all I know, the simple matter of resuscitating a travel-weary patient. The melons often reach their destination in a shrivelled state, after a long trans-desert haul in the back of an open truck, sometimes partly covered with tarpaulin, but more often open. The ingenious vendors then puncture them discreetly with a pin or skewer and leave them overnight in the local sewer to swell back to their original size. They look fine the following morning, but taste rather stronger than usual. The traveller would do well to inspect any melon closely for tell-tale marks before buying. (In fairness, I should add that the foreign tourist is most unlikely to meet this in better-class hotels of Kabul or Bamyan, as this custom is confined to some of the bazaars and roadside vendors.)

Despite the relatively minor problems of this nature, I was feeling on top of the world. I had already survived more in the way of hardship and rough living than the English doctors thought possible, and felt supremely confident of being able to face up to anything that might come my way. To date I had merely found it inconvenient on occasions, not to be able to climb stairs, and sometimes felt irked and wistful at being stuck in the car seat or wheelchair, when it would have been a joy to get up and scale a mountain, explore, help Jocelyn with the car and gear. I tried to dismiss such thoughts and apply myself instead to making the utmost of my limited mobility. I also had cause to be grateful for my iron constitution; Jocelyn had suffered repeatedly from diarrhoea, fever, stomach pain and minor bronchial troubles, probably caused by dust, but so far I had escaped scot-free.

In fact I was feeling so cheerful that I thought we might push our luck a little. I badly wanted to visit one of the remoter parts of Afghanistan, where I could gain an insight into the situation of the disabled in communities untouched by modern conditions. Nuristan seemed to fit the ticket perfectly, but I had been wary of mentioning this back in London. I was uncertain then as to how my health would hold up, and I knew that the Afghan government were wary of issuing the necessary permits to visit the more inaccessible regions. When I brought this up in Kabul, Mr Tarzi, head of the tourist office, was helpful, if guarded, in his reaction. 'The matter will receive proper attention.'

Nuristan lies in the shadow of the mighty Pamir mountains, north of the Khyber Pass. It is a province of mountains, forests, and a distinctive people who preserve a characteristic culture of their own. Tall, lean and blue-eyed, they are often thought to be the descendants of Greeks who settled at the time of Alexander the Great. With their distinctive dress, their carvings and not least their chairs – the Nuristans are virtually the only people in Central Asia who sit on chairs – I thought a visit could be eminently rewarding. In the meantime we were busy in Kabul: while Jocelyn overhauled the Gypsy and put the starter right, I visited the disabled and local hospitals. Caught in these activities, I had quietly given up hope of Nuristan, until the helpful Mr Tarzi told me, after about two days had elapsed, that he had been authorized to issue permits. He was merely doubtful as to whether I should undertake the journey. 'There are no facilities of any kind in Nuristan. We are not even too sure of the exact distances.'

'But that's all part of the fun,' I replied with a grin.

'Well, God be with you. At least we can provide you with a Nuristani guide.'

One further hitch developed, as we were preparing to leave. We were busy trying to rearrange the gear to accommodate our guide and the extra jerry cans of petrol when Mr Tarzi popped out of his office and said with a long face that our route was blocked by landslides. 'Come back in another three days,' he suggested. In fact this delay proved a blessing in disguise, and gave us more time to make suitable arrangements for the kit we had decided to leave behind.

Sure enough, the track was reported clear on the third day, and we assembled in the early morning to meet our guide. Promptly at six o'clock, he arrived – a thin-looking Nuristani, sporting several days' beard, a rather shabby jacket, trousers and shoes without socks. He stumbled towards us bearing two large bundles of gifts for his numerous relatives in Nuristan. 'Me Abdullah,' he said shyly, 'me Nuristan guide.' He spoke with the dignity of a Red Indian brave, and I took to him immediately. 'Salaam Aleikum.' 'Glad to meet you, Abdullah.' Without further ado, he climbed into the middle between us, and we set off, travelling first of all eastwards on the Khyber road, then sheering off to the north towards Nuristan.

For some twenty miles Abdullah sat quite still, without speaking, and I began to wonder if his dignity might not prove too much of a good thing, if he kept it up for ten days. But when Jocelyn and I began to sing, he began to thaw. I doubt very much if he understood the words of the Eton Boating Song, since his grasp of English was limited to a total of twenty-two words. But before we decided to camp for the night, we had covered a good sixty miles, over a track that deteriorated with every mile, and Abdullah had become a firm friend.

We set off early the next morning, along a track that flanked a mountainside, dipping awesomely on our left to the broad and swift-flowing River Kumar. There was no question of going back now, for the simple reason that the track was little more than eight feet wide for long stretches. After twenty-three miles, we stopped abruptly as we rounded a bend. The entire width of the track was buried under about five feet of mud, torn scrub and boulders, some of them two feet or more in diameter, while in the mountainside above us we could see a large yellow gash, exposing tree roots and mangled bushes. Jocelyn and Abdullah set to work with shovel and pick-axe, helped by some local people who appeared on the scene. Two hours later they had tunnelled their way through fifteen feet of landslide, using the boulders and bushes to rebuild some of the road that had been carried away. Using my hand controls, I slowly edged the Gypsy in four-wheel drive over the mud covered with brushwood, hugging the mountain-flank as close as I could, while Jocelyn guided me forward peering anxiously underneath to see how the mended part of the track was holding. It held.

Half a mile farther on, we met another landslide. After the third, which involved digging through at least thirty feet of clay, stones and uprooted bushes, Jocelyn returned to the driving seat with a grim face. 'Arthur,' he said in a voice that usually preceded an explosion, 'this is getting a little monotonous, don't you think?' I looked up at the mountain towering above us, its flank strewn with large boulders, and at the sky which threatened rain. 'Yes, I know,' I replied, trying not to sound too anxious, 'at least there was nothing diplomatic about the landslides they reported in Kabul!' Stony silence followed my feeble joke, an even stonier silence when we hit our fourth landslide in three miles. As I watched them struggling to remove the boulders and branches from the road, I suddenly felt mad that I could not join in. I had not felt so exasperated for years. There was nothing I could do, of course, but sit tight and pray that we would not hit any more. As Jocelyn edged the Gypsy past, we slithered badly on the mud, and we both glanced down at the river five hundred feet below. 'I wonder if there are many crocodiles down there,' he commented rather unhelpfully. 'Keep going, old man,' I shouted, anxious that he should keep his eyes on the job. Abdullah meantime had taken refuge up on the roof, presumably to jump off fast in case of trouble. 'Allah very good!' he called out as we reached firm ground again.

Allah was indeed kind to us that day, because after the sixth landslide the track was clear. When we reached the village of Barikot, we breathed an enormous sigh of relief, as we gorged ourselves on unleavened bread fried in mutton fat with huge chunks of unpunctured water-melon to wash it down. In fact I doubt if we would have either noticed or cared if they had been punctured. We were sitting outside a tea house that was gaudily painted in the most outrageous colours, with pictures of guns blazing, lions on the rampage, and centaurs. This exhibition of local art, combined with the meal and our tiredness after a hard day, made us more than ready to doss down on the *chaparkats*, which had been brought out into the lane for us to sleep on. I sprawled gratefully on the hard string ribs of my cot, perfectly at home in this unusual open-air dormitory, only vaguely conscious of the barking of the village dogs. Suddenly, just as I was dropping off, I was conscious that something was distinctly amiss at the bottom of my bed. In a flash, I realized that one of the mangy curs, evidently an indifferent marksman, had cocked against my foot missing the target of the bed-leg by at least ten inches. I instinctively leaned down to grab the nearest missile, and picked up what I thought was a large stone. To add insult to injury, it turned out to be a freshly-minted horse dropping, and I cursed my misfortune in a volley of unprintable language. 'Calm down, Arthur,' Jocelyn advised when I eventually paused for breath. 'Think yourself lucky that the dog didn't choose the other end of the bed!'

Next morning we sheered away from the Kumar, soon after we had left the village and its piddling mongrels, and entered the gorge of one of its tributaries, the Bashgul. We were now in Nuristan proper, and the scenery was wild and magnificent. The higher reaches of the mountain range towering above us were dense with primal pine forest, which gave way at lower levels to a belt of deciduous growth dotted with massive cedars. At the foot of the gorge, by the raging torrent, I noticed holyoak, mulberry, tamarisk, willow, apple, pomegranates, walnut and wild apricot. Small patches of cultivation appeared, and occasional villages that nestled high up against the mountain flank, blending so well with the rocks and trees that they seemed a natural part of the topography. After travelling for a day through this breathtaking scenery, which caused both of us to fall in love with Nuristan, we stopped for the night at the village of Mundegal.

Abdullah, born in the Darai Lahman valley of Nuristan, had never visited here before. But he was so happy to be back amongst his people. He pressed his forehead down to the gnarled hands of the grey-haired patrician elders, hugged the middle-aged notables with grave decorum and shook hands with the younger ones. This ritual completed, he set off hand-in-hand with a couple of the local men up the steep alleyway, set with rough, uncut stones.

Left to our own devices, we exchanged greetings with the elders, bowing our heads with solemn propriety, our right hands on our chests. Formality satisfied, we were invited to share a pot of tea and some rather stale, sugary biscuits that smelled of mutton-fat.

Few, if any, of the two hundred-odd souls in the village had ever set eyes on a Westerner before, and so we attracted our share of attention. The men came to take a look at us with curious if restrained dignity. The children giggled self-consciously, while the women, who wore baggy cotton pants down to their ankles and full black smocks, quickly drew the edge of their kerchiefs across their unveiled faces, and walked hurriedly past, casting furtive glances whenever they thought we were not looking.

After a couple of hours of this mutual if wordless contemplation, the food arrived and we all settled down in the shade of a huge walnut tree to a meal of the standard bread fried in mutton fat, preceded by chicken-gut soup. We tucked in ravenously. I caught Jocelyn's eye when I had scraped the platter clean and we exchanged an anxious query. Unfortunately that proved our lot. From Jocelyn's wistful expression I guessed that despite all the arcadian charms of Nuristan, right then his thoughts were riveted on the family dining-table back in England, or even the mess-tin full of that fatty and tepid chelao pilav we had despised so often in Iran.

After supper, the sleeping drill followed the usual pattern, except that the chaparkats were laid out for us on one of the flat roofs of the village houses. This meant that poor Jocelyn, aided by two hirsute Nuristanis, had to lug me up steep ladders carved out of tree trunks. But the beauty of the night from the rooftop took our breath away, and more than compensated for these privations. The moon was full, bathing the village in cool ghostly light. The Bashgul raged incessantly beneath us at the bottom of the gorge, accompanied only by the peaceful murmur of cicadas and a soothing wind from the forest.

When we awoke the next morning, I noticed three Nuristanis below us in the lane carrying long bunches of bamboo. There must be fish in the river, I reasoned. Perhaps we could improvise a fishing rod? The thought of fish for breakfast drove away immediate hunger; beckoning to the men I managed to persuade them to carry me down to the river. Sure enough, I saw plenty of silvery fish darting about, and my mouth began to water. 'Abdullah, we catch fish?' I suggested, pointing to what I thought were trout below us.

'Yes, yes,' he replied, 'fish in river office.'

Abdullah was fascinated with the word 'office'; having recently graduated from the simple life of Nuristan to the comparative sophistication of Kabul, he was only too anxious to take the 'office' along wherever he went. So we travelled in the 'car office', ate in the 'eat office', and slept in the 'sleep office' and so on.

The fish were undoubtedly in the 'river office', but how were we to get them out? 'Abdullah, if no plenty eat, Jocelyn . . . ', I folded my arms in an expressive gesture for going on strike. 'Jocelyn eat fish good.' Abdullah grinned helpfully, but didn't seem to know what to do about it. So I tried to take matters in hand. With a length of bamboo, some string and cork we found in the Gypsy and a hook contrived from a safety-pin, we rigged up a fishing-line. Abdullah dug some worms, and we tried our luck. Two hours of futile casting and we felt hungrier and more frustrated than ever. The fat fish swam leisurely by, disdaining the bait. We often went hungry in Nuristan.

Our final destination in Nuristan was the village of Bargamatol, which is dominated by an observation tower reminiscent of a medieval baronial keep. When we approached the village late in the afternoon, we found that it lay on the other side of the river, which we had to cross by a precarious bridge of logs. The logs were lashed together in the best Nuristani do-it-yourself style, with ropes made of twined creeper; Jocelyn took one look at it and grabbed the handbrake. But Abdullah was brimming with confidence. 'Go, go! Bismillah!' he shouted from the back, 'in the name of Allah! Allah very good!' Having learned to respect Abdullah's trust in Allah, Jocelyn edged the Gypsy forward until the front wheels were riding the first logs. Looking down, I could see that they were creaking and swaying with our weight. Gingerly we edged forward, until the whole vehicle was supported. The logs groaned still further, but held. We crept across like a snail. A throng of children and youths were waiting to welcome us. As usual on such occasions, I deliberately stayed in the car at first. It wasn't so much the unbridled curiosity that mattered, as the choking dust kicked up by the dozens of bare feet. With no breeze to get through this human phalanx, the dust would billow up so thick that I would cough and splutter, gasping for breath. But as I looked around, I couldn't help but think that life here must have gone on unchanged for hundreds of years. Some of the crowd that had gathered were still carrying their bows and arrows; by a cottage farther up the slope, others were busy threshing wheat, holding on with both hands to the eaves of the house, rotating the sheaves with their feet. While I watched this peaceful scene with half an eye, an old blind man shuffled up. Evidently he was the village bard, because he began to improvise verses of welcome to the visitors from the wide world beyond, accompanying himself by thumping an empty oil-drum. Before the crowd could close in around us, we got out and followed the bard quickly to the headman's cottage, where it was customary for visitors to stay.

As the evening shades began to draw in, they lit a large log fire; the bard now began to recite in a sing-song voice the plaintive ballads of Nuristan, swaying rhythmically back and forth as he sat cross-legged on the ground, turning his large, sightless eyes towards the stars. His expression was full of yearning and pathos like a saint in a vision from a painting by Giotto. Looking up, I saw that a number of the village men had begun to dance; as the evening wore on, the songs gradually became gayer, and the men warmed to the dance.

The chant and the dance were an integral part of the timeless scene around us: the thrumming Bashgul, the sky bright with stars, the lofty peaks in the distance, the almost palpable sense of peace and eternity with which this scene was imbued. As the lilting voice rose and fell, I sensed how it expressed the very stuff and rhythm of their existence. Together with the men's graceful, swaying dance, it embodied the spirit of this place so well that I felt I could have described it just from listening and watching. Never before had I experienced this feeling, certainly not from modern music as we know it. Perhaps we have wandered too far away in the West from the grass-roots of creation. As I watched entranced, I tried to remember what it was that they reminded me of. Suddenly it came to me. I was once in Greece, in Delphi, and had got out of bed at daybreak to climb Mount Parnassus. Before setting off, I had sat alone on the deserted terrace of my taverna, munching my breakfast, watching the early morning sun chasing away the puffs of mist that had drifted over the vineyards deep below. Suddenly I had looked up, to find that I was no longer alone. A young Greek, with a red rose clenched between his teeth, was dancing a hymn of praise to the beauty of the dawn, gracefully fluttering a kerchief. His arms were raised above his head, as he clicked his fingers; his steps were measured, then quickened in sudden bursts and leaps. Beyond the haze, I could see in dim outline the mountains of the Peloponnese, whilst the waters of the Gulf of Corinth glittered far below. Oblivious to all but the glory of creation, my unknown companion fixed that scene in my memory for ever.

At his initial briefing from Mr Tarzi back in Kabul, Abdullah had been told about my work with the disabled, how I wanted to see how they lived in Nuristan. I reminded him of this while we were in Bargamatol, and he promised to find out what he could. Meanwhile, I could see a lot with my own eyes. Wherever I turned, I was confronted by the sickly pallor and consumptive cough, splotches of bloody spittle on the ground. A doctor in the hospital at Mazar-i-Shariff in Northern Afghanistan had told me that in some areas in the north of the country an estimated thirty per cent of the population suffered from TB. From the evidence in front of me, I reckoned that in Nuristan the incidence rated as high, if not higher. From the rarity of old and even middle-aged people, I gathered that the life expectancy here was low, that few people lived past the age of thirty. This was hardly surprising, considering that no doctor or proper medical care was available in the entire region. Malnutrition was evident in many of the skinny children.

But when people came up to me, pointing to their various complaints – severe ulcerations seemed to be particularly common – there was precious little that I could do for them except to cleanse and bandage up some of the sores, and administer iodine, anti-worm pills, penicillin and the like from our medical chest. As for the disabled, I think that their situation could best be summarized by the reaction of one village elder whom I asked about this. When I had eventually made myself clear, by indicating my own emaciated and immobile legs, he merely pointed up to the sky, murmured 'Allah', and then lowered his head sideways so that it rested on his open palm. He was obviously puzzled as to why I should ask about such a simple thing; but his miming of a merciful death was only too clear.

Death remains the one drastic solution to the problem of disability in Southern Asia; as a doctor in Turkey put it to me rather
forcefully, 'Had you been a peasant in this country, you would
have been dead long ago.' For the less severely disabled, of
course, much depends on whether they can take up the occupation
they followed before they became afflicted, or perhaps do something that is normally associated with an infirmity (such as the
blind bard). The one and only positive aspect of the situation
seemed to me to lie in the close family bonds. Virtually all over
Asia, particularly in rural areas, relatives, even distant relatives –
or the village community in the rare cases where no kith and kin
are left – will consider themselves bound to give them food and
shelter. For a while at least.

On our second day at Bargamatol I was being pushed back by a
dozen children from a visit to the local school, when Abdullah
came rushing up to me, grinning broadly. Seizing the handles at
the back of my wheelchair, he began to push me at high speed
towards the outskirts of the village. The children came along, too,
together with about twenty villagers; but since I had long since
abandoned all hope of being able to conduct my interviews in
any semblance of privacy, I made no effort to dissuade them.
When we arrived at the shack, which stood a little beyond the
main cluster of dwellings, I saw why Abdullah was so excited.
In front of the shack, a man lay flat on his back, on the bare earth,
his only comfort the bare shade of a nearby tamarisk bush. He
watched our procession approach without the faintest expression
of surprise. As I wheeled myself up to him, one of the villagers
reached out from behind me and lifted one of my legs, letting it
fall again with a little thump, to show him that we shared a
common misfortune.

Over the next three hours, I pieced together the story. His
name was Ali, and he was in his late twenties; until about a week
previously, he had been perfectly fit, working as usual on this
rather poor and stony land, grazing a small flock of sheep on the
mountain pastures. Quite suddenly, he had felt this pain in his
back, and had started to run a high fever. Paralysis had followed
soon afterwards, and was still spreading. Now he could not move
without help; all he could manage was to lie outside, in his
tattered clothes, and resign himself to fate. Despite Abdullah's
agitated questioning, and the active participation of the other

villagers, all talking volubly and often picking up and letting drop any inert limbs, he never betrayed any emotion whatsoever; his face remained a mask of dignity. He just lay there, with his legs tucked under him.

I remembered my own experiences in Penang and Singapore where my legs were stretched daily and put through the entire range of movements a leg is normally able to do. This was essential to prevent contractures from setting in; otherwise the muscles in the limb affected by paralysis contract as if they were shrinking, eventually leaving it rigid in a permanently flexed position. Thus apart from the paralysis the victim becomes deformed, condemned to being fixed in disfiguring and awkward postures, which only drastic surgery can attempt to rectify.

Sadly I realized that the only real crumb of comfort for Ali lay in the relative security of his hut and relatives, despite the slow death to which this existence, without any medical attention, condemned him. But I wanted to find out if the thought of any alternative had crossed his mind. I wondered if he had considered fighting back. I decided to put it to him bluntly. 'Ali,' I said, 'you sick. You come back with me to Kabul, see doctor.' As Abdullah translated this simple message, simple enough even for his limited English, I watched anxiously for the reaction. Ali just looked at me blankly, as if I had asked him to accompany me on a trip to the moon. Then he muttered something indistinct to Abdullah. 'What does he say?' I asked impatiently. 'He say Will of Allah.'

Ali's relatives insisted that, as an honoured visitor, I should take tea with them inside. Whilst I sat sipping the hot liquid, I looked at them squatting on the bare floor in the dim light, and wondered to myself what sort of life Ali could expect, lying there week after dreary week. According to Abdullah, the family cultivated about two *jereebs*, or four acres, of land; hunger was seldom far away. Once the novelty of Ali's misfortune had worn off, they were more than likely to look upon him as an unproductive drag on the family food supplies, and treat him accordingly. In the summer, he might drag himself outside, and lie in the shade of the tamarisk tree; in winter, he would be confined to that cold earth floor. Bedsores, urinary infections, hyperstatic pneumonia or pulmonary œdema would inevitably follow.

It was time to leave, to start back to Kabul. Seeing my long face, Jocelyn enquired as to how the case looked. After I had described the situation, he asked how long I expected him to last. 'Two years at the most,' I replied morosely, 'and there, but for the Grace of God, go I.'

In fact this research was still causing me much heartsearching and many sleepless nights. Back in London, success seemed to revolve around efficiency, on making thorough preparations, establishing the right contacts, and leaving the rest in the hands of the Almighty. Now, with a daily quota of dust, dirt, heat, bugs, being shaken around in the car, lousy food and language problems, something more than efficiency was required. Discipline, of course; I needed all the discipline in the book to tackle this research, in an area of such appalling human wretchedness. Jocelyn could hardly be expected to help overmuch here; very understandably, he was increasingly reluctant to be closely involved in this aspect of expedition life. I could hardly blame him for such normal reaction of recoil; but the fact remained that this made my task the more lonely.

Something more than discipline was required. I kept reminding myself that my brief was to 'assess' the condition of the disabled and not to attempt the impossible at this stage in trying to change it. But regardless of whether this was reasonable or practicable, I had a compulsive urge to help, to start *doing* something.

It was relatively easy to find them. People would come up to the car, wherever we stopped, offering to show us the local museum or ancient ruins. Declining as politely as possible, I would explain that we had really come to visit the handicapped, whereupon their faces would assume a bewildered expression. But as soon as they saw that I was handicapped myself, their surprise would disappear, and they would fall over themselves to help, leading me all over the place, into the most awful slums to meet pitiable pieces of human wretchedness lying in the dank twilight of the houses.

To discover the true facts was less easy. Fact-finding is an acquired art in the East. Often I would discover that two relatives held quite different ideas as to the individual's age, the year of the onset of the infirmity, its symptoms, and so on. To get at the facts, reconstruct the true sequence of events, isolate the salient incidents, let alone attitudes, often proved virtually impossible. More often than not the villagers of South Asia set little store by the Western approach to situations, which endeavours to isolate and categorize events, to arrange them in some logical and distinctive pattern. They prefer that sense of harmony with the totality of creation, both manifest and spiritual, instead of inclining towards the particular. When I think of the volumes of distorted opinion and information which have been poured out about Asia in books and speeches as a result of this fundamental discrepancy of attitude, I shudder.

Even so, this part of my interviewing was still relatively easy, in comparison with the last stage, that of taking my leave. Over and over again I felt at a loss for words. To many of them I hailed from a magic land, where everything was possible. In most cases, of course, the disabled person would be resigned to fate, seemingly indifferent to my presence; but the relatives would cluster round looking into my eyes with hope and expectation for the first time in years. What could I say? 'Thank you for inviting me. I think you are wonderful?' They would turn away, crushed. After trying various permutations, I fell back on my status as a journalist. 'Thank you for seeing me; I shall write about you,' I said as cheerfully as I could. Writing about them was one thing, but what I desperately wanted was to be of practical help there and then.

When we returned to Kabul, I discussed our trip fully and frankly with Dr Aziz Seraj, one of the most humane and enlightened doctors in the country. Trained in the USA, Dr Seraj was not only Chief Medical Officer to the Kabul Municipality and President of the Department of Health and Hygiene at the Ministry of Education, but a practising physician with a successful private practice. Dr Seraj had been out of town when we first reached Kabul; we met now in his office in the Kabul Municipality building, and I soon discovered that he was not only deeply conscious of the problems of the disabled, but a remarkable organizer into the bargain. Sitting in his office with its beautiful red and black Afghan carpets, he asked me numerous questions about the expedition, particularly about our time in Afghanistan. I warmed to this quiet, rather shy doctor, and told him how desperately I wanted to be of some practical help. 'Ah, but this is the East', he sighed.

He told me how some five years previously he had battled to set up day-nurseries for the children of married women teachers, so that they could carry on teaching. The country was short of trained personnel, particularly teachers, and he had been struck by the wastage involved when these women had to abandon their teaching to look after their husbands and children. Custom and tradition demanded that women should remain unseen under head-to-toe veils, called *burkas*, to all but the immediate members of their families, and stay indoors for the most part, especially after marriage. For two years Dr Seraj battled against the weight of custom and apathy on the part of both officialdom and the general public. 'I persevered and eventually succeeded in getting some support from the government. Now there are six such crèches in the country. But it was a tough, slow process.'

The more we talked, the more I came to admire the determined approach behind his easy, unassuming charm. An idea suddenly flashed through my mind. There were, as yet, no rehabilitation facilities whatsoever in Kabul; could we not, somehow, between the two of us, start such a centre, on however modest a scale? There was no time like the present, and so I asked him point blank. 'Oh yes,' he replied with a warm smile, 'these things can certainly be done if you are willing to make the effort, and for long enough.' He paused, and rummaged in his drawers, pulling out a sheet of paper. 'As a matter of fact, some of us had already thought of something like what you mention, for about fifty out-patients.'

I studied the notes with the keenest interest, trying hard to restrain my excitement. Here at last, I felt, was something positive; a project moreover that maybe I could help in some way. I saw that on the basis of a simple, single-storied building with the barest minimum of equipment and local furnishings, the basic cost would work out to around £4,000; that moreover Dr Rahim, Minister of Health, had already granted the project some six acres of land in a central area of Kabul; that some of the diplomatic wives had formed themselves into a group to raise funds and that about 160,000 Afghanis (about £1,000) had already been secured. 'This is wonderful,' I said. 'But I see this has been on the table for about two years now.'

'Ah, that's the trouble. It's a long story, but what we really need is someone like you to help get things moving again.' 'But we have to leave in five days time.' 'Why don't you try all the same?'

I said that I should be only too delighted. After discussing the plan in detail that evening, I left with a sheaf of notes and a list of contacts.

When I realized the next morning what I had agreed to undertake, I was filled with excitement and apprehension. How could I, a peripatetic Westerner, help overcome, even in such a relatively narrow field, the permanence of centuries? How could I possibly achieve anything in five days? Dr Seraj had told me how he had waged another of his wars over the provision of spectacles for students with poor eyesight. After almost a year, he had eventually organized a system with the help of some of the university staff and students whereby he collected two Afghanis (about threepence) from all university students. Owing to the lack of efficient local organization, he himself had to remain the driving force behind the scheme. But it saved the eyesight and the careers of the students concerned. How could I tackle this much more complex problem?

I asked Jocelyn to help me get out the case with our shirts and the one lounge suit we had each taken. He looked mildly incredulous until I explained the reason for the sudden transformation from scruffy, blowzed yobbo to distinct respectability. Feeling clean and tidy for the first time in weeks, I called on Mr Tarzi. I knew that the kindly Mr Tarzi, with his wide connexions in the country, and a telephone on his desk, would be an ideal ally and mentor for what I wanted to do.

'But of course! Please use this as your headquarters.' Mr Tarzi knew all the Ministers, and would be delighted to help.

I quickly discovered when I got busy on Mr Tarzi's telephone (a rare amenity in Kabul) that I held one ace in my own hand. Everyone seemed to have heard, through the press or some grapevine, of my own disability, that I had come a long distance to help those similarly afflicted. 'You can rest assured of my eager cooperation,' said Dr Abdul Qayum, the Minister of the Interior. 'I come from a modest background myself, and am no stranger to poverty.'

This was an excellent start. Though the creation of such a centre didn't strictly lie within his ministerial province, both Dr Seraj and myself felt that the interest and support of his dynamic and influential personality would matter a great deal. When I saw Dr Rahim, the Minister of Health, I was put through a searching cross-examination about the facilities I had found for the disabled in Turkey and Persia. Fortunately I had the details fresh in my mind and was able to paint an accurate picture of what was going on in these countries, which face similar problems. Dr Rahim assured me that he would now make a point of speeding things up with the Prime Minister when he saw him next.

One of my last calls was on Dr Kassim Rashtia, Minister of Finance, Press and Information. 'Minister,' I began, 'I do hope that you will not construe my concern in these matters as meddling.' 'Of course not, dear friend,' he replied. 'It is wonderful that you should come so far on this noble mission. I shall consider it an honour to see that a sum is set aside for this scheme in our next budget.'

For five days I raced from one government department to another. From the response I received from ministers, the medical authorities and the press, I felt confident that the plan would now go forward. This was a tremendous boost to my morale; when I wrote to my mother on my last day in Kabul, I told her that I felt that this small victory alone justified all the years of preparation and hard work. I also wrote to Dr Rusk in New York, asking him if he would consider sending Dr Kassim Rashtia a letter of appreciation from the World Rehabilitation Fund. When I had sealed the letters, Jocelyn took them to be mailed in the central Post Office.

It was time to leave, via the Khyber Pass, for Pakistan and India.

CHAPTER 9

Courage and Fatalism in India

*

ONE afternoon in December 1964 I was wheeling myself down the orthopaedic ward at the King Edward Memorial Hospital, Bombay, when I looked up to see a small body encased up to the pelvis in white plaster. The head was crowned with a mop of black, unruly hair; but what really held my attention was the eyes – huge liquid eyes that were striking in their beauty, but the gaze that fell on me was wistful. As I wheeled myself to the side of his bed, I asked him what the trouble was.

'My legs,' the boy replied, grinning mischievously. 'But I'm going to walk again soon, like everyone else.'

'Well, not quite everyone,' I replied, slightly taken aback. 'I can't walk, as you can see.'

The grin disappeared as he stared at me disbelievingly. 'They failed with you, did they?'

There was something refreshingly direct and uncompromising in his attitude. With the help of Mr Manik Shahani, Superintendent of the Physiotherapy School, and the hospital social worker, I gradually pieced together his story. Maruti Shivaji, it turned out, had been the youngest of four sons of a humble truck driver from Poona. While he was still an infant, he had contracted polio, which had left his legs and part of the lower trunk paralysed. The inevitable contractures set in. His mother nursed him devotedly; but when he was three, she died.

The father's job as a truck driver kept him away from home for long periods. There was no question of changing the job to allow him to spend more time with his family – he was lucky to have a job at all. But the four boys managed somehow, the three older ones taking it in turns to look after the crippled Maruti. After about three years of this precarious existence, the two eldest decided that it was time they left to try their luck. For the next two years, Maruti lived quietly at home with his one remaining brother, who was two years older. But when he had just turned eight, disaster struck yet again: one day the father returned very sick from one of his trips. Four days later he was dead.

Since the parents were not native of Poona, there were no relatives to care for the two young orphans. No welfare handouts, no pension nor children's allowances, of course. Faced with the grim prospect of a slow starvation, they put their heads together and decided that they, too, should try their luck, leaving home as their elder brothers had before them. They packed their belongings into two small bundles, a head-scarf, tattered shirt and shorts, a cotton blanket riddled with holes and a little food. Helped by his brother, Maruti crawled painfully to the railway station.

Neither of them had ever left home before, let alone travelled by train. When someone asked them where they were going, they looked at each other blankly, trying desperately to remember the few names of far-away towns that their father had mentioned. Reasoning that they might fare better if they split up, the brother announced that he was going to head for Bangalore. 'Very well,' Maruti said, 'I'll head for Bombay.'

When the train drew in, willing hands reached down to help him aboard. Preoccupied with finding a square inch in the corridor, he never managed to wave farewell; before he realized what was happening, the iron monster was hurtling along the track. He crouched in the corridor, trying to make himself as small as possible, too bewildered even to cry. When the inspector demanded his ticket, he looked up at him blankly; the inspector turned a blind eye, having encountered many such pitiful bundles before.

When the train eventually pulled in to the Victoria Terminal at Bombay, Maruti stumbled out on to the platform in to bedlam. There were more people scampering about, jostling and pushing each other, than he had ever seen in his life. But no one took the slightest notice of the small figure shuffling painfully on his bottom. Since he had nowhere better to go, he decided to curl up in a corner. Somehow the station offered him a scrap of security; it was like clutching the end of a long thread that had started with another life, that led back to the home he had left earlier in the day. So he stayed in his corner all night and all the following day. During the days, weeks and months that followed, Maruti lived on the station, only varying his nightly corner when someone else got there first.

The terminal, with its vast halls and platforms of concrete, became a jungle, fraught with both danger and opportunity. To survive as a beggar, Maruti had to learn the laws of this asphalt jungle the hard way. He not only had to learn the subtle art of how to induce the passer-by to part with a coin or a *chapati*, but how to avoid the police and railway officials, the baggage trolleys, the porters carrying huge loads on their heads. There were other hazards too: other beggars, too hungry and vicious to think twice before snatching a hard-earned rupee from a child; and worst of all, the gangs on the look out for attractive children to pressgang into their beggar syndicates.

In time, Maruti found himself friends and allies through his own bravery and through keeping his wits about him. There was a fraternity living on the station, or at least spending most of their time on it: in addition to a whole army of beggars, there were the pickpockets, the touts, shoeshine boys, prostitutes, newspaper sellers, barrow boys of one kind and another. There were also the Wolves, a group of young urchins who became his friends. Despite his handicap, the Wolves accepted him into their midst, partly because he could hold his own despite his handicap, which earned him their respect, partly because there was little that he could not do in his own way, which was useful to them. What he lacked in mobility, he made up in ingenuity and initiative, and soon developed a remarkable flare for directing his little pack to where the spoils would be most rewarding.

But his greatest friend and ally was Bagherra, an old newspaper seller. From his pitch on the sidewalk outside the station wall, Bagherra used to hold the Wolves entranced with tales of his former life. Long ago, in the days of the British, he had worked as an errand boy in an office. The writing on the papers he was often sent to carry had fascinated him so much that he had taught himself to read and write. Bagherra was literate, a rare accomplishment in the asphalt jungle.

One day Maruti came up with one of his bright ideas. 'Why don't we learn to read and write?' 'Bah! Why d'you want that fancy stuff?' cried one of the Wolves. 'That won't help wheedle another paisa, and that's for sure!' 'Oh but it might,' said Maruti pensively, 'have you ever wondered what all these sign-boards say? Perhaps they tell of secret ways of getting more money.

Those who can read seem to have more money than we do, don't they?'

This clinched the argument. Without further ado they all went to share their new ambition with the old man. 'Ho, ho! So we want to get on in the world!' he teased. But next day Bagherra brought a slate and some chalk; setting up a classroom on the sidewalk by the station wall, he started to teach the urchins to read and write. Brushing the dust away, the boys copied the letters laboriously after him on the paving stones, holding the unfamiliar chalk close to the tip so it wouldn't break. They all chipped in to pay the old man twenty-five paisa (about threepence) for an hour's lesson.

Engrossed in this work one afternoon, Maruti looked up to see a figure hobbling past on a pair of crutches. He had seen such people before, but had never taken much notice of them. But the new world of the alphabet had excited his curiosity, so he asked the old man how these crutches worked. Bagherra laid aside his slate, and told him of hospitals, where clever doctors made people walk again. Maruti listened closely. The more he heard, the more determined he became to find out more for himself.

Shortly after, Mrs Lakshmi, the social worker, was sitting in her office one morning when the office boy announced that a patient had arrived to see her. Without looking up from her paperwork, she asked the boy to show him in. 'Then I saw these remarkable eyes, looking up straight into mine,' she recalled. 'He must have crawled all the way from the station, until he reached the swing door of my office.'

She had asked him what he wanted, and he had replied that he had heard that the hospital treated people and made them well again. 'Would you make me well?'

Intrigued by this unusual visitor, she had pushed her papers to one side and invited Maruti to tell her his story. He had related his experiences without self-pity, almost without emotion, as if it had all happened to someone else. Amazed at this mixture of innocence and maturity, so unexpected in a boy of eleven, who had no home, no security and no shelter worth the name, she asked him if he was sure that he wanted to undergo painful treatment at the hospital. 'When you have stayed for a long time with your legs in plaster, you will be able to walk again – but only with the aid of crutches and braces.'

'Won't I be able to walk like everyone else?'

Disappointed as he was, Maruti nevertheless was determined to go through with it. Mrs Lakshmi promised to help, and arranged for him to see a doctor, and reserved a bed in the hospital. Meanwhile, she found a place for him in a private orphanage, until the hospital bed became available.

When the time came, Mrs Lakshmi took Maruti to the orphanage, and introduced him around. 'But when I said I must leave, all the bravado dropped like a mask. Tears came into his eyes as he asked me when I would come to see him.' But the training in the asphalt jungle stood Maruti in good stead. Thanks to the skill and care he received in hospital, and frequent visits from Mrs Lakshmi to boost his morale, he survived the numerous operations cheerfully. Thanks to his indomitable cheerfulness and courage he became something of a special patient, loved by all the staff. 'I've now had the last operation,' he announced to me, cheerfully thumping the plaster on his legs. I looked at Mrs Lakshmi for confirmation. She nodded agreement. 'Yes, it's true,' she said. 'What's more, we've managed to persuade one of the Bombay charities to pay for some leg braces. Also, we've found a place for him at the School for Crippled Children here.'

Maruti was one of the lucky ones, one of the fortunate few. Just how lucky he was quickly became apparent as we plunged into our field work.

By the time we reached India in September 1964, we had clocked up 10,000 miles; by the end of that year, the mileometer showed 21,000. Although I always made a point of calling in at hospitals, normally in the larger cities, we spent most of our time in the country, well away from main towns and trunk roads. After a while, we felt that we had never known modern conveniences. We camped out wherever our fancy took us, a long way from camping site regulations and restrictions; we shared the simple life with the villagers we met, and felt honoured when they invited us in to share a meal, or to spend the night with mud walls and thatch around us.

But there was no inverted snobbery about this. Since four Asians out of five live in villages, in conditions that would strike most Westerners as primitive beyond belief, it seemed to me that if my 'random sampling' of the disabled was to be fair and acceptable, we should spend roughly four times as much time off the beaten track as we spent in the cities. But as the weeks turned to months, I realized that the pattern was very different from what I had visualized, sitting in the cosy warmth of a London flat.

As I talked with cripples, day after day, from early morning until late at night, in their homes or in the streets, sharing their hopes and problems, I entered a new world, a world of hopelessness and misery that few Westerners have ever penetrated. This may sound conceited, but most visitors from abroad seldom stray far from a well-worn path, scurrying busily between their tourist hotel, some ancient monument and perhaps the clinical, germ-free atmosphere of the modern hospital ward.

The more immersed I became in this work, the more I found that my own values and outlook were beginning to change. Meeting an orphaned child lying on the pavement with both legs amputated, my own problems and worries appeared ridiculous in comparison. After all, what does a tax demand, or a better flat, or a vacation abroad really mean when confronted by someone who is literally starving, whose last meal several days previously consisted of undigested grains rinsed from cow droppings? What price a smart kitchen, or a new car, when you meet a crippled girl condemned to a life of begging because her parents can't afford tuppence a day for her busfare to school? Many argue that such comparisons are unrealistic and unfair. Up to a point, they may be right. But they have never lived, I suspect, in the East, and have never had the opportunity of finding out for themselves how the less fortunate live, how little is asked of life.

In this connexion, I shall always remember Azad Bhat, a beggar whom we met in the village of Tangmarg, in the Himalayan foothills of Kashmir. We met him by the side of the road, sitting cross-legged in his tiny wooden cart, little bigger than a doll's pram, pulled by a helpful neighbour. When we stopped for a chat, Azad talked uninhibitedly about his legs, which had been paralysed since he was two years old, how he had lost his parents, and laughed uproariously at the tattered shirt that he was wearing, which was his only real possession. He even invited us back to the one-roomed, dark, dirty hole in which he lived. It was painfully true; he had nothing else, barring that shirt, his cart and a dish of half-eaten cold rice carefully saved for next day's meal. I asked him if there was anything in particular that he wanted. 'Oh no,' he replied, shrugging his shoulders. 'Just enough food. Enough to eat.'

'But surely there must be something else,' I persisted. 'If you had the chance, for example, would you go to hospital?'

'No, I wouldn't. I'm all right as I am,' he replied.

All he wanted out of life, the sum total of his ambitions, was enough to fill his belly. The inevitable crowd had gathered as we were talking, and as I turned to leave, a voice mentioned the word *baksheesh*. I fumbled in my pocket, and Azad's smile vanished; the fun was over, this was business. A well-rehearsed look of pathetic dejection came over his face, while the eyes watched my hand, like a hawk about to drop on its prey.

Considering that there are as many diverse languages, customs, traditions and cultures within India as in the whole of Europe lumped together, it is rash to generalize about anything. But during the past two or three centuries, the Indian people have endured increased poverty, not least through the humiliation and exploitation they have endured at the hands of the colonial powers. A tradition of hardship, coupled with one of the world's oldest continuous civilizations, have helped to nurture a pessimistic outlook on life and, more often than not, a disdain for the value of worldly pursuits. There are numerous other factors, of course, but poverty always loomed largest whenever I pondered the predicament of the disabled.

You can never escape it, even in hospital. I was discussing this one day with Dr T. P. Srivastava, a surgeon at the hospital in Benares, when we were touring his wards. We suddenly came upon a bed which was conspicuously empty, in itself a rarity, and I asked him the reason why. 'Oh, that's Bokai's,' he replied with rather a sad smile. 'He was here, off and on, until yesterday. But I doubt if we shall see him again.' When I pressed him to explain, he related how Bokai had met with some ghastly accident nine weeks previously, and had been admitted with the sole of his foot torn off, leaving one huge festering wound. With treatment and care, his condition had begun to improve, whereupon Bokai started to slip out of hospital during the daytime. Ripping his dressing off, he squatted on the pavement exposing the wound to passers-by, hand outstretched, until he felt that he had earned enough to return for a night's rest in hospital. 'I told him yesterday that I was going to make a skin graft,' the doctor added wryly. 'I

Taj Mahal seen from the Agra Fort

Gol Gumbaz mausoleum (famous for its echo), Bijapur, Mysore State

Details of the
Channakesava
temple in Belur,
Mysore State

The King's Balance in Vijayanagar, Mysore State (according to legend the King was weighed against gold which was then distributed to the poor)

Kandariya-Mahadeo temple in Khajuraho, Uttar Pradesh

explained that this would probably heal the wound completely. But this would have killed the goose that laid the golden egg. We haven't seen him since.'

He would have earned between five and ten rupees a day, as a beggar with a suitably horrible wound. About one and a half rupees back at his old job, as a sweeper. It all added up. I asked about his chances of survival. 'Very poor, I would think,' he replied, 'Gangrene, most likely.' A hopeless, inescapable poverty will sometimes drive a desperate parent to fearsome lengths. I once knew a blind beggar called Yussuf, who lived in the wretched slums of south Tehran, in Persia. Yussuf was cheerful enough; being talented in his profession, he was relatively well fed. I asked him once how he became blind, and he told me of how his family had lived in a one-roomed hovel . . . how eight children lived and mostly starved there, how his father had worked as a porter in the bazaar, and how five of his brothers and sisters had died of malnutrition. 'When my mother returned from burying the fifth,' he said, 'she called me into our home, and poured arsenic into my eyes.' He paused for a moment, reliving the pain maybe, his hands gripping his gnarled stick until the knuckles showed white. 'She loved me very much,' he added, 'and now I understand. It is better to be blind than always hungry. Most probably I should never have survived, if it had not been for my blindness.'

But when attempting to analyse the predicament of the disabled in Asia, I seldom, if ever, found a case of poverty uncompounded by some other factor. Poverty, by itself, is relatively easy to understand; poverty by itself can be fought, if there is a will to fight. But poverty compounded by fatalism, by acceptance according to God's will, is something much more formidable. As the Indian scholar Abid Husain explains in his book *Indian Culture**: 'the basic wants of the people were few and the natural resources for supplying them ample. The economic factor was, therefore, not as important in their lives as in colder countries. The mainstay of their life was tilling the soil and a good harvest depended on favourable monsoons which they believed to be subject to the will of the gods. So their talents and energy were devoted not so much to the invention of efficient ways and instruments of production as to the search for efficacious prayers

Indian Culture p. 2, Abid Husain (Asia Publishing House, London 1963)

and sacrifices. And if these failed to please the gods they had no alternative but to submit to their will ... Events which disturb the normal routine of nature are rare. There are no volcanoes and earthquakes are mild and infrequent. No stronger natural calamities than storms and hurricanes of moderate intensity are experienced by the people. The most important effect produced on the Indian mind by the observation of the regularity and the continuity of natural processes is the feeling that the operation of the moral law is just as regular and continuous and the moral consequences of every action as definite and inevitable as the succession of seasons. The determinism or the so-called "fatalism" of the people of India is not based on the idea that man is a mere tool but on the belief that in initiating action he is free within certain limits, but once he has done something, a chain of reactions is started which is not in his power to stop or change. So he must accept with patience the consequences of his action.

'The Indian people did not have to carry on a struggle for existence against the ruthlessness of nature. They had only to wait for the rain-bearing monsoon to come and pour rain upon their fields. "The rain, the rain, the welcome rain." This was another reason why they failed to develop vigour and vitality. Their philosophy of life did not aim at contending with nature to wring its mysteries out of it or to conquer and control its forces but to submit to its inscrutable ways, to be initiated into the spirit of the Reality permeating it and to live in harmony with it. Their ideal, in short, was not struggle but peace, not self-assertion but self-abnegation.'

Such an ideal has helped breed a fatalistic attitude towards disablement. Usha was eleven, when I met her in the slums of Jamkhandi, squatting on the threshold of a murky one-roomed dwelling in the back streets. Other children were running about, playing their games, on their way home from school; Usha looked at them wistfully. She looked so thin and bedraggled that I asked Jocelyn to stop the car and enquired if her parents were about. After a moment a small, mousy man appeared from inside the shack and I asked him about Usha. 'It is very hard to make ends meet,' he complained, avoiding both my eyes and the question. 'As a clerk, I only earn a hundred and fifty rupees a month.'

Hordes of children were now running in and out of the doorway, and I asked how many were his.

'We had thirteen,' he replied, his face twitching nervously, 'but three died, leaving us three boys and seven girls.' He paused a moment, stroking the week's growth on his chin. 'But last week we were blessed with a baby boy.' He stood before me, grinning sheepishly. I wondered if I would count this a blessing, to exist with eleven children on a hundred and fifty rupees a month. 'But what about Usha?' I asked, determined to have my answer. 'It is very sad,' he sighed. 'It is the Will of God.'

When I asked about school, he replied that she could not possibly go to school, because she could not walk like the others to get there. But I had already discovered, from my researches the previous day, that a Kindergarten school collected children in a tricycle rickshaw, converted to take a large vanlike box on the rear. I was sure, in fact, that this rickshaw passed close to them every day. I described how the system worked, but the father's face remained unmoved.

'Well, why don't you ask them if they can collect her?' I asked, goaded to desperation by his ineptitude.

'Ah, perhaps,' he replied, never having thought of it. Never intending to know either, alas. Life is harsh under such circumstances. Who am I to blame him for concentrating his resources on his healthy children? After all, Usha, to him, was a write-off.

Such a fatalistic attitude permeates existence throughout South Asia. The older the civilization, the more ingrained the fatalism; and – as embodied in the Gandhian philosophy – the greater the distaste for unbridled material pursuits. Such fatalism is by no means peculiar to the field of disability. But it tends to make the lot of the disabled doubly hard, as I found to my sorrow and distress. Sensing that to struggle against the inexorable serves only to tighten the noose, the disabled themselves rarely possess the will to fight back. Their motivation towards self-improvement or finding work is minimal, by and large. This is inevitable in a part of the world where a great deal of material and social progress still remains to be attained before self-improvement and a measure of control over material conditions becomes a realistic goal for the individual.

On the reverse of the coin, the relatives and friends of the disabled, representing society at large, usually regard disability, even its more minor manifestations, as crippling to the point o-outright rejection from the ranks of the employable. Although I found many instances of the disabled performing a worthwhile job of work, to their own and their employers' satisfaction, there is a widespread feeling within society generally that the disabled man or woman is totally incapable of doing a job of work.

The role played by religion can hardly be underestimated, particularly in areas where Buddhism and Hinduism is predominant. Like the cycle of sowing and reaping in the fields, the soul is believed to transmigrate in countless, if not infinite, rebirths, and may reappear in the next incarnation in a variety of forms, human, animal, semi-divine or even insect. The status of any particular incarnation is not so much influenced as strictly determined by the balance of merit, or the opposite, that the soul has built up, and carried over on the balance sheet, from previous incarnations. This is the unrelenting, inexorable 'cause and effect' law of karma, one of the most pervasive and tenacious laws governing human behaviour that society has ever devised. Karma, together with poverty and the minimal control over the physical environment of a pre-industrial society, underlies the much-maligned, much-misunderstood concept of 'oriental fatalism', which most people in the Western hemisphere dismiss with a wave of the hand as mere spinelessness or indolence. But in its context karma is quite different, and can be explained in terms of plain acquiescence to the facts of the situation. When you play a game of cards, you have virtually unlimited opportunities of exercising your skill, depending of course on the game. But you have absolutely no opportunity to influence the cards you are dealt to begin with. Similarly with karma; how you lead your present life is up to you, but the kind of rank and existence you have been born into, the cards you have been dealt to begin with, lie outside your control, having been predetermined by the merit balance sheet of your previous incarnations. No wonder then that the Ushas of this world mutter 'Will of God', when they talk about their predicament. It is not easy, especially for those brought up on the maxim 'God helps those who help themselves', to realize how deeply this acquiescence is ingrained. It is not true that you need only drive and diligence to live by this maxim. No less essential is that sophisticated grid of social and economic amenities which we in our society have come to take for granted, but which provides an invaluable springboard under our feet.

Our Expedition covered South Asia from west to east, an enormous area. Before leaving I expected the condition of the disabled to differ widely in countries as distinctive in history, geography, climate, religion and social traditions, as, say, Persia, India and Thailand. Yet, as we soon found out, where the lot of the disabled was concerned, virtually no difference was observable. Thus it follows, to my way of thinking, that if the similarity is so striking, it must be rooted in factors that are common to these countries, which are otherwise so disparate.

What are these factors? Broadly, age-long poverty and the scant command over physical environment, characteristic of a traditional, pre-industrial society. Thus the predicament of the Asian disabled, with all its wretchedness, despair and prejudice, hardly differs from what prevailed in pre-industrial Europe. This also indicates how relief may come, and local governments are well aware of this, on the whole. If, before Independence, the situation was virtually stagnant or deteriorating, much progress has already been achieved in the short span since self-determination. That progress would seem even more impressive, had not much of it been nullified by the population explosion, paradoxically its by-product. Thus in the field of health and medicine, in the years since the country attained Independence, life expectancy has been raised in India from thirty-two to fifty years; the number of hospitals and dispensaries from 7,400 to 14,600; hospital beds from 73,000 to 240,100; doctors from 47,400 to 86,000; nurses from 7,000 to 45,000. Rehabilitation facilities, virtually non-existent in 1947, have received a share of this effort.

Yet the magnitude of the task ahead remains enormous. I was once touring the wards of the Medical College Hospital in Allahabad, when I came across a pitiful figure in one of the beds, staring silently at the raw amputation scars on both his wrists. The bandages had just been removed for the first time, and Ram Lal had only just realized the extent of his injuries. As he lay back on his bed, his arms bent at the elbow, his eyes flickered unnervingly from one lacerated stump to the other, like a spectator at a slow-motion game of table tennis. I asked my host, Dr R. C. Gupta, what had happened. 'So far as we can make out,' he replied, 'his hands got caught up in some machinery at the flour mill where he worked. His employer dumped him on the hospital steps, only half-conscious with pain and loss of blood, and ran away.'

When I approached, Ram's eyes stopped flickering for a moment, and his eyebrows puckered when he noticed my wheelchair. 'God give you happiness. May you walk again,' he said, in a strangled voice. I was deeply moved, but before I could reply, he had retreated once more into his private terror. 'Have faith in Almighty God,' I said. Somehow the words rang hollow. 'This is my karma, this is my karma,' he kept repeating, mesmerized by the hovering stumps. 'What will happen to my children?' Expecting no reply, he pressed his stumps into his eyes, unable to bear the sight any longer. The tears began to trickle down his cheeks.

I wheeled myself out of earshot, and asked Dr Gupta about his background, and what his prospects were now. It appeared that he was a poor, landless villager, earning about thirty rupees a month, until the accident a month ago. His job was not pensionable, nor would he receive any compensation. There were no facilities locally for fitting him up with artificial hands, nor any institution or orphanage to care for his five children. 'There's little hope except begging,' the Doctor concluded. 'A short life of begging at that, before malnutrition or disease puts his body to rest.' I found Ram's wife outside, squatting in the dust by the back entrance of the hospital, clutching their youngest child in her arms. I noticed, with a sinking heart, the familiar look in her eyes, a glazed expression that reached through and beyond pain and suffering, an expression that I had seen stamped on all too many faces during the Expedition already. When I tried to express my sympathy, she merely echoed her husband's words in a hollow monotone, 'This is our karma, our karma.' When I enquired after the other children, she directed us towards a village eighteen miles away. We found them there, squatting dejectedly inside the small mud hut. Some neighbours of the same caste had evidently brought them food; but the blackened hearth was cold. They knew that their father had met with an accident, but that was all. When I asked the eldest boy what they were going to do, he replied with the time-worn phrase: 'Bhagwan ki khel', or, 'it's all God's whim'.

This reaction is hardly surprising when you consider local conditions. When calamity strikes in the West, or in some economically advanced community, the person involved can call upon a sophisticated network of controls. If the house catches fire, he telephones immediately for the fire brigade, which comes tearing to the scene in mechanized vehicles, pumps water from hydrants, and puts the fire out, with any luck. If he is unlucky, and the house burns to the ground, he can claim insurance money. But an Asian fire is a very different kettle of fish. No telephone. No fire brigade, anyway. Certainly no hydrant, and no insurance. Instead, the villager grabs a pail from somewhere, and laboriously draws a bucketful of water from the nearest well; by the time he has staggered back, the house (probably thatched) has already been reduced to a pile of cinders. No wonder, when faced with such impotence wherever he turns, he hangs his head, and mutters 'This is the Will of God', or 'This is my karma'.

It would be wrong to dismiss insurance out of hand, if only because I found that the so-called joint (or extended) family system – and in any event the sense of a blood relationship, even when physically tenuous as between tenth cousins – is still a force to be reckoned with, especially in the more primitive, tradition-bound areas. The joint family system usually operates on a strictly hierarchic basis, the members pooling their earnings, like some socialistic society in miniature, the males having the say and the elders firmly ruling the roost. Thus blood-bonds are woven into a fabric of security and protection amidst conditions of economic precariousness. In case of any misfortune, sickness, unemployment, feud, litigation or moral predicament, the member can count on the assistance of his relatives.

I had always assumed, along with the authors of the various books on the subject, that this system would take care of the rural disabled. Not so, at least not necessarily so. Although it is always dangerous to generalize, I would say that this is because the system, like more modern forms of insurance, is not entirely free from considerations of self-interest, and does not really lend itself to the care of severely and permanently handicapped members of the community. The man who is sick, or out of work, can call upon help from the joint family; but his affliction or predicament is short-lived, by comparison; anyway, the odds are that he might be giving, not receiving, one day. But the cripple who is permanently incapacitated will never be in that happy position. He will never be able, in all probability, to shoulder his part of the burden. Instead, he will have to share living space that is already over-crowded, eat food that is already insufficient, perhaps even tie down one of the able-bodied, because he needs someone to attend to his basic needs. When the novelty wears off, the rest of the family recognize him as a permanent liability, he can expect a dog's life, especially if his affliction is regarded as a shameful product of his karma. A badly disabled woman might even be thrown out, because women are generally regarded as less important than men. No detailed research has ever been carried out; but from my observations I would say that the common attitude towards disabled villagers, whether male or female, is depressingly similar to the cruel way in which Hindu widows were once treated. Except that the handicapped have the additional burden of feeling useless, and being a physical encumbrance.

Very few of the rural handicapped ever receive medical attention; relatively speaking, Ram Lal was fortunate in this respect. India has been training many more doctors in recent years, but at the time I was travelling, there was still only one doctor to every five thousand population. The target is to reduce this ratio by 1974 to 1 : 4,500. But of the doctors in practice, and of those recently qualifying, four out of five choose the relative comfort of the urban area. As one doctor told me ruefully: 'A rural practice exposes one to greater hardships and drawbacks than it is fair to expect of anybody short of a saint. Often most of the basic amenities are absent, there are hardly any people of similar education and interests to mix with in one's free time; schools are poor, not of the standard where a reasonably ambitious middle-class parent would wish to send his children. To gain peoples' confidence, to break through the prejudice and suspicion, takes years of effort. Such practices are virtually dead-end jobs, with little opportunity for becoming known and established professionally.' Communications between town and village are either poor, or non-existent; I have spent many hours of exquisite frustration in attempting to telephone from outlying townships in the country. Few of my disabled friends, on the other hand, would recognize a telephone, if they saw one, let alone have enough money to pay for the call, if they knew how to use it. The village is their whole world, the one source of security.

If only a small percentage of those who need help receive it, fewer still receive it in time. 'If only he'd come in earlier' was what we kept hearing from doctors everywhere. All too often the patient arrives when his condition has deteriorated beyond hope.

I remember discussing this with Dr M. L. Gupta, Orthopaedic
Surgeon at the Medical College in Srinagar, Kashmir, as he
carried out a pre-operative examination on a man with a severely
crippled hand. 'Look at this hand,' he sighed, trying to flex
fingers hard as stone. 'Had he come to me in time, I could have
operated. He would have been back at work within a month as
good as new. Now, well, whatever I do, the man will remain
partly crippled for the rest of his life.'

I felt intensely in sympathy with this quiet, dedicated doctor
battling against scarcity of funds, facilities, equipment, short-
comings at every step, besetting his task with almost insuperable problems. I asked him what he would concentrate on if
he had better facilities, more money, more staff. 'Getting
them in quicker,' he replied without hesitation. 'Or at any
rate finding some way of treating them at an earlier stage.' I
looked at Ali Shah, Dr Gupta's patient, who would probably
never be able to work again, because he arrived too late, and I
wondered.

A comprehensive analysis of this whole problem would fill
several volumes, and I must restrict myself to mentioning two
other factors only, which I believe to be basic to the condition of
the disabled in India. The first of these is the question of caste.
Although caste discrimination was outlawed after Independence
and equality enshrined in the new constitution, the fact remains
that many features of the caste system have survived, virtually
as powerful and pervasive as ever. This has given rise to
much heart-searching in India.

To many in the West, caste has been associated essentially with
some of its more notoriously sensational aspects, such as untouchability. In fact, the caste system over the centuries has
ordained the daily life of everyone from the highest to the lowest,
down to the smallest detail on the personal level. As Ronald
Segal puts it, in *The Crisis of India**: 'Caste penetrates every
aspect of living. It conditions how and when and what and
where a person eats and washes and talks and prays; from whom
specific foods and drinks and specific utensils may be taken, and
to whom offered; the way the hair is worn, the kind of clothes, the
shape of ornaments, the form of funerals, the frequency of sex . . . '
In fact, the caste system ensured that society was conducted like

**The Crisis of India* p. 34, Ronald Segal (Jonathan Cape, London 1965) a well-disciplined symphony orchestra, with each player bowing or blowing precisely the right note at the right time for the right duration. But unlike the symphony orchestra, whose individual members retain their individualism off the concert platform, caste tends to produce within each sub-caste a human stereotype, or as near a stereotype as makes no odds.

Another, if related, concept fundamental to traditional Hindu society is that of *dharma*, the natural or pre-ordained function. It is the dharma of a river to flow, of a fire to burn, of things born to die; extended into the human realm, it is the dharma of a sweeper to sweep, of a cobbler to make shoes, of a washerwoman to wash clothes. However lowly one's dharma, it is not only a duty, but indeed a blessing to perform it; to pursue another's dharma is dangerous, according to one of the holy Hindu scriptures. Thus, in terms of occupation, society is almost static, sons following doggedly in the footsteps of their fathers. When linked up with caste, which ordains the minutiae of everyday life, it is hardly surprising that the individual possesses a highly developed sense of his 'place', of his role to play in the grand symphony of creation. I remember once, listening to a senior official in India discoursing about the brotherhood of man. As he warmed to his theme, telling me how all men were brothers to each other, all children of God, he began to wave his arms in the air to emphasize his feelings. With one of his more exaggerated sweeps, he knocked a pencil eraser off his desk on to the floor. He looked at it for a moment, as it lay by the leg of his chair. Pressing the bell, he ordered the servant to pick it up and replace it on his desk, before returning to his theme.

Attitudes towards disability vary widely according to the caste, but nearly always to the detriment of the disabled member. Much of the caste mentality endures. Let me illustrate this by repeating the words of Mrs Kumeran, whom we found lying desolately on the floor of a mud hut in East Kerala, at the foothills of the Western Ghats in Southern India. It was a familiar story. No furniture, no windows; total possessions consisted of three cooking pots and two small bundles, tied up in a corner of the earthen floor. Lying there, day after day, with no strength to drag herself out, even to beg. Of her eight children, only three had survived, a son and two daughters. When the son married, he brought his wife back, too poor to set up home on his own. Five adults and now two small grandchildren were sleeping, eating, cooking, living after a fashion in a space of about twelve foot square. 'Have you ever seen a doctor?' I asked.

'No, Sahib. It is the Will of God. Besides, what doctor would want to touch me?'

'But there's no such thing as untouchability now.'

'But it wouldn't be right, sahib,' she replied. 'We belong to the Pulayan people. It wouldn't be right.' (The Pulayans were regarded as the 'lowest' outcasts in the region.) Nothing that I could say would have the slightest effect, and so I gave up.

When I arrived in India, in September 1964, I had high hopes that I might be able to make some impression on the problem of infirmity, that I might be able, somehow, somewhere, to do something to help mitigate it. But the more I saw, the more disabled people I talked to, the more I realized I could never achieve anything very substantial on my own, single-handed. The problem was immensely complex, and had existed, to all intents, as long as man himself. After a while, I began to rationalize this, on the grounds that if I was unable, unlike David, to fell Goliath with a single pebble, at least I could try more gently, with a little push here, a little there. I began to notice, for example, that many of the facilities that already existed to alleviate suffering were often not fully utilized and even neglected. Some of the doctors who were qualified in this field had abandoned it, while others complained that they were so overloaded with paperwork or other jobs that they had hardly any time left for the disabled. Hospitals were hamstrung by lack of funds, or red tape, or both; if shortage of funds was inevitable, the bureaucratic morass was surely amenable to improvement.

I began to formulate ideas for publicity campaigns, using the mass media of radio and the cinema, to try to combat the public prejudice and apathy towards disability. I had ideas for making cheap orthopaedic appliances, suitable to local conditions and pockets; ideas for training disabled villagers in basic handicrafts, and for setting up small-scale manufacture adapted to rural areas, by reserving for the disabled a quota of places in the Training Institutes which cater for such education; for selling the products of home-bound rural disabled through special counters in village co-operative stores. The more miles we clocked up, the more the ideas fermented in my mind. None of them involved huge capital expenditure, none seemed too far-fetched. 'Where there's a will, there's a way.'

But as the weeks turned to months, I realized that I was fighting a lonely battle. I had never imagined that my self-imposed task would be easy; but the more deeply immersed I became, the more I became convinced that the greatest stumbling block lay deeply embedded in the collective subconscious, in those stalactites of quiet endurance, of numbed suffering, of doubt in the very worth of living and the possibility of true earthly happiness. There was no denying that much could be done in the short term along the lines I had been planning, in tapping and adapting existing amenities. But the biggest enemy was apathy, apathy not only amongst the able-bodied public towards disablement and re-habilitation, but the apathy of the disabled themselves. There was a look in the eyes of the disabled that haunted me night and day, a look that frightened me to the very core of my being, in comparison with which the worst injury or disfigurement seemed relatively trifling.

I shall never forget the eyes of a small nine-year-old boy called Gulu, staring at me from a hospital bed in Jagdalpur. As I wheeled myself up the ward towards his bed, the eyes watched me calmly and steadily, huge limpid brown eyes fixed in a vice of ageless melancholy. A few inches below, the skin glistened, taut to breaking point, under the strain of a huge evil growth, half the size of his head. I could tell at a glance that Gulu had cancer in its final stage. He must have been in terrible pain, and yet his face and expression remained composed.

'Does he know that he will die soon?' I asked the doctor quietly.

'Yes he does.'

'Does he ever cry, or complain?'

'Never. He regards it as his fate.' From the tone of his voice, I realized that to the doctors and nurses, Gulu's endurance was nothing exceptional.

'Is he constantly in pain?'

'I am afraid so,' the doctor replied. 'Moreover I am afraid we do not have enough suitable drugs to mitigate it.'

I felt myself shivering before this numb gaze, which seemed to sum up not only his own agony, but the wretchedness of un-counted millions in India, the silent, unknown millions. If only they could fight back with the same courage!

I may have been somewhat over sensitive to Gulu's particular predicament. Two weeks previously, in Calcutta, I had received Tadeusz's telegram bearing the news of my mother's death. Though I had expected it, the news left me numbed and shattered. I couldn't help reproaching myself for being 7,000 miles away. The next day several letters reached me with details of her last days.

Though in very severe pain, till the very eve of her death she had insisted on cooking, cleaning and keeping up with her correspondence. When Tadeusz protested that he would be only too glad to do whatever was needed, she replied that it gave her great satisfaction to remain active and useful. There was something truly awesome in her quiet, gentle, unbreakable will-power and self-command; it had been typical throughout her life. She remained in control of her person in the teeth of her terrible affliction, right up to the threshold of death itself.

The end came on the 14th of February 1965 when the cancer affecting her head and neck gnawed through an artery, causing slow but unstaunchable bleeding. She knew this was the end. She requested a priest and the presence of several of the closest friends and relatives, asking some of them personally over the telephone by her bed. Feminine and aesthetic to her last, she asked Tadeusz for a mirror to tidy her hair and face. She had willed her eyes for a corneal graft; knowing that the pupils have to be removed within an hour or so of death, she realized that Tadeusz, who was mustering the last ounces of self-control as he sat beside her, might not be in a position to call the hospital. She therefore asked a cousin to do this, giving her the telephone number. Apart from a reminder that she wished her ashes to be buried in Poland at the foot of her mother's grave, her words were concerned with the lives and well-being of her nearest ones, especially Tadeusz. She thanked him for the wonderful years of happiness she had shared with him and enjoined on all those present to help him in the days of shock and loneliness in which her departure would leave him. Two hours before death the loss of blood caused her to lapse into unconsciousness. Her last words were about the happiness which the love of Tadeusz, the beauty in life and nature had given her.

Over and over again I read the letters in which those final hours were described. I sat in a friend's garden. The temperature was in the eighties, and golden orioles scampered about the lawn; the letters mentioned frost and snow in London. At times I felt this was only a bad dream that would prove as unreal as the frost and snow were in that green, sunny garden. The person whose loss I found so hard to admit had been much more than a mother to me; that relationship had been superceded in my adolescence by one where she had primarily become my closest and most respected friend.

For generations cancer has been a relentless scourge in her family. Her aunt, mother, brother, sister and many others had died of it, often after particularly painful illnesses. But invariably the affliction had been faced with unflinching fortitude, with what was set up above all else, inculcated in each of us from our earliest days, the twin patrician virtues of courage and self-command.

An ardent patriot, she had been awarded the 'Krzyz Walecznych' (Cross of the Valiant) in recognition of her outstanding bravery and service to the Resistance during the Second World War. Yet she never lost sight of the stupidity of war that divides us into friends and foes, never allowed hatred to blind her to the opponent's humanity. Finally, when in the aftermath of war and the Communist invasion she lost everything material, she retained her innate grace, wit and nobility intact, carrying these with utter naturalness even as she swept the floors and washed the dishes. And so she died, *en grande dame*, in a manner that befitted her life.

I found that my mind had clarified. Perhaps it takes a shock of this nature to make a man realize that he cannot take on the whole world singlehanded. Whatever the reason, I found that when I began to pick up the threads of my work again, I was drastically rearranging my priorities or streamlining my ambitions; whereas before I had struggled to find the answers to the whole problem, in all its complex manifestations, I realized now that I must concentrate my energies and resources. I would have to find one particular area in which something small but positive needed to be done and could be done; then I would endeavour to move heaven and earth to see that it really was done. After all, even the greatest palaces are built of single bricks, as the Polish saying goes. But which area?

Some pessimists have claimed that a country like India, faced with so many priorities of desperate urgency, would be better advised to forget rehabilitation of their physically handicapped for the time being and concentrate its resources first in other directions, for instance in that of preventive medicine. But I reasoned that problems like this would hardly ever get tackled if they were neatly pushed into a queue. Before my eyes, the disabled were subsisting in conditions that could hardly be imagined by those who hadn't seen what I had seen. For me, that was enough. Rather than question the principle of help, I decided I would concentrate my attention on evolving the most practical methods of rehabilitation, the methods best adapted to the local environment. In short, how best to 'Asianize rehabilitation in Asia'.

But where was I going to lay my brick? That was the question that now kept me awake at nights.

CHAPTER 10

'Chief Fool' at the Holi Festival

*

CAR travel in Asia is anything but dull. Often we drove over jungle tracks frequented by all manner of wild beasts, from jackals to tigers. From time to time, well-meaning villagers would come up to the car with a worried look on their faces. 'If you meet an elephant,' they would say very seriously, 'you must stop and stay quiet until elephant go. Elephant dangerous beast, trample car, kill!' Although I hate to admit it, we drove for hundreds of miles through such wild beast country in various parts of south-east Asia, but never encountered anything more alarming than a panther. Jocelyn was changing a wheel one day, shortly after dusk, when I saw this panther sitting placidly by the roadside, about twenty yards away. As soon as I shouted, the beast slunk away into the forest. It never even growled.

All the same, I was often alarmed at the thought of such an encounter. It was all very well for Jocelyn, who could shin up the nearest tree if the worst came to the worst – always assuming that the enemy was not a faster tree-climber. But my tree-climbing days were over.

Travelling the length and breadth of India, we encountered all types of scenery, from the flat, endless plains of the Gangetic Valley to the breathtaking forests of Orissa, the Western Ghats and the Terai as the jungle tracts of the Himalayan foothills are called, with their flowering trees and lush tropical vegetation. Whilst we were primarily concerned with the disabled project, we deliberately tried to offset this with visits to palaces, temples, ancient ruins, tribal encampments and craft centres. Many of these trips were return visits for me, to places I had seen years previously when touring on foot or by bicycle. The fact that I was seeing them again never failed to cheer me, and I fear Jocelyn had to put up with a good deal of surplus culture. But he never complained. Nearly every day we managed to see something unusual whether by accident or design, something well and truly off the beaten track. I remember how heartened I was one evening when he told me that he had no regrets about coming. 'You never know on this lark what you'll be eating next, or where you'll be sleeping. But at least there's never a dull moment!'

Most of our time was spent in the outback of course. Sometimes we stopped in Dak bungalows. In India these are designed to offer basic accommodation to minor officials on tour. Bedding is not normally provided; water sometimes comes out of a tap, but more often is brought in a pail. More often than not, however, there was no such rudimentary shelter available, and we would stay with the village headman, some rural development worker, or simply camp.

Travelling for most of the time through hamlets and villages, our diet was similar to that of the villagers. This was partly a matter of 'Hobson's Choice', no other food being available, but mainly because our budget did not allow anything more fancy than a simple diet of the cheaper kinds of food. I was glad that this should be so, and made it a cardinal, vigorously enforced Expedition rule that we should live frugally to the point of harshness. I firmly believed that by living close to the ordinary people of Asia, we would gain a much deeper insight into their conditions and attitudes and the place of the disabled in society. The food varied from region to region. In South India it was mainly rice and curries, burning hot with chilies, in the north the unleavened pancake-like bread together with lentils, onions and other vegetables, chased down with strong tea usually boiled in the kettle together with the milk and sugar. The resultant brew doesn't taste like anything associated elsewhere with tea. Once this led to an impassioned argument.

'What do you think this is?'

I tasted the brew. 'Hmm. I think it's coffee.'

Jocelyn took another sip. 'It's tea. No, I believe it's coffee.'

By this time I had changed my mind. 'Bet you two rupees it's tea.'

'You're on. I say it's coffee. Let's drink up what's in the kettle, and see who's right.'

Nobody won the bet. At the kettle's bottom there were tea leaves, coffee grounds, and much else besides.

To quench the thirst we usually had to rely on water. We did so reluctantly, as the risks of infection, even to such hardened constitutions as ours, made other beverages preferable. But aerated waters were unobtainable in the smaller places; elsewhere, often only local preparations are to be found, syrupy, dusty and hot from the sun, with names such as Lavo, or Pi-Cola. (As Jocelyn once remarked caustically, 'tasting of it too'.)

The driving itself was an acquired art, an experience which is inclined to be nerve-racking for those with an impetuous temperament. The chronic over-population of India is only too evident on the roads, with people walking all over the place, totally indifferent to motor traffic vainly trying to honk its way through. The age of the motor car may be coming, but as yet there are few signs; bullock carts creak mournfully down the centre of the road, while the supercilious cows stop and stare, defying you to try and pass. Cyclists riding five abreast, look at you over their shoulders in surprise, if you sound the horn, and swerve still further into the road, making it even more difficult to pass.

It was a miracle, in fact, that we escaped as lightly as we did. I often wondered what would happen if we hit someone, if only because in the more primitive areas the people are inclined to dispense a rough and ready justice on the spot. We nearly put this to the test one day, approaching a village in Bengal. Jocelyn slowed down, as we approached a group sauntering along the road, and began the usual steady honking on the horn. Just as we drew level with the last of the group, two of those in front made a wild dash for the other side, right across our front wheels. Jocelyn braked hard, so that we both hit the windshield with our foreheads. 'Bloody chicken maniacs,' he swore, as he rubbed his bruise. 'Next time I'm going to put my foot hard on the accelerator, and to hell with the bastards!'

We were driving southwards at the time, along the Bay of Bengal. We were on our way to the former State of Bastar, where the Maharajah had invited us hunting, to film the extraordinary tribal war dance of the Bison Horned Murias, and to visit a *gothul* or communal hut shared by young Gonds in pre-marital permissiveness. Before we sheered off inland just north of Visakhapatnam, we drove through a region dotted with some of the most beautiful villages in the world. The whitewashed earthen huts are small and circular, with conical rice-straw thatch. The thatch in that region is carried out with enthusiasm, to within about three feet of the ground; this makes for interesting architecture, because the doors have to be cut out of the eaves before anyone can get inside. The huts themselves are dotted about all over the place, which would drive a town-planner to drink; but from a distance, the effect is quite charming, as the villages resemble Lilliputian colonies or fields of mushrooms.

On the road between two such villages, we encountered a large white temple bull, leading a procession of drummers and dancers. 'Shivratri!' someone shouted. Since Shivratri is one of the principal festivals of the Hindu calendar, we pulled off the road and grabbed the cameras.

The bull swayed on towards us, nonchalantly chewing the cud, whilst the crowd of onlookers pressed forward, prostrating themselves on the ground, touching its hooves in salutation. Escorting it came a dozen men carrying flaming torches and gyrating frantically, the sweat streaming off their faces, in a temperature of over 110°F. The inevitable band followed, the trumpets and drums helping to whip up the frenzy. They were entirely successful, because I saw one of the dancers collapse in a trancelike swoon. A bucket of water soon brought him back to his senses.

As we got out of the car, I saw more drums and tambourines approaching, followed by a group of four men and four girls bringing up the rear of the procession. The girls were gorgeously dressed in colourful flouncy dresses, and heavily made up. They were dancing with that spirited, soft, swaying motion so characteristic of India. I was spellbound: but something, I knew, was wrong.

'Jocelyn, be careful!' I called out, furiously photographing. 'Careful of those girls!'

I knew from experience that girls never took part in such ceremonies. Jocelyn had no such qualms, however. 'What's biting you?'

The anklet bells tinkled seductively, as one of the girls sidled up to me, swaying her hips. Lips parted, teeth flashing, she advanced and retreated, large eyes beckoning, hands weaving a suggestive pattern. There was a whole world of experience in those flashing eyes, a sensuality that any woman would envy. I held my breath, feeling the sweat trickle down my back. I knew this was no woman, and yet my senses refused to acknowledge the fact.

Sensing my dilemma, she came right up to my chair, and took hold, quite gently, of my hand, still dancing. I was being invited to feel her breasts. Not trusting myself to speak, I nodded, trying not to appear too eager. I put my hand over the bodice . . . the chest was flat. I pulled my hand away, grinning stupidly.

'He's only fifteen! Give him a chance!' somebody yelled. The crowd roared with laughter and carried on with the dance.

One day in March 1965, we were in the small town of Mathura, some ninety miles south of Delhi. We decided to call in at the museum; as Mishra, the young curator, was showing us some of the beautiful statuary, dating mostly from the early post-Christian period, I noticed Jocelyn eyeing his *dhoti*, which was streaked with bold streaks of blue, red and orange. Knowing that the great spring festival of Holi was celebrated with much fervour in this area, I asked if he had been getting in some practice. 'Oh yes,' he replied laughing. 'It's already started. I'm going to watch the fun at Barsana later today. Why don't you come along too?' He looked rather dubiously at my wheelchair. 'It gets a bit rough, you know.'

Having calmed his fears, we set off after lunch to drive the twenty odd miles to Barsana, talking animatedly about Holi, busily comparing notes. I discovered to my great pleasure that our new friend was a mine of information about the local variations. Basically, Holi means that 'it's all over'; the old year is done, so let yourself go, throw everything to the winds in an orgy of the three R's, *Rang*, *Ras*, and *Rag*, colour, dance and song. In antiquity, rather similar spring festivals were celebrated with great zest across most of Asia and Europe and even our Easter is related to them. Nowadays such festivals are celebrated in a rather attenuated, rudimentary form, except in Northern India and particularly in the country of Braj, as the area around Mathura is called.

Parking the Gypsy on the outskirts of the little town, we locked it carefully and made our way through the dense crowds towards the centre. Some of the unpaved streets were no more than eight or nine feet wide, and I noticed Mishra looking nervously at the wheelchair as we forced our way through the throng.

'Don't worry,' I said cheerfully. 'We're used to boisterous crowds.'

'Yes, I'm sure,' he replied. 'But we must press on. The streets will soon be jammed solid.'

When we reached an intersection, we decided that this would

be the best vantage point. Fortunately, there was a narrow, raised plinth in front of a shop; after straining and grunting for a moment, my two companions managed to heave the chair up, so that I could not only see the fun, but avoid being trampled by the thousands below. We were only just in time. As the tumult below swelled by the minute, with people shouting and jostling for elbow room, I saw the vanguard of the procession in the distance. Teams of men were pulling carts bearing huge, six-foot kettle drums, while to either side, a dozen youthful 'lictors' forced a passageway through the crowd. True to custom the womenfolk in the crowd, dressed in bright *saris*, were the prime target as the men shouted bawdy remarks about their fertility and appearance. Not to be outdone, the women taunted them back about their virility.

Milling through the crowd came groups of *sadhus*, traditionally the poker-faced holy men of India. They were wearing only loin-cloths, bodies liberally smeared with ash, but were now grinning cheerfully as they stomped their tridents. As our cameras clicked and whirred, we saw several groups of clowns; some were waving large staffs, decorated with bells and coloured cloth, while others leaped about in a rhythmic hop and dance, and a third group stalked the women like satyrs, busily fluttering their eyelids.

All hell was breaking loose. Most of the vast crowd that crammed every inch of road, ledge and parapet had come equip-ped with syringes and pailfuls of coloured water. Thousands of excited revellers were now busy dousing and being doused; as well as water, handfuls of coloured powders were being tossed into the air, the plumes of greens, yellows, reds, blues and pinks criss-crossing each other like some psychedelic kaleidoscope gone berserk. The streaks of coloured powder and liquid became so dense that little besides the swirling rainbow of colour was visible. As I aimed my camera unwisely at a man covered all over with multicoloured streaks, I received a syringe of pink liquid full in the face. Mishra watched, grinning mischievously. 'Stop spluttering,' he cried, handing me a pailful. 'Get your own back!' I hesitated, because the culprit was now well out of range and a group of dignified elders had taken his place. 'Go on. It's Holi.' I lifted the bucket and poured, hoping for the best. 'Holi-ka ki jai,' ('Long live Holi!') they yelled delightedly, throwing two buckets over me for good measure. As I choked and spat, drenched to the skin, I saw Jocelyn laughing. 'Good God, I'd never recognize you, if it wasn't for your wheelchair!' he shouted.

Although we gave as good as we got, the climax was still to come. At about five o'clock, a group of women veiled in orange saris forced themselves through the crowd. Brandishing six foot poles, they cheerfully belaboured anyone who stood in their path. Almost immediately they were joined by men wearing turbans and thick cloth bandages wrapped firmly around their hands. The men carried leather shields, about eighteen inches in diameter, which they held above their heads as they squatted on their haunches in the dust. Now the fun was really on, because the women, having selected their opponent, began thrashing away with their staves, hitting the shields with every ounce of muscle in their bodies. Though wearing saris that reached to the ankle, the force with which they belaboured their opponents was truly awesome; we watched, breathless and spellbound, as the men hopped frantically like frogs, trying to dodge the next blow, while the sharp thump, thump, thump of the blows continued to crash down.

'They train for weeks ahead,' Mishra was shouting in my ear, trying to make himself heard above the deafening noise of the crowd. 'They stuff themselves on milk and cream. Good way of getting their own back after another year of marriage!' He looked at us with eyebrows raised, expecting agreement. Neither of us was married, as it happened, but we grinned and nodded approvingly all the same. At that moment, one of the leather shields began to disintegrate rapidly, shedding bits of leather and metal. It was a tense moment; if the man stood up, the women should stop beating him. But to our horror, he continued hopping around, frantically dodging the blows, warding off the poles with his padded arms.

'Good Lord,' Jocelyn shouted. 'They'll kill him!'

Suddenly he darted out into a porch; somebody handed him another shield, and he rejoined the fray. We breathed again.

'Look, he's taking on seven women now!' Mishra cried. 'Tomorrow he will be the great hero in Barsana!'

As we returned to the Gypsy late that evening, we were buttonholed by an All-India Radio correspondent, who insisted on recording an interview. He was flabbergasted that I had deliberately exposed myself in Barsana to the danger of getting caught up in the stampeding revellers. 'How on earth did you manage?' he asked. This seemed an excellent opportunity for a little propaganda, and so I waded right in, saying that with a little self-confidence anyone in a wheelchair could lead virtually as full a life as those on two feet, even during Holi. 'So please spare a thought for the disabled in your midst,' I concluded. 'Many are languishing in their homes right now. Help them to rejoin the rough and tumble of life. Help them to enjoy Holi. The surprise, I promise you, will not be entirely one-sided.'

I was quite used, in fact, to this type of off-the-cuff interview by this time. But I was pleasantly surprised to hear that it had been transmitted in full about two days later. Mishra heard it. 'Many others heard it too,' he remarked. 'I think you did much more good that way, by describing how you enjoyed Holi, than you could have done in years of speechifying and theorizing.'

My one regret was that we had evidently missed the Fool's Parade. Traditionally, this used to conclude the Holi celebrations, and everyone within miles used to foregather in a central town for the finale. When I mentioned this to Mishra, he seemed disappointed. 'You are quite right, it used to be hilarious. But we have not had one here for the last two years.' The next evening, he was back in the travellers' bungalow where we were staying, grinning like a Cheshire cat. 'Good news, my friend! The Fool's Parade will be held after all. Because you were so keen, we decided to organize it. Moreover, we have chosen you as chief fool!'

I realized that I had been deeply honoured. No non-Indian had ever been chosen to play the leading role in the long history of Mathura. When the big day arrived, we climbed into our Holi-stained clothes and arrived at the moving-off point promptly at two o'clock. A distinguished local poet had been elected President and was already lording it over the assembled company from a high chair on a dais, wearing an outsize peaked cap and feathered mantle. 'Very strange, I know,' he announced, as he placed the two foot dunce's cap on my head. 'I acquired them in Berlin. But there you are, fool of fools!'

With garlands of marigolds and beggar-heads around my neck, a drawing of a large owl pinned to my chest, I was lifted out of the wheelchair into an open horsedrawn carriage. Fortunately the seat had a back and armrests, all upholstered with padded leather. Remembering what I had said about 'self-confidence' during the radio interview, I tested the armrests and surveyed every likely support and hold in the carriage, determined not to make an even greater fool of myself by falling out.

'Are you all right?' the President was frowning with concern.

'Piece of cake!' I said airily, crossing my fingers.

Preceded by the President, sitting regally in his elephant's *howdah*, we eventually lurched off through the courtyard into the streets. The moment we left the sanctuary, the water started to fly, hurled from windows, roofs, balconies. Bucket after bucket of coloured water drenched us to the skin within seconds. As the pushing, jostling crowd screamed their delight, innumerable hands reached out to shake mine. Smiling, wearing my best idiot face, I obliged as best I could, one hand clutching the dunce's cap, leaning as far out of the carriage as I dared. 'Hold on to me tight,' I yelled to Mishra, sitting beside me. 'They'll pull me right out, given half a chance.'

By this time we were all sitting in puddles of water and the carriage was rapidly filling with other projectiles. Every time that the President stopped ahead to cut another ceremonial ribbon, opening another stage of our progress into Fool's Paradise, the crowd seized the opportunity of a sitting target to pelt us good-humouredly with carrots. There were carrots all over the place, presumably because of their erotic symbolism. Every shop that we passed had something to offer, sweets, betel nuts to chew, maybe a stick of cotton wool dipped in musk to sniff, or a garland of dried cow-pats. Cupful after cupful of liquid refreshment was passed up, usually of *bhang*, a local narcotic made from hashish and other ingredients, that would make any self-respecting medical man shudder. Apart from etiquette, the searing heat made any liquid welcome and I opened and shut my mouth like a fish, hoping for the best.

Eventually, bruised, battered and rather more than a little drunk, we reached a large open space on the outskirts of the town. Having survived over two hours of the procession, I was hoping for a breather. But a dais had been erected in the centre; one by one the principal participants made short speeches, amid much guffawing from the crowd. I was beginning to hope that I had completed my duties when I felt a sharp dig in my ribs.

'Your turn next,' Mishra hissed in my ear. 'I'll translate for you!'

As they lifted me out of the carriage up on to the dais, I prayed for guidance. I stared nervously at the sea of faces below, wondering what on earth I was going to say. 'Ladies and Gentlemen . . .', I began nervously. Immediately a voice from the crowd contradicted me. 'No women here,' Mishra explained, giggling unashamedly. 'No women fools?' I said, 'And shall I tell you why? Because they're all so busy producing fools like you! They've no more foolishness left in them!'

I was away. The crowd roared with laughter. I was accepted.

Thailand

*

THE 4th of April 1965 found us at Madras Dockyard, loading the Gypsy on board the British India Steam Navigation Company's SS *Rajula*. With the monsoon only a few weeks away, I had decided that it would be asking for trouble, even in the Gypsy, to continue with our work in India for the meantime. Besides, I was anxious to see how the disabled fared in south-east Asia.

The five-day voyage made a welcome break, not least on account of the food on board ship. We had almost forgotten what a decent meal tasted like, after months of our meagre, coarse diet in the villages. It also afforded me an opportunity to collect my thoughts, to take stock of how the Expedition was shaping up. While Jocelyn took an inventory to check if we had lost any vital kit, I sat up on deck, bringing my notebooks up to date and ruminating. We had covered a lot of ground, but as yet I was no nearer the mark in identifying a precise target. Wherever I turned, there was a crying need for dynamic action on someone's part.

One of the saddest stories that I had heard in Calcutta concerned the Basus, who farmed all of two acres in the remote Tripura region of Assam, not far from the Burmese border. The Basus were poor and they were illiterate, but they were content with their quiet life, with their seven children: until their seven year-old son, Girish, contracted polio. They watched helplessly as the paralysis crept slowly up his small body. By the time the disease had finished, both his arms and legs lay useless and he was breathing with difficulty.

Neither of the Basus had ever ventured farther abroad than the neighbouring village; but they had heard mention of Calcutta, a huge city far to the west, where the streets were paved with gold, where wise doctor-sahibs performed miracles. They loved little Girish whole-heartedly, and would stop at nothing to help him. If only they could transport him to Calcutta, he would be cured in no time! There seemed no hope, until the day when the father looked up from his work in the fields to gaze at the big silver aeroplane humming slowly across the sky. Of course it was presumptuous of them. But if that was the only way, they would sell nearly everything.

Leaving the other six children in the care of some relations who lived nearby, they eventually reached the airport. They had been forced to sell most of their meagre possessions, both their bullocks and half their land, to pay for the tickets. Everything seemed strange, but they comforted each other, arguing that the miracle of regained health and strength was now only a short step away.

But when they stood at the reception desk at the B. C. Roy Polio Clinic at Calcutta, the lady receptionist merely frowned. Hands folded in the *namaste* greeting, they bent low once more. 'This is our son Girish,' they said. 'Please make him well again.' 'But I cannot find your name on my list,' the lady replied. 'Are you sure that you reserved a place here?'

The Basus looked confused. 'We don't know of these things,' the father said humbly. 'Please make Girish well again.'

The doctor was summoned. He explained as gently and as sympathetically as he could. They had fifty places in the clinic and a waiting list of at least three hundred and fifty. Most of the latter were at least as bad as Girish. 'I'm afraid the clinic is full,' he said despairingly, 'and I just cannot let you in out of turn.'

They pleaded with him. Girish was so small, he would take up no space, he would be no trouble. Perhaps the kind doctor would take him for just a few days, so that he would become well again. But their pleading was in vain. Without the remotest idea why the miracle had failed, they trudged wearily away towards the Howrah railway station. They lay down on the bare concrete with other refugee families as the wind blew clouds of dust and litter over them.

Every day, for ten days, they returned to the clinic to plead. The miracle seemed so near, yet so far; maybe, if they persevered, the doctor would relent. On the tenth day they realized that they were beaten, and took the plane back home. They had lost virtually all their worldly possessions and had gained nothing.

'I cried when I was born and ever since I have been learning why,' the father muttered, quoting an old Indian proverb.

When the SS *Rajula* docked at Penang, I disembarked with

mixed feelings. Almost seven years had elapsed since I had been taken off the Rangoon-bound boat, strapped to a stretcher. As we drove now along the familiar route to the hospital, down streets heavy with crimson blossom, I wondered if I would recognize anybody. My hopes were dashed: none of the doctors or nurses I had known were still there. But the ward where I had spent three months of pain and terror still looked familiar enough; as I lingered by the bed I had occupied, I let impressions and associations carry me away, unchecked. Absent-mindedly I let my eyes explore the cobweb of tiny cracks in the paintwork on the ceiling, a pattern that had held my gaze over those long hours of despair. Sumangalo, the Buddhist monk, had been right when he predicted that I would come back after a number of years. 'You were moving slowly, with difficulty, in pursuit of some worthy mission.' I had come back indeed; in a strange way I was thankful that I was alone and unrecognized, able to spend a minute in the quiet privacy of my thoughts.

Before I left the hospital I was happy to see the efficient-looking physiotherapy department which had been created since my days there. As an attendant helped me out of the building, I noticed a sweeper by the steps. Something about him was familiar; he stared back at me for a moment, before rushing over to my chair, grinning from ear to ear. We both jabbered away, trying to express our pleasure at the reunion; I had never managed to understand much of what he said, but the expression on his face was heart-warming. After tut-tutting at my legs and the wheel-chair, he insisted on grabbing the handles and pushing me over to where Jocelyn was waiting in the Gypsy. While I heaved myself up into the cab, he broke off a twig of frangipani blossom, handing it up to me with a smile. I had tears in my eyes as we drove off, waving good-bye.

Jocelyn kept his foot hard down, as we were hoping to drive the thousand-odd miles to Bangkok in three days. It was a rough track most of the way, flanked by a tangle of lush tropical vegetation and majestic rain forests, and the heat was withering. For some reason we encountered many more snakes here than on Indian roads; on the second day out from Penang, we ran over a particularly large one. I looked back over my shoulder and saw it lying motionless on the road. 'Let's stop and have a look,' I suggested. 'It looks dead enough.' But when Jocelyn backed up to within a few yards, and opened his door, the snake, stunned but still very much alive, slithered at high speed under the chassis. Jocelyn looked at me accusingly as he got out to investigate.

'Can't see the brute anywhere,' came a voice from under the car. 'I think it must be in the undercarriage somewhere.' Grabbing a stick, he began to prod gently, but without success. 'Perhaps it's got through a crack, and is lying amongst the gear in the back.' The thought sent shivers down my spine, as I had little chance without any legs against a vituperative snake. 'Impossible,' I said. 'Try starting the engine.'

No amount of stopping and starting had any effect. In desperation, I got out and joined Jocelyn in laying about the car, thumping every panel inside and out. By this time, a small crowd had gathered to watch the two mad Englishmen, beating their car in the full heat of the noonday sun. 'Why you beat car?' a passing motorist asked, curious to know what the attraction was. 'Car not going, huh?'

'Car going fine, fine,' I replied grimly. 'But snake under hood not going. Huh. Huh.'

He looked at me piteously and laughed. 'I have elephant in my car. You beat him, too, huh?'

Jocelyn's face was redder than ever when he stood up, having peered hopefully under the chassis once more.

'Nothing for it, old boy. There's only one place left. Under the seat panel.'

The thought of sitting by the side of the road in my wheelchair, at the mercy of an extremely angry snake was anything but reassuring. With baited breath I watched him unscrew the four screws and lift off the panel gingerly. 'Here she is,' he cried, pointing to the snake neatly coiled on the emergency petrol tank. The crowd fell back a respectful distance, while Jocelyn insisted, with true British phlegm, on photographing it for posterity. From what the crowd were saying I gather that it was a highly venomous green pit-viper, which can kill within the hour. Gingerly replacing the panel, Jocelyn took his stick and gave it an almighty thwack. The snake obligingly slithered away into the undergrowth.

We ran over several other snakes, but decided not to stop.

When we reached Bangkok, in three days flat, I plunged into work straightaway. I was delighted, in particular, to meet Princess

Prem, a member of one of the foremost Thai families, who was
deeply involved in the cause of the Thai disabled. On the day that
we arrived she came in person to the YMCA where we were
staying. Most of what she told me was only too familiar. Public
indifference and apathy condemned the disabled member of the
family to a life of hopelessness and despair. Surprisingly, however,
she pointed out that India, while a poorer country than Thailand,
was ahead in rehabilitation facilities. 'They have many hospitals
with at least rudimentary facilities,' she said in her charming,
vivacious voice. 'But here, outside Bangkok, with the exception of
Chiang Mai, we have none. But we are making progress slowly
but surely.'

At her suggestion, I visited a residential school for severely
handicapped children on the outskirts of Bangkok, built largely as
a result of Princess Prem's efforts and fund-raising. The school was
a model of its kind, equipped with a good gym, neat, airy class-
rooms and an excellent playing-field. I came away with the
laughter of happy children ringing in my ears.

Our stay in Thailand was officially sponsored by the office of
the Prime Minister, and the officials who helped arrange our
programme organized a press conference for me. So one afternoon
I found myself facing eleven Thai press and TV correspondents,
in the offices of the Ministry of Foreign Affairs. After the usual
barrage of questions about the British National Health Service,
they moved on to more personal questions. 'How did I like Thai
food?' 'Was the weather too hot for me?' 'What monuments did I
plan to visit?' and so on. Of the Thai disabled, the main purpose
of our visit to the country, there was no mention. After about half
an hour of this I began to grow hot under the collar. I had met,
earlier the same day, a diligent, hard-working clerk in the
prosthetic department of the Siriraj hospital near by. He had been
born without legs below the knee, or arms below the elbow; but
thanks to artificial limbs, he was now one of the most useful,
dependable employees in the hospital. He had told me rather
wistfully that he had appeared no less than ten times on TV;
every time he appeared, he was represented as a freak. 'In fact
I'm almost beginning to feel a freak,' he told me. 'But I'm not a
freak really, am I? Anybody can work, given a chance.'

It annoyed me intensely when the disabled were treated like
this, when they were merely showing what could be done, given a

helping hand. I was beginning to feel that the pressmen in front of me were treating me likewise, and decided to move in to the attack. When one of them asked if it was *really* true that I could get about without help, I seized my chance. 'A disability need not be such a total handicap as you think,' I murmured. 'For instance, you could have conducted this interview perfectly well sitting in a wheelchair, just like I am.' Judging from the copy that appeared next day, my tactic had hit the mark. I had made them think, at any rate.

From previous experience, I knew that visiting hospitals and disabled in their homes all day and every day, week in and week out, was apt to be dispiriting. So we deliberately took a certain amount of time off, and managed to help celebrate Songkram, the Thai Water Festival, in the small town of Pakhlat, just south of Bangkok. From the amount of water that was thrown, this bore a strong resemblance to Holi in India. But instead of hurling the coloured powders, they smear a white paste, rather like gypsum, on each other's faces. They also elect a Miss Songkram who rides at the head of the procession on a float, flanked by gorgeous Thai attendants in their ravishing national dresses.

At first, my wheelchair seemed to attract almost as much attention as the gorgeous Miss Songkram. I was not only offered sweetmeats; everyone politely made way wherever we appeared. This was not my idea of joining in at all. 'Give me a bucket!' I cried. Once I had thrown and received a couple of buckets, the politeness dissolved into shouts of laughter, and I had to ask Jocelyn to hold on firmly to the handles of my chair to prevent it from keeling over in the mêlée. I was suitably soaked within minutes, whilst the prettiest girls took turns in applying layers of gypsum to my face.

All manner of wildly exaggerated stories were circulating next day about my antics in Pakhlat. As before, my appearing in person in the midst of such a boisterous mob had broadcast the message much more effectively than a hundred speeches.

When Princess Prem announced that we had been invited to a Royal Garden Party, we were suitably flattered, if rather apprehensive about our formal clothes. However, we fished out our suits, crumpled after weeks in a battered suitcase, and managed to borrow an iron in the YMCA. The party was being held to celebrate the sixtieth birthday of Princess Suvabhanas, a consort

of the late King Rama VI of Thailand; when we arrived at the
Princess's villa in Bangkok, we found ourselves amongst the cream
of Bangkok society, dressed for the most part in traditional Thai
court dress, which somehow made me think of the French formal
attire at the time of Louis XV.

As they stepped elegantly from their sleek Cadillacs, we parked
the mud-spattered Gyspy alongside. When we had joined the
throng around the sumptuously decorated stalls, we were soon
wading cheerfully through a mountainous meal of exotic lotus
dishes, endless oriental delicacies, aromatic duck and birthday
cake, washed down of course with an endless supply of champagne.
The royal barge, complete with orchestra, floated majestically on
one of the ornamental ponds, while the fountains changed colour
as hidden lights played on the jets. It was quite a scene, all the
more enjoyable because, for a change, no one stared, or tut-tutted
at my wheelchair.

One by one the guests were introduced to our hostess, who sat
on a stepped verandah. I watched with some misgivings as each
one mounted the steps on all fours, squatted one step below the
Princess's chair, talked for a moment, and then accepted a
monogrammed wallet from her hands. Folding their hands in the
Thai salute of *swadhi-krap*, they touched the ground with their
foreheads, and withdrew backwards down the steps. As I wondered uneasily if this routine would be expected of me, an official
came up. 'You will be presented now,' he said quietly. 'Please
remain in your wheelchair.' I was grateful that court etiquette,
stiff as it was, could be flexible on occasions. I pushed myself to
the bottom of the steps, whereupon the Princess got up, smiling
graciously; after exchanging the formal pleasantries, she thanked
me touchingly for what I was doing on behalf of the disabled. 'I
hope very much that we shall have better facilities here in Thailand
soon,' she said, handing me my beige wallet. I thanked her
warmly, folding my hands in the swadhi-krap; bowing solemnly
with as much dignity as I could muster, I pushed myself away.

After the presentations were completed, a group of delicate,
willowy Thai girls performed one of the classical Thai dances. We
watched spellbound as they swayed and swirled in formation,
moving with infinite grace in their gorgeous costumes. There was
such exquisite refinement in every gesture, such control and
meaning in the supple twist of the hand, in the angle of a long,

A group of Sadhus

Local festival in Rameshwaram, Madras State

At the Pushkar Fair, Rajasthan

Jain pilgrims in Satrunjaya, Gujerat

Snake charmers at Molar Bund, near Delhi

Villagers by a wayside station

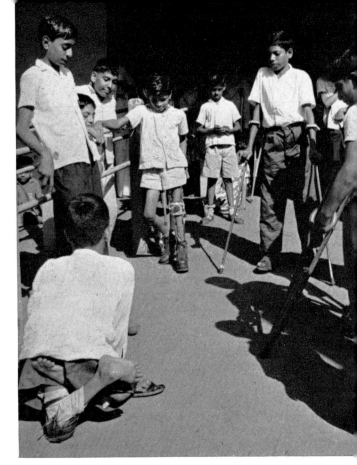

Maruti at the
School for
Crippled
Children in
Bombay

Ratanam on his
home-made
wheelchair

elegant finger. But the moment they had made their bow, a very different form of entertainment was announced. The girl had peroxide hair, piled up on the top of her head into a crow's nest, a face that was liberally coated with war paint, and eyes heavy with mascara. She wore what I can only describe as a bathing suit sprinkled with red sequins. Grasping the microphone to her bosom, she crooned a couple of numbers about love and lovers, jigging with her feet, buttocks wobbling, sequins twinkling. As I looked around, I realized to my astonishment that the assembled company were entranced by this apparition; whereas they had watched the classical dance politely, this riveted their gaze. When I commented on this to a Thai standing beside me, he seemed faintly amused. 'East meets West,' he replied with scarcely concealed irony. 'This comes from the civilized world, and so we are curious.'

This was by no means the first or the last time that we encountered such cultural miscegenation. For reasons that would take too long to explain here, I was determined whilst we were in Thailand to film the traditional sword dance of the Lë tribe. According to my researches, the Lë had many fascinating traditions in addition to sword dancing, such as sacrificing pigs to the spirits of the fields, and pairing off couples for marriage by throwing wooden balls between the ranks of boys and girls. After considerable difficulties, we eventually found some of the Lë, in a remote village near the small town of Chiang Kham, a hard day's drive south east of Chiang Rai. As it happened, the filming was a flop, because when we eventually persuaded the old men of the village to perform the sword dance, they were so out of practice that they collapsed with exhaustion after two minutes. The swords were rusty; their turbans kept falling off their heads for they had forgotten how to tie them. We watched sadly, wondering what the Lë had gained for the loss of their cultural heritage. However expeditioners have to expect such disappointments.

Getting to Chiang Kham in the first place, however, was quite an adventure. The road from Chiang Rai was just a dirt track, and we ground along in low gear, hour after hour, over potholes, stones and protruding roots. To either side, the jungle rose in a wall of impenetrable greenery, which made our journey seem like a trip to the end of the world. No one on this earth knew where we were, except an American missionary at Chiang Mai. If the engine failed, or if we met with some dangerous beast which decided to attack, our chances of rescue were small. But this type of adventure is the very stuff of expeditioners, and we were too exhilarated by what lay ahead to give a thought to the risks. Eventually we rounded a bend, and there in the distance lay the peaceful little teakwood township of Chiang Kham. We decided to stop for a moment before driving in; as we quietly slaked our thirst, I suddenly heard a familiar sound. Amongst the jungle noises of monkeys and geckos came an unmistakable beat. 'Yea, yea, yea' they cried, their voices echoing off the sturdy teaks, with the full power of a transistor radio. The Beatles had beaten us to it.

We soon discovered that whatever might be distinctive about Thailand, it wasn't the condition of the handicapped. I remember the sad, empty face of a tribesman in the Chiang Mai hospital. His left arm had been shattered by a gun, fired at point blank range. To staunch the flow of blood, he had tied the stump with creeper and had walked through thick jungle for five days, without food or assistance, to reach the nearest road and eventually the hospital. Now he lay on that bed, fatalistic resignation carved deep into his face. To most of us in the West his apathy would appear as incredible as his initial feat of endurance in reaching the hospital.

Some days later we visited the hospital in the town of Phitsanulok. The orthopaedic ward with twenty-five beds, was over-crowded with forty-four patients, of whom twenty-five were cases of gunshot wounds. From one bed a sallow face stared at us briefly before relaxing back into apathetic torpor. Dr Cham Long, the orthopaedic surgeon, told me that his name was Moi, that he was thirty, and used to work as a lumber-jack. 'Four years ago a log fell on him and broke his back, which left him paralysed from the waist down. He's been here ever since, for he has simply nowhere to go.' His two brothers apparently weren't much concerned with him. 'The last time they came to see him was over two years ago. They refused to have him back.' Meantime many others in critical condition could not be admitted for lack of space.

'Would you like to be taught some practical work?' I asked Moi.

He glanced furtively at Dr Cham. 'Yes, I would but there isn't anybody here to teach me.'

This was unfortunately true. But it was also quite clear to me that Moi's chief aim was to adopt whatever attitude he believed would ingratiate him most successfully with Dr Cham and assure his permanent stay in the hospital. Probably for the first time in his life his basic needs, particularly enough food, were being met, and met without any exertion on his part.

On the other side of the ward lay forty-five-year-old farm labourer, Sein. Two years previously a bullet had broken his spine.

'At least we got him early,' said Dr Cham. 'Usually they only come to us as a last resort, after the quacks and monks have failed.'

Sein had worked for a rich landowner; following an old custom now dying out, he had been paid only in kind with food, shelter and clothing. He had been married, but his wife had divorced him when it became apparent that he wouldn't recover. Nor would his family have him back. 'They say, perhaps with some truth, that they are too poor to support him.'

As I was about to leave a nurse rolled Sein on his side and attended to the bedsores on his seat. These were in a very advanced condition, with the bone exposed. When she had applied fresh dressings, she rolled him on his back again. Sein had remained impassive while this was done; now he rolled a cigarette, inhaled deeply, and stared up at the ceiling. Most probably he would continue to gaze at that white hospital ceiling for the remainder of his life.

One of my greatest ambitions in south-east Asia was to visit one of the Tom Dooley hospitals in Laos or Vietnam. During the last years of his life, I had followed Dooley's work with the keenest interest, as he steadily built up this growing network of small jungle hospitals, bringing medicine and hope to the people where it was most needed. I had often wondered what had happened since his tragic death from cancer in 1961. Whenever I asked about visiting one of the hospitals, my question always met with a shaking of the head. 'Ah yes, Ban Houei Sai perhaps. But it is very difficult to get there.' Or 'You will need visas to cross the Mekong into Laos.' Or 'There are many bandits and Pathet Lao about, which makes the journey very dangerous.'

The greater the difficulties, the more keen I became to have a go. I was well aware of the hazards, if only from touring the orthopaedic wards in the provincial hospitals. At least half the beds were always filled with gunshot cases, and for once I felt a twinge of sympathy for the officials in refusing to take any responsibility for us. But we set off regardless, avoiding open roads after dusk, and reached Chiang Saen, in the extreme north of the country, safely enough. Ban Houei Sai lay about sixty miles downstream on the other side of the Mekong.

Scouring for information along the muddy quay-side, Jocelyn duly reported that a small passenger boat was due to sail early the following morning. When we showed up, we were slightly alarmed to see four Thai soldiers, rifles cocked, take up their positions fore and aft. As we set off, the jungle closed in on us once more, and I found myself gazing with a blend of awe and fascination at the walls of huge trees garlanded with lianas that towered above the banks to either side.

For the first few hours the water remained slow and sluggish, the serenity of the scene only shattered by the occasional rifle shot in the far distance. But as we approached Chiang Khong, the river began to froth over angry-looking rapids. I positioned myself by the railing, gripping it firmly, as the little boat shuddered, swayed, then rushed forward. The water level was at its pre-monsoon lowest, so the jagged rocks, inches away, looked deadlier than sharks; I just hoped that the helmsman would prove up to the task. However he was obviously used to these waters, steering the little craft with sharp but sure twists of the wheel, his face calm and expressionless.

We breathed a sigh of relief when we finally tied up at the muddy mooring at Chiang Khong; it was a very small town, with a pioneering air about its one street, which was unpaved and flanked with wooden houses, like something out of a Western. But our troubles were not over, in that we still had to find someone to ferry us across to the other side. Once more Jocelyn came back from his reconnaissance with a gleam in his eye. 'Found a boatman,' he said with a grin. 'Sixpence a head and no questions asked.'

Having crossed visa-less into Laos, we hired a bullock-cart on the bank from some local tribesmen, and slowly creaked up the bank towards Ban Houei Sai. A fortnight previously, we had experienced another equally bizarre ride when we made our way on a rail trolley, propelled by hand, over the notorious Japanese 'Death Railway' in western Thailand, past the famous Bridge on the River Kwai. But nothing can beat the traditional bullock-cart; it wends its way imperturbably, so slowly that even pedestrians overtake it, hard, unsprung wheels whining and groaning over stones and pot-holes. Sitting on my wheelchair cushion to soften the bumps, I watched the patient, lumbering, supercilious animals in front, whilst keeping half an eye on the nearby forest, wondering what to do if we were attacked. We were not only illegal visitors, but quite defenceless into the bargain.

When we lurched into the hospital compound the neat barrack-like building stood out in striking contrast with the squalid shacks we had passed on the way. The first person I saw was a trim, brisk figure in a spotless American nurse's uniform. Stepping down from the verandah, she never batted an eyelid at seeing two scruffy Europeans emerging from the jungle. 'Hi there!' she called out breezily. 'Come on in!'

'I'll just fix the chair,' Jocelyn said, goggling unashamedly. 'Wheelchair, actually.'

'Oh, let me help.' She helped lift the chair from the back of the cart, as if complete strangers dropped by in wheelchairs every day of the week. When we were safely installed on the verandah, she introduced herself as Nurse Pat Cherpees. There were two others, she said, one other nurse from the USA, Nurse Martha Villander, and Dr Jose Costelanos from the Dominican Republic. 'You'll meet them soon. Meantime, will you please sign the visitors book? We don't get too many visitors here, and we always ask them to say how they came.'

While I was busy writing *by Austin Gypsy overland from England, by boat in a wheelchair down the Mekong, bullock-cart from the river bank*, Jocelyn was equally busy making up for lost time.

'Pat, how come a pretty girl like you is in a place like this?'

'Well thank you, young sir,' she replied with a smile. 'Actually it's very simple. I was an air hostess with TWA, who run a scheme for those with nursing experience to work in countries like Laos. I volunteered – so here we are!'

'It must have been a bit of a shock at first.'

'Oh, sure, it was kind of bewildering for the first few weeks. But you get used to anything out here. You have to . . . '

Leaving Jocelyn to the tender mercies of Nurse Pat Cherpees, I wheeled myself off in search of Dr Costelanos. I found him in a simple, barrack-like ward at the back, tending a Laotian soldier who had received a bullet wound in the thigh fighting the

Communists. He greeted me warmly and apologized for the overcrowding. 'As you see, we have thirty beds and thirty-four patients!'

The ward was spotless. The beds were tidy, the sheets clean, even if the facilities were basic. The patients looked well fed and cared for; everything pointed to a place that was run with efficiency and care. Coming to this from the conditions of south-east Asia was like jumping on a time machine for a thousand years, all the way from resignation to hope.

When I asked him how they had fared since Tom Dooley's death, he took me outside to show the gutted shell of the original hospital, burned down in a Pathet Lao attack of 1960, and told me how Dr Carl Wiedermann and Al Harris had opened the hospital again, after months of neglect, in 1962.

'Of course, we are pretty desperate, but we do what we can.' He stared wistfully into the distance. 'We need plenty here all right. I just wish everyone back home could see how desperately we need things like equipment and drugs. How much even a small amount of money, like the price of a pack of cigarettes or an ice cream, can buy. Do you know, we can often save a life out here for the price of things like that?' He continued to stare thoughtfully at the wrecked building and the wall of jungle that stretched for miles on end to the north, east and west, a jungle that had seemed quiet enough when Jocelyn and I creaked along its edge an hour or two earlier, but which sheltered enemies who struck without warning. Sensing the direction of his thoughts, I asked if he was worried about another Communist attack.

'They are never far away,' he replied, waving his hand towards the jungle. 'But they haven't bothered us recently. Anyway, we've too much to do to spend our time worrying about them.'

Later the same evening, I spent an enjoyable hour with Dr Costelanos talking more generally about the problems of south-east Asia, social as well as medical. He showed the keenest interest when I told him about my ideas for 'Asianizing' rehabilitation, and asked me a number of searching questions. I asked him to tell me frankly how much he had been able to do for the disabled. Instead of answering, he suggested rather enigmatically that I come down to the village with him next day.

We awoke the following morning in our pleasant, if sparsely furnished room. The view, during breakfast, was peaceful and enchanting – seen across a small yard dotted with frangipani trees in blossom were delicate clumps of bamboo in a morning haze, which resembled a Sung etching. When we set off, the distant ribbon of the Mekong was streaked with mists, softening the sombre bulwark of the jungle beyond. We had not moved more than half a mile towards the village when the doctor stopped. 'There he is,' he said quietly, pointing to a crippled beggar slowly pulling himself along on his bottom, dragging lifeless legs behind him as he cried for alms. 'When a surgeon visited us here, I had him come up to the hospital, and we offered to operate. I told him we could probably improve his condition considerably, and that eventually he might even walk with crutches. But he refused point blank, saying that it was his lot, and that his condition helped him to earn a living. Does that answer your question, my friend?'

As we returned to the hospital, the conversation reverted to the question of adapting rehabilitation to village conditions. I told him how I was now beginning to feel my way towards the idea of some modest centre that would help train the disabled in village crafts, possibly in agriculture. To my great delight Dr Costelanos began nodding in agreement. When I had finished expounding my ideas, rather incoherently perhaps, he said that this reminded him of a dedicated young American, Robert Wulff, who had set up pioneer villages for burnt-out leprosy patients near Chiang Mai in Northern Thailand. According to the gossip on the jungle grapevine, Wulff had spent many years in the East, and had been deeply moved by the hopeless plight of disabled lepers. Having bullied the government into giving him some raw jungle, with the minimum of funds, he had now helped the patients clear the jungle and build settlements.

'I think he's created about three villages now,' Dr Costelanos concluded. 'I'm afraid I've never had the chance to see any of them myself. Why don't you drop in there and have a look?'

I looked at Jocelyn, who nodded his approval. It was time for us to depart anyway. Having thanked the good doctor for his hospitality and encouragement, I waited rather impatiently while Jocelyn said good-bye to Nurse Pat. Eventually he joined me in the back of the bullock-cart, and we creaked off back by the jungle down to the Mekong. Recovering the Gypsy intact at Chiang Saen, we made steady progress over the rugged tracks. Four days later we were knocking at Bob Wulff's door on the outskirts of Chiang Mai.

It was a neat house, built mostly of teak, set amidst shrubbery at the end of a quiet avenue lined with scarlet flame-of-the-forest trees. To either side, bungalows lay in pleasant gardens, secluded from the roadside. I had never penetrated what I assumed to be suburban Chiang Mai, and I wondered for a second, as we waited by the door, if we had not come on a wild goose chase.

The door was opened by a lanky man in his mid-thirties, who looked at us shyly behind large, black-rimmed spectacles. As soon as I had explained our mission, the gentle face broadened into a welcoming smile. 'Yes, I'm Bob Wulff. Glad to see you. Come right in.'

As we entered, I noticed that he had installed a number of Western-type appliances and gadgets; but the general feeling was one of spartan simplicity, with Thai scrolls decorating the walls, and teak carvings on the tables and shelves. As we passed into the living room, Bob introduced us to his wife Ajana, a petite and strikingly graceful Thai lady, with their small son clinging to her skirts. 'I am sure you would like a cold drink,' she said in her soft lilt. 'I'll fetch something.' I apologized once more for bursting in on him in this manner, hot and dusty from a long, hard drive. 'Don't be silly,' Bob replied with a grin. 'We don't stand on ceremony out here!'

When I asked what had led him to this work, he told me briefly how his family were deeply religious Lutherans from Albert Lea, Minnesota. Sitting comfortably in his large wicker armchair, sipping an iced Coca-Cola, he told us how, after graduating from high school towards the end of the Second World War, he found himself posted to the Marshall Mission to China. Confronted every day by the abysmal wretchedness of the people, which appalled his sensitive conscience, he returned to the States when his tour was completed, with a burning conviction that his vocation lay in helping somehow to alleviate this misery.

It was almost by accident that he began to work with lepers. Having graduated from college, he drained his savings account and found his way by a devious route to northern Thailand, (China was already in Communist hands), where he met up with Dr Richard S. Buker, who ran a leper colony near Chiang Mai. Despite his revulsion, which is common enough for anyone encountering the ravages of leprosy for the first time, he pitched right in. 'I was the guy who came to dinner and stayed for a year!' Having started off with no knowledge or experience, he not only picked up the necessary know-how about leprosy itself, but learned a great deal about social conditions in rural Thailand into the bargain.

On his next trip back home, he started telling anyone who would listen about the conditions in Thailand, about the need, about his plans for starting up a village where burnt-out lepers could earn their living, and so become rehabilitated members of a community. He stressed that however useful leprosaria were, they coped mainly with the medical aspects. What was needed was a village where the social and economic aspects could be catered for, and he was determined to strike out in this direction. His local Lutheran men's group, from the Trinity Lutheran Church in Albert Lea, chipped in with five hundred dollars; he raised more through lectures and appeals, and returned to Chiang Mai in 1955, itching to get started.

'I was absolutely clear about one thing,' he said. 'I knew that if any rehabilitation project was going to be effective around here, it had to be firmly tied to the land, to farming. After all, farming is all most of them know, the only life they understand.'

'I couldn't agree more,' I commented. 'Although we've been looking primarily at the physically handicapped, we've come to the same conclusion over and over again. An urban based institution, however well endowed or equipped, simply isn't the whole answer.'

I was only too keen to pursue this further, and to hear how he started his villages. But it was getting late, and we had no wish to overstay our welcome. 'Perhaps you could tell me the rest another time,' I suggested hopefully. 'Sure. I tell you what. I'm going out to Li village tomorrow. Why don't you two come along?'

Having spent the night in a small hotel, we picked him up early the next morning, and drove for five hours along a fiendish track, corrugated in small ridges like a washboard. Conversation was impossible, thanks to the vibration, the dense red dust and the heat. Eventually we rumbled over a wooden bridge, crossing the River Li.

'Solid enough,' Bob shouted above the noise of the engine. 'This was our first major success here.'

So far we had only paid a few brief visits to leper colonies, and I was slightly apprehensive about Jocelyn's reaction. To his credit, he never batted an eyelid as the patients began to swarm around the car. Their affection and devotion to Bob were quickly evident. Chatting volubly in Thai, he asked each one about some particular problem, the onion crop, the peanut blight, or the new baby.

Surrounded by this happy, gesticulating crowd, we began to wander around, to admire the crops, to greet the womenfolk placidly suckling their babies on their raised verandahs. The heat was overpowering, and the thirty-odd dwellings scattered over a wide area. Pointing to the blackened stumps, Bob told how everyone had thought him clean out of his mind when he started the first village, with twelve patients in August, 1955. But despite the snakes, scorpions and wild animals, they had stuck it out, and soon had the first plot cleared, and planted, the first huts raised up on stilts in the traditional manner. 'But the worst thing was the condition of the recruits. Most of them were all so completely unfit for such back-breaking work. A leper's hands often become anaesthetized, so that he cannot feel pain if he cuts himself. Every day someone would come up, holding up a bleeding stump, imploring me to help, saying he couldn't cope. I had to steel myself to refuse, because if someone didn't force them to stand up to this tough life from the start, sooner or later they would go under. I could help them set themselves up as farmers, but I knew I could never be a permanent source of help and support. I just had to say no, and watch the tears running down their cheeks.'

With Jocelyn helping to push me over the rough plots and paths, we passed a group of men placidly harvesting an onion field, others busy making charcoal, while a third party sat cross-legged under an awning engrossed in carving various objects in teak. We stopped for a moment to admire their work, bowls, fighting elephants, decorative bookends and other traditional designs for which northern Thailand is famous far and wide. Many of the carvers were crippled, but a few seemed able-bodied. I asked Bob the reason.

'Not all our people are lepers,' he replied. 'This is deliberate. If we had set up a village exclusively for lepers, it would have been much tougher for them – social stigma, ostracism, even difficulty

selling their produce in the market place. So we have always
taken good care to hold the door wide open, to the homeless,
beggars, mentally retarded, even ex-prisoners. They seemed to
shake down all right!'

It seemed to be working pretty well, even if nobody showed
much inclination to hurry. But this was the dead season of the
year, the period before the monsoon when farmers haven't much to
do in the fields. Instead, as in our wintertime, they take the opportunity to repair their implements, and tidy up behind the scenes.
Soon after the monsoon, the fields would be bursting forth with
cabbages, peanuts, vegetables, fruit. Now was the time for
relaxation.

It was a peaceful, happy scene. As the time drew near for us to
leave, I took one last look at the mother suckling her child on the
verandah. She looked happy enough, smoking a corn-leaf cheroot.

'Bob, you know something? It looks just like any other Thai
village. But don't get me wrong . . . '

'No, indeed! It's a compliment.'

The phrase kept turning around in my mind as we drove back
to Chiang Mai. All this, and yet it looked just like any other
village. Surely this was the measure of his success; surely, too,
there was a pointer here for me.

CHAPTER 12

Japan and the House that Toichiro built

*

It was early in the morning of the 3rd of May 1965 when we touched down at Tokyo Airport. The rush hour was at its height. As I gazed out of the taxi, I saw everyone hurrying purposefully to work, with a look of determined efficiency, like the components of an intricate, well-oiled machine.

It was quite a change after nearly a year of the soporific, slow-motion life of Southern Asia. Having checked in at the Tokyo YMCA, we plunged straightaway into work, heading for the offices of Justin W. Dart Jr, President of Tupperware Japan, Inc. As the taxi pulled up before the Tupperware offices, I wondered what sort of man to expect. All I knew was that he was a native of Texas, that he had contracted polio at the age of eighteen and had been confined to a wheelchair ever since.

'Welcome to Japan!' he cried, wheeling himself swiftly to the doorway of his large, well-appointed office and shaking my hand in a vice-like grip. 'Come right in. Tell me all about this expedition of yours.' Justin was around thirty-five years old, with a broad, muscular physique and an alert, determined face topped by a crew-cut. An example to all of us of what a courageous, resourceful man can do despite a handicap. When he had taken over Japanese Tupperware it had been a very small affair with a handful of employees; after introducing American business methods, not to mention Justin's own drive and personality, sales had rocketed and the firm now employed around ten thousand men and women.

'Are any of them disabled?'

'They certainly are,' Justin replied. 'Not too many, as yet, but we've made a start.' He looked at his watch. 'They should be in the gym right now. Why don't we go over there so you can see for yourself?'

As we raced down the corridors, tyres squealing on the polished parquet, Justin explained how he now had ten disabled on his payroll and had hired a gym where they could play basket-ball during off-duty hours. 'We even have a coach now, Richard Maduro,' he said over his shoulder. 'You'll meet him in a moment.'

As we entered the gym, two teams were playing a vigorous game from wheelchairs. They raced about the floor like dodgems, bumping into one another, bouncing the ball deftly as they charged along. There was certainly nothing 'invalid' in the way these young men were playing. 'There's Richard over there,' Justin said, pointing to an athletic, powerfully-built man playing a fast, aggressive ball. When the whistle blew, Richard came over to introduce himself. I admired his pupils' skill. 'Well, they're certainly coming on now. I guess this is as good a way as any of giving them confidence after all those years of being cooped up.'

He drew my attention to Koike, a cheerful thirty-two-year-old throwing the ball up into the net, practising by himself. Koike, now employed by Justin as a clerk, had been bed-bound a mere eight months previously, after no less than sixteen years in hospitals. 'Look at him now,' Richard said proudly. 'No more moping for him. Justin is doing a great job here!'

On our way back to the office, I told him how impressed I had been, not only by the gym, but by Richard. 'He's really mastered his disability,' Justin replied. 'He lost both legs in a motor cycle accident back in Texas. He sure went through it at the time. But he fought back; I first met him when he was representing the USA at the para-olympics in Rome, in 1960.'

I saw quite a lot of Justin during the next day or two, and he introduced me to his charming Japanese wife. His crowded schedule never prevented him from finding time to help the disabled whenever he could. Although he didn't care for public recognition, he was *ex officio* chief fund raiser and publicist in the Tokyo area. We discussed the problem of appliances and he questioned me closely about the cost of artificial limbs and wheelchairs. I pointed out that in most countries of South Asia an artificial limb, even if it was available, could cost the equivalent of a year's wages for a lower-paid worker. When he pulled a face, I described how one day Jocelyn and I had met Musa in September 1964, outside Peshawar in West Pakistan. Musa was cutting grass by the roadside, one hand grasping his wooden crutch, the other a sickle. As we drew nearer, I saw him place his sickle on the ground, so that he could gather up the cut grass and put it in a large wicker basket nearby. When we stopped for a chat, I noticed that his leg had been amputated below the knee. After the customary greetings, I asked him in sign language why he didn't have a simple peg-leg, which would allow him to stand on both legs, to use both hands for his work.

Musa had looked at me sadly. From the exchange that followed, I gathered he was only too glad to earn a little money this way, hard work though it was. As we drove on, I had turned my head back, to see Musa struggling to lift the heavy basket on to his head, still holding his crutch. He staggered a few feet, and fell on to the road, spilling the grass.

Justin remained deep in thought. 'But surely he could have gotten himself another job – maybe as a night watchman?' I explained that where unemployment was rife, especially amongst the poor, for unskilled people to have any sort of job was a great privilege.

Justin could not have been more kind and helpful. When he heard that we were thinking of hiring a car, he insisted on placing his comfortable office limousine at our disposal, complete with driver and English-speaking secretary. As we toured Tokyo, I realized that I had already fallen in love with Japan. Despite all the dynamic growth, she offers a delicate beauty and charm, particularly in the most mundane, everyday things. I shall never forget the time when I popped into a large department store to buy some batteries for my camera flash. They not only recognized what I wanted; within seconds the small parcel was politely handed to me neatly wrapped and tied with a blue ribbon. 'But you can't use that!' Jocelyn said, as I fingered it admiringly. 'You should put it up on the mantelpiece for decoration!'

As we drove slowly along the congested highway to Osaka, luxuriating in our unaccustomed comfort, I wondered to myself if I should find the same picture, where the disabled are concerned, in major cities outside the capital. Rehabilitation facilities in Tokyo had been impressive, echoing with the 'one, two, one, two, fall, stand up, go on, go on' that was so familiar to me from my time in Camden Road. Although they could only cope with a small fraction of those in need, they seemed to be well organized; in addition to the physical side, the authorities provided a wide range of job-training from dress-making and handicrafts to watch repairing and TV assembly.

In South Asia the physiotherapy department of a provincial hospital would usually be tucked away in cramped premises, apart from the mainstream of hospital life, the Cinderella of hospital departments. With notable exceptions, I had often found the staff to be embittered by their conditions, half-heartedly trying to coax their patients to exercise; while the patients, as often as not, would react passively, preferring the array of electrotherapy gadgets (the more dials, buttons and flashing lights, the better), hoping that technology would restore them to instant, effortless health.

When we reached Osaka, the noise of the sweating, grunting patients was even more awesome than that I remembered from Camden Road. I remarked on this to Mr Nagai, director of the Hyogo Rehabilitation Center in Kobe. 'But things aren't all that rosy here,' he said. 'We've still a long way to go before the disabled are given a proper crack of the whip.' He explained that their whole rehabilitation process was geared to active exercises, leading to job-training, which was all very well for those who could stand the pace. 'It's the drop-out rate that I worry about.' Those who were too severely handicapped or too emotionally disturbed to undergo the rigorous exercises, fell by the wayside. Poor prospects for eventual employment, they were sacrificed on the altar of the great god Productivity.

There were still plenty of other problems. The supply of appliances was grossly inadequate, so that patients sometimes had to wait up to two years for delivery. Moreover the attitudes towards disability were only beginning to move away from the apathy and indifference I had found in South Asia. In the remoter areas, such as Hokkaido, Kyushu or the Tohoku District, where tradition had hardly begun to crack, the disabled still languished in the age-long conditions of charity, acquiescence and a home-bound existence.

But in places like Tokyo, Osaka, Kobe and other large industrial cities in the mainstream of the technological boom, attitudes were changing fast and the disabled were now given a place amongst the working population. Disability in itself was no longer a bar to employment. When we stopped to fill up with petrol in Kobe, I noticed that the pump attendant walked with a pronounced limp:

possibly he had one partly paralysed leg. We were on our way to visit Mr Hashimoto, Director of the Vocational Training Center in Osaka and I mentioned how deeply I had been impressed by this simple occurrence. 'Ah, but then we are far luckier,' he said with a broad smile. 'Here we have full employment. When there is no other labour available, employers are only too quick to throw prejudice out of the window!'

Pursuing this line of thought a stage further, I told him of Bawa, a garage mechanic I had met in Kerala, in South India, who had been unlucky enough to contract tuberculosis of the knee. The knee was perfectly all right after treatment, except that Bawa found it a little stiff. He could still crawl easily under cars; but although he had worked faithfully and well for his employers for ten years, the firm refused point-blank to re-employ him. 'We don't employ disabled,' he was told every time he asked. 'But I'm not disabled,' he pleaded. 'But you limp, don't you? There must be something wrong. Nothing but trouble from disabled.' Bawa had almost given up in despair; when I talked to him, he was still hoping that the labour exchange would find him a job of some sort, but he said he was branded by his limp, branded worse than a criminal; he was disabled. Of course, as I told Mr Hashimoto, there are many who take a more enlightened view and thousands of disabled around India have found jobs to the satisfaction of everyone concerned. But attitudes such as the one Bawa met with still remain more of a rule than an exception.

We talked at length about this type of prejudice, in the context of employment. Mr Hashimoto told me that over thirteen hundred disabled had passed through his hands during the past year, having graduated after a year's job-training. Few had failed to get a job straightaway; fewer still had proved bad risks for their employers. 'Employers may seem unwilling at first. But when they see our people at work, they usually tell me that they wished they'd employed handicapped labour before. If you give the disabled a chance to prove themselves, reservations melt away – like the snow in spring.'

'No complaints about poor productivity?'

'Quite the reverse. Often they report that the atmosphere on the shop floor has improved once they've taken on some of our people. And a good atmosphere usually spells high productivity.'

Disabled people are accepted much more readily in Japan;

unlike their South Asian counterparts, the Japanese seldom stop and stare. Whenever I wheeled myself along South Asian streets, numerous people would stop, tut-tutting at my chair; nobody stopped in Japan – I had to push with the crowd.

Despite the vast improvement in rehabilitation techniques and employment prospects, life is hardly a bed of roses. We stayed in Osaka in a typically Japanese home, with one of Justin's friends. It was a delightful house and our charming, solicitous hostess went out of her way to make us welcome. She cooked the most delicious *tempura*, *sukiaki* and other delicacies, much to Jocelyn's appreciation. But while I watched him tackling his third or fourth helping, to the delight of all concerned, I could hardly help thinking how unsuitable such a dainty house was for a disabled person. Although I had enjoyed every minute of our visit, I felt like a bull in a china shop amongst such delicate furniture and frail partition walls. As I lay down that evening on a mattress spread on the traditional *tatami* mat, I thought how infinitely frustrating these beautiful, doll-like houses must be if you have to live in one permanently and are confined to a wheelchair. Stairs tend to be steep, doors narrow; lavatories are of the Eastern, squatting type, with the bowl let in flush with the floor; even the small details of everyday life must be worrying. I was lucky, of course, in that our hostess was so sympathetic; but how do less fortunate wheelchairers cope with crossing a threshold? Shoes are taken off, before entering, to avoid soiling the precious, sacred tatami mats. How can a stranger enter such a house, in a wheel-chair, or wearing a brace?

If the disabled of Osaka fare relatively well, they may well have Mr Hayakawa to thank for it. When I met him in the offices of the Hayakawa Tokusen Kinzoku Company, of which he is President, I asked him why he took such keen interest in their welfare.

'I have always been interested in such things,' he replied modestly. 'Ever since I was a child, in fact.' He told me how he was orphaned at the age of thirteen, and left at the mercy of a step-mother. She made his life such a misery that eventually he ran away, and slept in the streets, homeless, tired and hungry. 'A poor blind old lady found me. She not only fed me and gave me shelter, but eventually found me a job. I have never forgotten her, and that is why I try to help people in need.'

When I asked him about his company, he described how it had

grown over the years, until they had reached their present size, employing over fifty workers, of whom half were disabled. I raised my eyebrows. 'Yes, I know that it's a high percentage. But they are good workers, often better than the able-bodied. I find that when a man has a disability, he has to strive to work that much better. It brings out the very best in him.'

However, facilities in Osaka were still most inadequate; according to Mr Hayakawa, they would have to be increased fivefold to meet the need. 'All the same the opportunity to find work is here. That is the essential, for only a fool or a hero will strive for something which isn't there. Where there is no flame to grasp there can be no Prometheus either.'

This reminded me of another unassuming hero in India, who, when a glimmer of hope appeared on the horizon, plodded after it in the face of formidable odds. I told Mr Hayakawa how Jocelyn and I had been driving towards Vellore when we met Mr Ratanam on his way to work. Shielding my eyes against the blazing sun, I had noticed a small, frail figure on the road ahead, laboriously hand-peddling himself along in what was obviously a home-made wheelchair. When we stopped, I saw that it had been produced from three bicycle wheels and was propelled from the front wheel with a kind of a hand-operated crank.

'Where are you heading for?' I asked.

'Katpadi,' he replied with a youthful, engaging smile. 'But speak Engleesh very bad.' It was 104°F in the shade; no wonder the sweat was running down his body, falling in drops over his bare, emaciated legs. Katpadi was a small village about a mile from where we met him. Since his large cumbrous wheelchair wouldn't have fitted in the Gypsy, there seemed little point in offering him a ride. 'See you there, then!'

As it turned out, we were both heading for the Swedish Red Cross workshop, where fifty disabled men made typewriter components. When I had introduced myself to Mr Subramaniam, a supervisor who spoke fair English, I asked if he could throw any light on the thin, smiling figure in that home-made contraption.

'That must have been Ratanam,' he said. 'He lives about nine miles away with his old mother. He has to travel eighteen miles a day in that chair – but he's never been late for work!' When I gasped in amazement at such a superhuman feat, the supervisor told me how Ratanam had contracted polio when he was small, and had become paralysed below the waist. His parents were desperately poor; he never attended school, or received medical care. Shortly after the Red Cross had opened the workshop, he arrived on the doorstep, pleading with them to employ him. His mother, now a widow, would starve to death if he failed to earn something.

'The problem was the distance. When various people offered to buy him a wheelchair, he refused and quietly set about building one himself with odd bits of wood and bicycle wheels.'

When Ratanam wheeled himself into the loading bay I went over and shook him warmly by the hand. As he shuffled out of his chair on to the ground, he told me proudly that he had used bits and pieces from no less than five different countries. I suggested that we exchange chairs for a moment, but Ratanam looked dubiously at Mr Subramaniam: the bell had already gone. He nodded approval. I got into the Gypsy to allow Ratanam to climb into my chair. He raced off down the road like an excited school-boy. 'It is very much easier and more comfortable' he cried over his shoulder, as Mr Subramaniam translated with a smile. 'It moves very fast.'

I saw what he meant when I clambered into his. The seat consisted of a rough, narrow plank, almost twice the height above ground as in my standard Western-type model. 'He wheels himself for eighteen miles a day in this?' I exclaimed, finding it hard to keep turning the crank for more than a few yards. 'Yes, in all weathers too,' Mr Subramaniam said. 'In fact, we can judge the weather outside by what state he's in when he arrives, whether he's merely caked in dust, or plastered with mud.'

So much for human courage and endurance.

One of my final calls in Osaka was on Professor Mizuno, whom I had met at a symposium in Bombay six months previously. He welcomed me like a long-lost friend; after spending the afternoon talking shop in his office, the Professor invited us out for an enjoyable evening at a Japanese cabaret, watching the show and enjoying some delicious local food. It was a welcome break after a heavy programme of visits and discussions during the previous fortnight.

'I know how interested you are in meeting the disabled,' he said as we were leaving the cabaret. 'Tomorrow I will take you to meet my friend Toichiro Fujikawa, near Kobe.'

When we met the following morning, I noticed that the Professor had a twinkle in his eye. But he said virtually nothing during the twenty mile drive. I asked him why Toichiro was so exceptional and he replied that I would be able to form my own opinion in a moment. We stopped outside a house in the Ashya suburb, a middle-class semi-detached dwelling set in a little garden. I noticed a slender figure in outsize blue working clothes, repairing a gutter at the top of a long ladder. The moment he saw the Professor he scrambled down, bowing and greeting us shyly with grave decorum in Japanese. I observed immediately that his face twitched, that his arms and legs jerked spasmodically; he was evidently suffering from cerebral palsy.

The Professor walked over. 'Well, what do you think of the house?'

It looked solid enough, an ordinary-looking three-storied house. 'It looks just fine to me,' I said, for want of anything better to say.

'Precisely. Isn't it remarkable? He built it himself.'

I could hardly believe my ears. 'But he can't . . . he couldn't have . . . '

'Oh yes he did. He built it all. Now you will understand why I brought you here!'

Anyone who has ever seen a cerebral palsy victim trying to drink a cup of tea, or hold a pen to write, can sympathize with my reaction. Spasticity plays havoc with muscle co-ordination; the simplest task becomes fraught with problems. To build a house single-handed seemed impossible, totally unbelievable. But as Toichiro led the way inside, blinking shyly at us behind his spectacles, I noticed an unmistakable look in his eyes. Unfortunately he spoke no English; I couldn't help looking at him and this large, solid house with unconcealed admiration.

Few things were 'impossible' when Toichiro put his mind to it. He had been born congenitally afflicted with the disease. His family had done everything they could for him; he had successfully completed secondary education, and was at an art school when war broke out. The years that followed were tough, but they survived cheerfully enough, until a major air strike left them homeless and destitute, one week before Japan surrendered.

The father was a carpenter by trade and they all helped him to build a new home – little more than a large shack. A major typhoon lifted it from the ground in 1947, smashing it into small pieces. While his father grimly set about rebuilding it, Toichiro took any job he could find to help out, on the land or in factories. His courage was admired, up to a point. 'Why do you bother?' his fellow-workers would say. 'You shouldn't be working, you should be at home where your family can look after you.'

It is only too easy to sound condescending to a CP victim; I had nearly fallen into this trap myself. The more people were 'kind', the madder Toichiro became. He was determined to prove that he was not a good-for-nothing. In 1954 he seized his chance. He had worked hard, and saved some money. His father offered to provide the materials. Toichiro began to build a house of his own, a ferro-concrete structure that no typhoon could touch.

Neighbours and passers-by would stop and stare, as the slight figure bravely mixed concrete, or attempted to lift the heavy steel rods. But he persevered, struggling uncertainly up ladders with heavy loads. Frequently he would fall, hit his fingers with a hammer or injure himself with a saw. But he'd pick himself up, wipe the blood away and carry on. Gradually the walls rose higher, none too straight, but solid as a rock. It took Toichiro four years before the nine rooms in the house were habitable.

As the others went upstairs, I waited in the roomy studio downstairs scattered with Toichiro's abstract carvings and paintings. His young wife joined me, smiling and bowing as she served the green tea, her movements graceful and refined. I bowed and smiled back, wishing that I could express my admiration more adequately. When the rest of the party came down again, I asked how much all this had cost. From the conversation that followed, I gathered that when the father's contribution had been allowed for, the total outlay was only about ten per cent of what such a house would have cost if it had been constructed by a firm of builders. Four thousand pounds of cement had been used, and twenty tons of steel rods. Despite working hard on the construction for eight hours a day, Toichiro had still found enough energy in the evenings for his sculpture.

Now he was already setting up his easel. The Professor turned to me. 'He would like to make a sketch of you.' 'I'd be delighted,' I replied. His hand twitched in an occasional spasm, but the line was unerring. In fifteen minutes the sketch was ready, an excellent likeness by an accomplished artist. Toichiro handed it to me, bowing and beaming. 'Domo arigato!' 'Thank you!' I said in my best Japanese, switching my gaze between the sketch, the sturdy walls and large windows opening onto the garden gay with red roses.

'What was the hardest part?' I asked, as we were taking our leave. 'Was it the plumbing perhaps, or wiring it all for electricity?'

When the Professor had translated my question, I saw his eyes light up again. 'I am a carpenter's son, but the hardest part was fitting the window frames!'

CHAPTER 13

The Amarnath Pilgrimage: a Climb of 12,000 feet

*

W H E N we returned to India on the 10th of June 1965, the pre-monsoon heat was at its most intense. The moment the boat docked at Madras, the heat rose up to hit us like the blast from a furnace; we were dripping with sweat before we even reached the Customs shed. At this time of the year, India is stifling, even for those like myself who pride themselves on being able to stand almost any temperature. The combination of heat and humidity turns the simplest task into a burden, requiring concentration and effort. We decided to head for Kashmir and the coolness of the Himalayas.

Once we left Madras, we made good going on the 2,400 mile drive. I was glad to be back in India, and gazed happily at the fast-changing kaleidoscope of villages, fields and market towns. As the sun began to dip towards the horizon, files of women, graceful as Greek statues, moved towards the wells, the brass pots on their heads catching the mellow light. Homing droves of cattle sent trails of dust across the plain, and the soft and peaceful scene felt rich like old, old wine.

The towns still retained their bustle, with that chaotic, garrulous but somehow warm and confident activity that always reminds me of the dawn chorus. People lay perfectly relaxed on the hard street, while others dozed on the cramped seats of waiting rickshaws or spread over the boxes of merchandise piled high on rumbling bullock-carts. I marvelled at the ease with which their bodies adapted themselves to such tortured postures, and thought how typical this was of the ability of the Indian people to adjust to the most trying conditions and yet retain an enviable inner capacity for joy and contentment. Jocelyn's thoughts must have wandered in the same direction.

'I started another letter, trying to describe it here; but it's damn hard. If you mention what hits you first, the poverty, the awful hardship, they write back saying quite sincerely that they can't understand how people here retain the will to live, because they themselves couldn't stand it for a week, and they talk as though everyone went about sad, crushed and groaning. But it isn't like that at all, is it? In spite of everything, there's so much joy and laughter.'

'I know what you mean,' I said slowly, my mind's eye still lingering on a little shepherd boy with one arm missing whom we had passed about an hour previously. He was thin and bedraggled, wearing a pair of shorts that was full of holes. In his only hand he held a flute, and played like a little faun as he drove his flock.

'Unconsciously we place ourselves in their shoes. If conditions are crushing, we assume the spirit will be crushed – but that's a false equation. If it were true, to hope for better things would be as futile as trying to raise the dead.'

Despite his living conditions, the spirit of Trilok Parimoo was not crushed. To reach his house, I had to propel myself through the slummiest back streets of Srinagar, Kashmir, through lanes that were thick and slimy with nauseating refuse. When I eventually reached the house, I found that he lived in one small room, at the top of a steep flight of stairs. The two Kashmiris who had shown me the way carried me up to his room and eased me down on the bed beside him.

'It is very kind of you to have come all this way to see me,' Trilok said in impeccable English as I tried to wriggle into a more comfortable position. 'I seldom see anyone now.'

The smell of urine and pus was overpowering. Bugs ran freely all over the simple *charpoy*, or string cot, on which he lay, without sheets, with bedsores growing daily more painful. I glanced around at the chair that had seen better days, the table, and the few bundles of old clothing in one corner, the sum total of his worldly possessions. Around the walls were the usual Hindu religious posters. Above the string cot there was a faded photograph of a dashing figure, immaculate in the uniform of an Indian Army sergeant. When I asked about this, his eyes lit up. The haunted, self-conscious, apologetic look dropped away, as he told me with pride that it had been taken nearly twenty years ago, in Quetta. He had been a sergeant then with the Royal Indian Army Service Corps; but in 1947, during the partition riots, a bullet had shattered his spinal cord. Paralysed from the waist down and incontinent, he had spent four years in various homes and hospitals. The doctors had been kind enough but could offer little in the way of treatment, nothing to help him rehabilitate himself. Wheelchairs 'were not commonly available' in those days. Eventually he returned to his native Kashmir and to the family home. He even succeeded in acquiring a second-hand wheelchair, which enabled him to get around a bit. But he could find no work; his relatives, fearing that he would become a permanent liability, edged him out of the house, although he owned a share in it.

His trials were not over. Having found himself the cheapest room in Srinagar, he tried to rally the local ex-servicemen, and started a local branch of the Old Comrades. He even set up a workshop, where disabled ex-servicemen could work together. He put not only enthusiasm, but virtually all his savings into these ventures. But most of the others were apathetic; the Association was wound up, the workshop never really got off the ground, and Trilok lost his savings.

'After that I tried everywhere to get work,' he said, the thick hair falling boyishly over the thin, sallow face. 'But I was knocking my head against a brick wall. No one wants to give any work to a disabled person.'

Although dusk was falling we continued to talk, and I questioned Trilok about his failure to obtain work. He confirmed many of my previous observations. There were literally dozens of able-bodied applicants for every job that became vacant; why should an employer bother to consider someone disabled? Besides, the disabled were frequently thought to be a liability, accident- or sickness-prone. Others believed quite seriously, even if they would seldom admit it, that the disability was a direct result of some devilry in a former incarnation. Caste was yet another factor, limiting both the field of employment and usually any philanthropy to within the given caste.

'Then there is the fact that for so many people work is no better than a curse,' he continued. 'Many, many people find only deadening drudgery in work – and with good reason. Usually it means a life of toil and misery, cut short by an early death. People feel that those like myself who have already been afflicted should not be exposed to further misery. It may be difficult for you to understand, coming from the West, but it's a fact of life here.'

I understood only too well. Science and technology have taken much of the back-breaking element out of unskilled work, as the word is understood in the West. Work for us has become not only the means to an end, the way in which we earn a living, but an end in itself: a pleasure perhaps, or at any rate a way of expressing oneself and 'getting on' in life. Few realize how new this concept really is.

In the falling darkness, the bugs were becoming really aggressive. I wondered, for a second, why he did not light the lamp; then realized that he probably had to economize on light. I asked if he managed to make ends meet.

'Well, not really, I'm afraid. I go hungry most of the time, except when I get an order for some embroidery. But that doesn't happen very often now.'

'But surely you get a pension?'

'Yes, I get thirty-nine rupees a month, plus an allowance of another fifteen rupees. But I have to collect it in person and so I have to hire coolies to take me to the office.'

So red tape cost poor Trilok six rupees a month, out of his fifty-four, leaving forty-eight rupees to keep body and soul together. 'Yes, I know it's not much,' he said, reading my thoughts. 'But I thank God that I can still live honourably. There's not much I can do now, except to help the children who come to see me with their homework. So many people in my predicament go out to beg; I'd rather kill myself than be reduced to that.'

Despite eighteen years of a living hell, the spark had not dimmed. As my two escorts lifted me back towards the dark staircase, I turned my head to admire the unquenchable spirit behind the sickness and squalor. Wheeling myself through the streets, back to the comparative luxury of our house-boat, I reflected that under such conditions it might often be better to die quickly than to become an invalid. The thought made me feel physically sick, and increased my determination to find some way, however modest, of helping to alleviate this misery.

Shortly afterwards we decided to go fishing. After driving about thirty miles along the road to Sonamarg, we stopped at a point where the glacial torrent came frothing down from the snows of the Himalayas. I sat dumbly on the bank, hopefully peering at the line, while Jocelyn pulled in one trout after the other. Our house-boatman wasted no time in preparing the fish and was soon frying the trout over a fire crackling by the side of the torrent; we sat quietly, enjoying our peaceful picnic, gazing up at the misty peaks.

'I'd love to get up there,' I said longingly. 'But I doubt if I'd manage a pony.'

'Well, perhaps we could strap you on, wheelchair and all . . . '

'We could try, couldn't we?'

The next day we drove to Pahalgam, the starting point for the arduous Amarnath pilgrimage. The main concourse assembles in August, when thousands submit to the rigours of a six-day trek at the time of the full moon; but ponies are also available throughout the summer and early fall, for rides in the surrounding forests and trails. As soon as we drove in, we were surrounded by grinning pony-wallahs, only too eager for business.

'You want ride, Sahib? Pony very good. Pony very cheap.'

When Jocelyn pulled the wheelchair from the back of the Gypsy, the hubbub died instantly. Business forgotten, they goggled, tut-tutting to themselves as I climbed in. In the earlier stages of the Expedition I had sometimes felt embarrassed by this show of unbridled commiseration, however well-meant. But I was used to it by now. When I wheeled myself over to the sturdiest-looking pony, they chattered in disbelief, shaking their heads with doubt and alarm. 'Sahib is joking!'

'No, no!' I replied gaily. 'First time for everything!'

The trail was dangerous, they argued, with snow and ice and landslides. The government would be angry, especially if there were an accident. I held my ground and eventually persuaded one of the rather more enterprising pony men to let me try his animal for size. The remainder watched intently as Ibrahim, the driver, and Jocelyn hoisted the empty chair. With the footplates folded, it straddled the pony's saddle pretty well. After the flanks had been padded with blankets as an additional precaution against chafing, Jocelyn strapped the lot together with yards of sturdy cord from the Gypsy. 'Now let's get you up,' he said, giving the knot a final twist.

When they heaved me into this singular perch, I found myself at least a foot above the animal's back but otherwise comfortable enough. It felt strange to be on horseback again, as we gently walked the ponies around the nearby woods. Apart from being a bit top heavy, it seemed safe enough, provided Ibrahim steadied it on the steeper slopes. Encouraged by this dummy run, we arranged to set off early the next morning from Chandawari, a few miles beyond Pahalgam, at the end of the jeepable trail.

To our surprise, Ibrahim was ready and waiting when we arrived at 5 a.m. Within half an hour we set off through the mist, grimly determined to do or die, following the path that zig-zagged steeply up the mountain. To our right, a torrent rushed down with a deafening roar. When the mist began to lift, patches of deep snow contrasted markedly with the intense green of the forest. As we slogged up the steep, rugged path, the trees grew more stunted, the vegetation more bushy, until we emerged on to the pastures of the high slopes. There we stopped for a breather, listening to the long calls and whistles of the shepherds reverberating in the clear air. I had never thought that I would taste once more the wild grandeur of a Himalayan summer. I breathed deeply. It seemed a triumph over my disability, which I felt I had shed far below in the valley.

Admittedly we had been on some tricky climbs before. Shortly before we had left for Japan, Jocelyn and I had spent three days exploring the ruins of Angkor in Cambodia. Built a thousand years ago as capital of the Khmer Empire, Angkor was conceived on a massive scale, roughly the size of modern Paris. Now the ruins rise up out of the jungle with huge pyramidal temple complexes rising from trees and undergrowth like fabulous wedding cakes left over after some Olympian celebration. More often than not steep flights of steps lead from one terrace to another, and so we had to leave the wheelchair locked in the Gypsy, while I clung like an outsize Koala bear onto Jocelyn's back. In places, the stairs were almost vertical, like Jacob's Ladder, with steps rising a foot at a time, so narrow after a thousand years of wear and tear that they only offered a slippery toe-hold.

But we scrambled happily up and down for several hours, occasionally taking the odd wall in our stride. Fortunately, there were few other tourists about, so we were spared helpful advice. I remember though meeting one small French boy, who was on his way around the world with his father. 'Regarde, Papa, ces espèces d'Angliches qui font les singes!' he said, his clear treble voice echoing off the jagged pinnacles.

Nepalese peasant

The grassy meadow behind us, I clutched the reins nervously as the pony strained to climb a particularly steep stretch. It was now about 10 a.m; the sun was high over the peaks, melting patches of snow, coaxing a riot of blue irises from their buds beneath the drifts. But the slush made the going even more hazardous for the pony, and I was glad of Ibrahim's steadying hand on the wheelchair, as he plodded alongside.

As the path became even steeper, I thought with awe and wonder of the thousands who make this ascent every August, one of the most sacred and arduous pilgrimages of Hinduism, comparable in its spiritual value to what the Jerusalem pilgrimage meant to Crusader Europe. We were now about 9,500 feet up, about half way to Lake Shish Nag, which we had agreed with Ibrahim as a reasonable compromise point. I was already beginning to feel the bitter cold through my thin jeans, despite the bright sunlight.

The object of the pilgrimage is a cave, at an altitude of over 12,700 feet, a full day's hard climbing over glaciers and a high pass from Shish Nag; at the far end of the cave there rises a stalagmitic pillar of ice. This column is regarded as the holy *lingam*, the manifestation of God Siva in his procreative aspect. Despite the painfully low temperatures, sadhus and hermits who have made the pilgrimage often sit almost naked on the icy shelves around the cave, or in the snow outside, deep in meditation. Having renounced the material world and its lures, they remain motionless for hours, seemingly unaffected by the snow and the freezing wind on their naked bodies.

According to Ibrahim, they chant hymns as they climb the stony path, shouting the name of God, 'Har, har, Mahadev.' Many climb barefoot, while some of the most intensely devout opt out of walking altogether and proceed up the mountain by 'measuring their length'. This involves prostrating oneself, rising again, moving forward to where the head touched the ground, prostrating again, and so on all the way. In times past a number invariably died of fatigue, exposure or falls; such a death was often regarded as welcome, since it ensured a short cut to salvation. Now, however, the government assists with an elaborate security system, providing a doctor, a mobile first-aid unit, a canteen dispensing free food, and tents for the needy all along the route; this has almost eradicated fatalities.

As the pony lunged, my wheelchair kept slipping backwards and Jocelyn had to keep making adjustments. At about ten thousand feet we reached flat ground, to the relief of all concerned, and decided to rest again. It was past midday. Jocelyn and Ibrahim helped me dismount to give the pony a well-deserved rest. While it grazed nearby, we compared notes, each believing to be more stiff than the other. We decided, in the end, that the prize should go to the wheelchair. 'Good thing Ibrahim didn't weigh you at the bottom!' Jocelyn chuckled, as we tucked into the rice curry we had brought in our mess-tins. 'He'd have made a lot more by charging you by the pound!'

'Don't you dare put the idea into his head!'

I always felt a little conscience-stricken when we spent money on these off-duty jaunts, even if such escapades almost always attracted publicity and focused public attention on the range of activities open to the disabled. It wasn't so much the cost, which in this case amounted to about two pounds, but the principle involved.

One of the rare exceptions we made to this rule was in October 1964 when we were in Palitana, Gujerat State in Western India, at the time of the annual pilgrimage to Satrunjaya. Satrunjaya is a sacred temple city of the Jains, a remarkable creed which accounts for some two million followers in India. Over the years pious Jains had cut or built over three miles of steps into the hillside, to enable pilgrims to climb to the sacred city at the top of the hill, two thousand feet above Palitana town. Looking up at the swarm of pilgrims, struggling up step by step into the distance, I realized that Jocelyn could never manage to help me up there by himself. I would have to hire a *doli* or sedan chair.

The last time I had made such a climb was in 1957, when I visited another cluster of Jain temples on the nearby Girnar mountain. Before setting off, I had noticed an extremely portly matron being placed on a weighing machine, which must have seen better days in some Victorian railway station. Although she protested loudly, she was unceremoniously dumped on the machine, to be charged per pound of flesh. I looked around for a similar contraption lurking somewhere at the bottom of the Satrunjaya climb. To my relief no such machine was to be seen. But owing to my wheelchair the bargaining proved louder and more acrimonious. Having opened our bids at five and fifteen rupees respectively, we eventually compromised on twelve rupees (about eighteen shillings at the time), and I was soon gently swaying above the heads of fellow pilgrims, men and women, old and young, as they trudged up the stairway, twisting towards heaven in a stream of bright colour.

'*Dharamlab*' they called out. 'May the faith profit you. But why don't you walk like us? A young, healthy man like you!'

'Well actually, I could explain, but it would take a little time,' I grinned, grateful for the backhanded compliment.

The four porters sweated and grunted for three hours. Suddenly we glimpsed the holy city, spire upon spire surrounded by tall battlements. There are no houses or human dwellings in Satrunjaya: just temples. Eight hundred and sixty seven temples, their pinnacles reaching up into the sky like a vision of Bunyan's Heavenly City. As we walked through the medieval gateway, we passed innumerable domes and shrines, all adorned with figures of celestial dancers carved in high relief. Prayers and chants mingled with the sharp clang of bells and the beating of drums, as the faithful bore flowers or other offerings, and laid them before the thirty-six thousand idols of Satrunjaya. We roamed about for the whole day, bemused, entranced, gazing at fabulous jewellery and intricate carvings, until the gates closed at dusk. Regretfully we set off for the plain below, leaving the city once more to the gods and the winds.

Ibrahim was urging us to get going again. Looking apprehensively at the gloomy peaks ahead, we moved on skirting a deep gully. At the foot of the precipice, about a thousand feet below, we could see the torrent gushing. There was no longer room for Ibrahim to walk alongside, steadying the wheelchair. When the pony began to stumble, I felt the chair wobble precariously. 'Look at path before you!' Ibrahim urged, as I glanced nervously, in a cold sweat, at the chasm less than two feet to my right.

Jocelyn trudged immediately in front, on the look out for treacherous snow underfoot. 'Reminds me of Nuristan, slithering past all those landslides,' he called back over his shoulder. 'Oh yes,' I replied hoarsely, too preoccupied with the problem of survival to make any further attempt at conversation.

Eventually the path left the edge of the precipice, and we began to climb into shrubless barrenness. Our relief was short-lived. Within twenty minutes we found a landslide of mud, stones and melting snow blocking the path for as far as we could see. 'We go by mountain,' Ibrahim suggested, taking the pony's reins and leading it straight up the steep slope. After half an hour of this cross-country work, our way was again blocked, this time by half a mile of packed snow, glistening with a veneer of ice. 'We go back now?' Ibrahim suggested hopefully. 'No, no.' I said. 'Let's press on . . .' We pushed on in silence, the pony's hoof-pads crunching loud through the brittle ice crust, or slithering danger-ously where it was thicker.

As the end of the pack ice came in sight, I saw Jocelyn stop again. He came back with a worried frown on his face. 'Sorry, fellows, but there's a fairly wide stream ahead. Looks bad to me.' I rode up cursing. The stream had undercut the bordering crust of snow into treacherous overhangs. It was around four feet wide, but allowing for the overhangs at either end, I should have to allow for six feet in all. I had jumped wider ditches in the past, and I was determined that this was not going to stop me now.

'No, no, Sahib,' Ibrahim pleaded, as I lined the pony up for the run. 'Please, no Sahib. Pony break legs. No pony, my family nothing to eat.'

This was too much. When Ibrahim offered to carry me on his back, I gave in. It was mildly ignominious to sit hunched over his back, as we inched into the icy water and scrambled up the far side. But we were rewarded within minutes, when the ground levelled out once more and the glorious vista of Lake Shish Nag opened out before us. The lake was about a mile long by half a mile wide, enfolded on three sides by bleak, inhospitable, snow-clad cliffs. Small icebergs on the still, emerald water appeared like swans bewitched into a dreamy stillness, banished from the impurities of earth to this remote fastness, free from all prospect of contamination.

'Good God!' Jocelyn said, as we paused, spellbound in admira-tion. 'It was worth it just to see that.'

He had summed it up to perfection.

The descent was a hard, numbing slog. The thought of having established a wheelchair altitude record at 12,200 feet was small comfort as we battled into a stiff wind lashing us with sleet. We were soaked to the skin before we forded the stream again and began to inch our way down the precipitous path. When we eventually returned to the starting-point, stiff and numbed with cold, we scrambled into the Gypsy; with Ibrahim galloping behind, Jocelyn sped down the narrow trail to Pahalgam, towards the relative luxury of hot rice curry in the rest house. When I handed Ibrahim an extra ten rupees, he grinned broadly. Neither he nor the pony seemed any the worse for the experience. We parted excellent friends.

The mountain road from Srinagar to Jammu is gruelling at the best of times. For about a hundred and fifty miles it leads over interminable loops, past blind corners, skirting precipices. Being the only road linking Kashmir with the rest of India, the traffic is heavy; besides trucks and cars, convoys of military vehicles use it coming and going from the powerful military establishment manning the disputed border with China and Pakistan. Frequently we passed lorry carcasses laying in mangled heaps at the bottom of ravines. To make driving still more hazardous, the road is frequently obstructed by grazing animals. The sheep we knocked was merely stunned and limped off almost as upset as we were. The chicken, alas, was less lucky; for all I saw when I looked in the mirror was a mangled heap of feathers. I am not superstitious, but I had an unpleasant feeling that we might strike a third time. Sure enough, as we dropped down from the mountains and entered the crowded suburbs of Jammu, a small child shot out of a doorway, straight into the path of the car. I gripped the dashboard with both hands as Jocelyn braked violently, and heard a sickening thud as the small figure disappeared underneath.

'My God, we've killed it!' I murmured, staring at a patch of blood that was sending small rivulets across the tarmac. Jocelyn sat silently, transfixed at the wheel. 'Don't you think you'd better have a look?' I suggested. Within seconds a crowd had sprung up, with relatives and friends screaming frantically. While Jocelyn investigated, I prayed hard for its life, hardly able to spare a thought to our own perilous situation. Ideally in such cases one ought to drive on and report to the police at least ten if not twenty miles ahead, for a hysterical crowd is sometimes capable of setting fire to the car or lynching the unfortunate occupants. But how could we drive on? The child was underneath us, possibly still alive.

After an agonizing delay, I saw the mother straighten up, clutching the wee mite. It was a girl of about eight and to my unspeakable relief, she was not only alive but gently whimpering. After a hurried conference, we decided to drive at full speed to the hospital; I made room for mother and child in the front, and we set off with a dozen others perched on the roof or clinging to the back.

I was still puzzled about the blood, because I could see no obvious wounds. When we spoke to the casualty doctor, he offered no explanation, diagnosing superficial concussion. 'I am sure she will be all right, but please stay until tomorrow all the same.'

After Jocelyn reconstructed the accident, we realized just how lucky we had been. As the car had hit her, with wheels locked by the brakes, she had fallen to the ground and rolled along in the same direction from the force of the impact. When the car came to rest, she was lying immediately below the front differential, with only two or three inches to spare at either end from the wheels. When we enquired at the hospital the next morning, the mother told us that the mite was about to walk home with her. She also resolved the one outstanding mystery. Evidently the child had been carrying a bowl of red soup, which I had mistaken for blood. I paid for the soup with a jumbo-sized bag of sweets thrown in.

Apart from this traumatic incident morale was high. We were now heading, albeit by a circuitous route, for the remote jungle village of Kandarya where some friends had asked us to join them for a short shooting vacation.

*

The influence of the traditional ayurvedic medicine is still extremely pervasive, especially in rural areas, as a brief glance at the figures will show: whereas the country has approximately 86,000 registered 'allopathic' doctors, the estimated number of 'practitioners of indigenous medicine' tops the 300,000 mark. Ayurvedic techniques have developed slowly over three thousand years; many of its practitioners tend to look back to an alleged golden age five or six centuries before the Christian era, when distinguished doctors and surgeons such as the famous Sushruta practised in India. Nowadays, although they can seldom compete with modern orthodox medicine in clinical terms, they still enjoy a degree of official approval and financial support.

We had come across some ayurvedics and had been quite impressed – for instance by the ayurvedic leprosarium run by an Indian ascetic on the outskirts of Benares. We had been to the Ayurvedic University there and also observed the selfless, dedicated work of Ram Prasad Mistry, a third generation bone-setter and ayurvedic practitioner in the village of Keshopur, Bihar State. Finally, we had seen a family of bone-setters at work in Puttur, a village in southern Andhra Pradesh, which patients flocked to from a distance of two thousand miles and more. Without anaesthetic, the practitioners in Puttur set not only single but multiple fractures, using a heavy stone to rebreak badly set fractures where necessary. Having set a fracture, they splinted the limb, applied a spinach-like paste made of egg-white and ground leaf (the identity of which is a closely guarded secret) and bandaged it up. The results were not at all bad, according to a doctor in the Christian Medical College in Vellore.

In this connexion, I had long wondered how the various diviners, mediums and hierophants that are sought after by many cripples fitted in. These arcane practices are surprisingly pervasive in the remoter rural areas and they fascinated me both in their own right and in the context of my work. Once again I thought that my own disability would offer an excellent pretext for experience at first hand. We decided to visit first of all the temple of Aavri Mata, in a small village east of Udaipur, where the sick and crippled are brought from far and near to lie before the effigy of this goddess.

When we arrived, sorely shaken after an exceedingly bumpy ride, the temple priest greeted us warmly. He was an elderly man with a stoop; eyeing me benignly, he suggested that I lie for a week on the temple floor. 'You might be helped as thousands have been,' he added encouragingly.

'Unfortunately we are a little pressed for time.' I grinned back.

The temple was a small, low, stone-built affair, picturesquely sited by a pond and an old spreading tree. He led us across the outer courtyard, with a cluster of red-painted tridents (emblems of God Siva the goddess's consort) standing in a corner, and through the narrow door. It was murky inside, but in the holy of holies at the far end I could just make out a rather ugly red-painted daub with two large, staring eyes, representing the goddess. The floor was chequered black and white stone; on it lay three old men, their heads pointing towards the effigy, covered with tattered brown blankets. They looked sickly and wan, with legs paralysed possibly as a result of strokes. 'Lord, the combination of that bumpy ride and this hard cold floor should be enough to finish them off.' Jocelyn said grimly. 'Maybe. But never underestimate the power of absolute faith,' I murmured.

A few days later we reached the remote desert village of Lamba, east of Jodhpur in central Rajasthan. Lamba's chief claim to fame is a plain, modest temple dedicated to the Goddess Chamundi, built on the outskirts of the village some thirty years ago by the votaries of the medium or *bhopa*, a well-built large man now in his late fifties.

When we arrived the bhopa, usually called by the diminutive *bhopaji*, was busy changing his clothes. A tense crowd of about forty, each having brought a handful of grain which they heaped before him, waited expectantly to hear what the goddess would tell them through her mouthpiece, the bhopa. We watched for half an hour as he put on an ankle-length skirt, blouse and head-scarf, and then began to darken his eyelids. Having decked himself out with various necklaces, bracelets, anklets, and a host of rings on fingers and toes, he sat quietly on the left side of the effigy in the inner shrine. The ceremony was about to start.

Small fires were lit in two earthenware pots; a thin boy with a long pigtail waved an oil lamp vigorously before the gaudy image of the goddess; another acolyte beat a gong; a withered old woman tossed her head furiously as she pounded a double drum. As if gripped by this convulsive beat, the bhopa's head began to shake violently. While the drums worked up to a mad crescendo, a woman from the crowd began to roll on the ground, yelling hysterically. Suddenly the medium leapt high into the air, to fall on a pile of cushions on his right. The noise stopped abruptly, so that you could hear a pin drop. Then he began to scream at the top of his voice, his arms and head shaking uncontrollably; the goddess had entered into him. Gradually over the next five minutes or so he calmed down; picking up an iron chain, he passed it through the flame from the nearest pot, then dipped his hand into the heap of grain. Letting the grain run through his fingers, he began to speak in a halting, mechanical and strangely feminine voice. As he called out their names, the petitioners approached, one by one, with suitable deference. Each one walked, or was

Sowing the first crop in a jungle clearing at Somnath

Harvesting chilis in Kashmir Valley

carried, to within a couple of feet and prostrated himself. Sifting the grain between his fingers, the bhopa would ask a few questions in a monotone, often anticipating the replies with garbled statements about the nature of the petition and the proposed solution. To some he would end by saying that if they persevered their condition would change; to others that if they worshipped regularly, the goddess would help them. Finally, after about five minutes, he would wave a bunch of peacock feathers at the petitioner and send him (or her) away with a pinch of holy ash from the fire.

One of those seeking help was a lawyer and member of the Rajasthan Legislative Assembly, who had suffered a paralytic stroke. Having spent some time in hospital, where he said nothing more could be done for him, he believed his present, slow improvement to be a boon of the goddess bestowed on him through the bhopa, whose seances he attended nightly. When I asked him about the other disabled present, he told me that they all shared a blind faith in the goddess; a few like he had come after having exhausted orthodox medical processes; many more had never seen a doctor or even tried to.

I was musing quietly to myself about the power of faith, particularly in the case of psychosomatic disorders, when I became conscious that all eyes were on me. 'There is a person from England here,' the bhopa was saying in his strained feminine staccato. As I wheeled myself forward, I thought of the countless disabled who approach such mediums. They were not merely curious, as I was, but in dead earnest, having nowhere else to turn to. They approached with a pathetic hope for a miracle. As two strong Rajasthanis from the crowd, heads tied with huge red turbans, propped me up into a standing position, I felt a trifle self-conscious, but above all tense with curiosity. While the lawyer translated bhopaji's words, I listened keenly. Most of the early questions concerned pigeons. Had I ever drunk pigeon's blood? Or been where the air is moved by pigeon's wings? I was baffled, until the lawyer murmured that in villages pigeons were regarded as helpful in curing paralysis.

'Have you visited the temple at Deshnoke?' 'Yes, but . . . ' 'Your left side is more paralysed than your right one.' 'That is true.' Presently he reached for the peacock feathers; having waved them the length of my body, he offered a generous helping of the holy ash which I received into a clean handkerchief. 'Rub it into your legs for two weeks,' he said as I thanked him. 'Take a pinch when you drink, too. Come back again if this helps.'

A minute later I rejoined Jocelyn, feeling happy but bewildered, as if I had emerged from the corridors of Hades itself.

*

The main purpose of our holiday in Kandarya was to enjoy a hunt with some friends, and if possible bag some big game. When we arrived at this remote jungle village we were mildly disconcerted to find that the tigers had been rare of late.

Our kind host, Jharkand Bahadur Singh, suggested that we try our luck with other game, particularly the wild boar that had recently been trampling the crops in the neighbourhood. 'They can turn very vicious though,' he said eyeing my wheelchair.

'I'll be all right, I promise,' I replied cheerfully. 'I was brought up with a gun in my hands.'

The estate covered about a thousand acres in all, two hundred of which were retained to meet his own household requirements. Admittedly it was a large household, with many relatives and servants – we never established precisely how large, partly because the women kept themselves strictly apart, partly because it would have been indelicate to pry. But Bahadur lived frugally in this feudal setting. He wore the *choti*, a small pigtail sported by devout Hindus, and retained the services of a Brahmin priest in a private shrine, set apart from the main quarters.

We were resting quietly in the small guest-room when he announced that our transport was waiting. As we emerged, blinking, into the sunlight, we found the *mahut*, or driver, standing stiffly beside Hathi, the elephant. As I looked up at the beast towering above me, I heard Bahadur laughing. 'Don't worry,' he called out. 'Hathi knows every inch of the jungle around here!'

When the mahut induced the animal to kneel, I realized that the howdah, the square wooden platform surrounded on three sides by a low balustrade, still loomed way above me. But when the mahut pulled from on top of the howdah, and Jocelyn pushed from below, I scrambled aboard. Bahadur, Jocelyn and another friend joined me on the howdah, whereupon the mahut gently rubbed his feet behind the elephant's ears, and Hathi ponderously heaved himself up.

It was now about half past four, or about two and a half hours before dusk. Since we had to take up our positions in the butts well before the wild animals came out on the prowl, we pressed on as fast as Hathi's thick, stubby legs would carry us, with the four of us riding in style, and five more, including two gillies, following on foot. The butts were scattered over a wide area, with about a mile between each, and the party dwindled as the members dropped off. Eventually, having watched Jocelyn disappear into the jungle with his hip flask and a twelve-bore slung over his shoulder, the mahut helped me dismount and retired on Hathi to a safe distance, leaving me alone with my gillie.

The butt overlooked a waterhole. It was no more than a lean-to scooped out from the slope of the bank, roofed with branches and faggots that had been cleverly tamped down with clay and grass on the outside so that you wouldn't notice it a few feet away. Having left the wheelchair on Hathi, I crawled like a mole through the small two-foot entrance. Inside there was just enough room for two; I laid my flask of gin on the straw, loaded my 303 Purdey rifle and a rifled sports gun with number seven cartridges and got ready to wait, sitting cross-legged with gun-butt between my knees. There were four small embrasures on the butt, so that our arc of fire covered the entire area of the pond and its approaches.

War experiences apart, a quarter of a century had elapsed since I had gone after anything larger than feathered game. But as I crouched on the straw, hardly daring to breathe for fear of betraying my presence, it seemed only a few weeks ago that I was back in Poland, waiting gun in hand for deer or boar in the forests near Dukla and Zaleze. The moon rose, filtering a chill light through the slits; in the distance I could hear the desultory cry of a peacock settling down for the night. I gazed out intently, listening for the crackle and grunt of boar.

Six spotted deer came to water. Alas, nothing else came out that night. Those who are familiar with hunting will appreciate that half the fun lies in the waiting; the fact that no wild boar crossed my sights was no real disappointment. A few days later, we learned on the jungle grapevine that a panther had been active in a nearby village, and had killed a bullock. Since there had also been a report of a tiger in a more distant village, we decided to try our luck. Once more we trudged through the forest, with four of us on Hathi, and six more on foot; for the last quarter of a mile, I rode on a tracker's back, to make as little noise as possible. Eventually we reached a small clearing overlooked by a *machan*, in this case a platform of branches laid across the boughs of a tree, about twelve feet off the ground. The machan overlooked a little clearing, with a goat for bait. A rough ladder, slapped together with creeper and branches, led up to the machan, and after several unsuccessful attempts they succeeded in hoisting me up. I sat with Pratap Singh, an old friend from Calcutta; when the others had gone off to their stands in different parts of the forest, we prepared for the vigil, adjusting the foliage around the machan so that we were well concealed from below.

'You'd better lean on me,' Pratap whispered in the failing light; 'these rifles give quite a kick.' Having no wish to be catapulted out of the machan by the recoil I did as he suggested, realizing with a surge of happiness that in the thrill of it all I had quite forgotten my disability. 'You fire first,' he murmured. 'I'll only fire if you nip him and he charges. An enraged tiger could get up here in no time!'

Hour after hour we waited, silent and motionless. The mosquitoes whined and bit, but we dared not even move a muscle to shake them off. In the distance we heard the shrill cry of jackals. A hyena skulked at the edge of the clearing, sniffing diffidently towards the machan and the goat, but apparently decided that prudence was best and faded noiselessly away into the thicket. A little later a brown bear came ambling by, gave the goat a disdainful sniff and padded off. But although we waited until eleven at night, neither panther nor tiger showed up. I must admit I felt a bit disappointed, but not for long. Jocelyn, who in his enthusiasm had aimed at almost anything that moved, was grinning all over, having bagged several sambur or spotted deer, a hare and a civet cat.

The following day, having lowered my sights, I too was more successful; my bag included a brace of partridge, quail, and a couple of large Siberian ducks which provided good sport and, even more welcome, a break in the monotony of the Expedition diet.

CHAPTER 14

I am exorcised in Ceylon

*

THE Kandarya holiday marked the culmination of Jocelyn's time with the Expedition. Soon after we returned to the south, he boarded a plane at Tiruchirapalli, bound for England and Cambridge University. We had been through all manner of adventures together; I was deeply grateful to him, and as I watched the plane disappear, I felt that a chapter had closed.

My new companion, Julian Ingram, had arrived a few days earlier, and had spent most of his time picking Jocelyn's brains about everything from the mechanical peculiarities of the Gypsy to the routine loading and unloading of our gear. Julian soon settled down to expedition life. He had prepared himself methodically, having taken a fortnight's course at BMC's Long-bridge factory in Birmingham before leaving. Fortunately for me, he proved tough, methodical and even-tempered, and showed a natural flair for tackling and solving the increasingly complex problems of the ageing Gypsy.

Shortly after we arrived in Nepal Julian developed toothache. When our first-aid kit failed to cure this, he decided to enlist help from elsewhere. He was shown to a temple in the Bange Mura Road of Kathmandu, where there is a large log in the courtyard: you get rid of toothache by driving a nail in. Oddly enough, such a belief in pain-transference was current amongst the Romans, who called it *defixio*. Anyway, this log was so full of nails that there was precious little room for any more. But Julian managed to drive one in, hammering with gusto – after which his toothache felt 'much better'.

Some of these observances and traditions can be entertaining or weird, or both.

Perhaps the strangest ceremony we encountered was the marriage of a little girl to a fruit, a bel-fruit to be precise. Since widows cannot normally remarry in Nepal, little girls are some-times made to undergo this ceremony. Later they may marry proper husbands. But should the man subsequently die, the woman is still technically espoused to the fruit. So she does not become a widow and remains free to remarry. It was from Kathmandu that we set out on our ten-day trek to Malamchi, described in the opening chapter. When we set off back, much of the conversation revolved around the subject of food. We were both ravenous on the scanty diet, and we comforted each other with vivid descriptions of what we'd order in the Globe Restaurant in Kathmandu. The speciality in the Globe was Buffalo Steak, costing all of one and a half Nepali rupees.

Kathmandu at the time was the beatnik Mecca, and the Globe was unlike any other restaurant in the world. Nobody quite knows why the beatniks chose Kathmandu. Perhaps because Nepal was remote enough to gratify anybody's anti-social instincts, because the country is beautiful and extremely inexpensive, and because dope, particularly hashish and *ganja*, is freely available and dirt cheap. From Istanbul eastwards we had met characters who'd wake up from their habitual lethargy at the mention of Kathmandu and the Globe. Only the hardiest, most determined ones made it to Nepal, those that outbeatniked their fellows in appearance, manner and odour: the Globe was always full of them. Some dossed down with their girls in a slum next door, where they slept on the floor, twenty to a room each paying one rupee a night. No water was available in the house, but there was a street pump not far off, which was seldom used. The story goes in Kathmandu that once that house was infested with bugs and lice, but that they all crawled out, unable to withstand the pong.

When we returned to Kathmandu, we were filthy but exuberant. Having spent a good hour with a scrubbing brush under a spigot trickling icy cold water, we felt human again, and hastened towards the Globe. We pulled up outside in the Gypsy and Julian walked eagerly through the door. Minutes later he reappeared, brandishing the dog-eared menu. 'The place is choc-a-bloc with beatnikdom, so you'll have to eat in the car. I've already ordered my buffalo steaks.' I looked through the greasy menu on which some nostalgic French beatnik had given vent to his hungry imagination. 'Champagne: 20 rupees; Paté de foie gras aux truffes: 15 rupees; Caneton à l'orange: 18 rupees' read the scribblings. 'I'll have Chicken Chow Mein, double portion,' I said. At four rupees a time this was a rare extravagance, but I felt it was deserved.

The steaming bowlful was soon brought out to me. I dug in, too hungry to be put off either by the greasy fork that slid between the fingers, or by the covey of women who squatted in the street and chatted, while de-lousing one another, their children and their menfolk.

Another of the major trips I made with Julian was to Ceylon. There was no ferry service linking the island to the Indian mainland as the harbours at either end had been destroyed by a severe typhoon. So there was no alternative but to leave the car behind and take the plane. Both in India and Thailand we had often travelled by train and local bus, apart from more exotic modes of locomotion, so the prospect was in no way novel; but even if we took some of the more valuable gear with us, I wasn't happy with the thought of leaving the Gypsy. Happily an acquaintance in Tiruchirapalli offered to store it under lock and key, and so, relieved of this worry, we boarded a Ceylon Airways Dakota bound for Colombo.

Having checked in at the YMCA, we took a cab to the Ceylon Tourist bureau. They couldn't have been more helpful. 'Ah, but you mustn't worry,' the director waved away my explanations; 'we shall be glad to place a chauffeur driven car at your disposal. Welcome to Ceylon!'

Ceylon is one of the most beautiful and interesting countries in the world, and small wonder that many legends associate it with the original Garden of Eden. Its kindly inhabitants are generous, easy-going and fun-loving. The country is indescribably lush; large areas are still covered with primal jungle roamed by elephants, panthers and other wild animals. Long beaches of fine sand, cool mountains opening across vistas of tea and rubber plantations or over the jungle, exotic and different at every bend of the winding road, remains of ancient civilizations that rival those of Egypt, spectacular festivals . . . Even if tourism wasn't our main purpose, we felt it would have been a pity to miss seeing many of these things through lack of suitable transport; and we were only too grateful to accept the offer of a car. Two days later a large if somewhat elderly Chevrolet pulled up by the YMCA and the driver, a rather thin man in his forties, stepped out to introduce himself as Karl, our chauffeur.

Karl not only knew the roads, the short-cuts and the cheap restaurants but was a veritable mine of information about local facts and customs. So with Julian in the back seat beside me for a change, we set out on my usual round of visits to hospitals, institutions, meetings with the handicapped, followed by a press interview, lectures and a talk on Ceylon radio. The situation of the disabled didn't seem to differ much from the one I was already familiar with, except that since Ceylon is not quite as poor as India, food was more readily available, and this showed right across the population spectrum, including the disabled.

In the remoter rural areas of the East, as in medieval Europe, disability is still often believed to be the result of a curse, a spell, or the possession by malevolent spirits. I was well aware that some Sinhalese exorcists continued to perform weird ceremonies to drive them out. These practices are on the wane; anyway even if their influence in rural areas remains greater than many would care to admit, their place in the spectrum of disability is a relatively minor one. All the same, I was curious, since these secretive practices have had such a powerful impact on countless cripples down the ages. I decided to grasp the opportunity of experiencing this at first hand: if I could find a *yakadura*, or sorcerer-cum-exorciser, I would offer myself as a guinea-pig.

My great ally was Karl, who was almost embarrassingly keen to find a cure for my condition. Characteristically, he managed to combine a fundamentalist allegiance to the Roman Catholic faith with a belief in all manner of gods and spirits. Before we set off in the morning, he would sit caressing the wheel of the car, mumbling prayers and incantations; before we joined a mountainous road, we would stop by the roadside and crack a sacrificial coconut to the denizens of the peaks. When I suggested that the ministrations of an exorcist could be worth harnessing to the cause of my cure, he jumped at the idea; wherever we went he kept looking out for the most suitable practitioner. His ingenuous, almost paternal concern was so touching that I felt a little bit of a cad.

Exorcists require a wide variety of 'aids', according to the particular tradition that they follow. One, it appeared, required cockerels for sacrifice, another several pumpkins to cut; and so I was glad to leave the eventual choice to Karl.

'If only we knew if the bad spirit is in you,' he said one day. 'That would make things much easier.'

When I suggested that perhaps a yakadura could try me out first, before getting involved in the full *tovil*, he shook his head doubtfully.

'Ah, dangerous. If devil is found in you, the yakadura's magic must be strong to make the evil one leave you. Might roll you in the dust, flog you – or rather flog *yaksha*, the devil, inside you. Might even have to light fire on your chest to make yaksha leave.'

It was important to treat all this seriously, for genuine exorcists are not found for the asking; no yakadura would have anything to do with someone suspected of bad faith. But the thought of a fire being lit on my chest was too much for Julian, who began muttering: 'You're crazy. They'll do you some real damage if you go through with this.'

Karl disagreed, claiming that it would be Satan who would get the punishment, and that I might even cry out for more as I felt him depart under the lashes raining down on my body. To make him leave less grudgingly, a cock or a goat would be kept close by to offer him a new abode.

All the same, I was beginning to feel mildly apprehensive as to what I had let myself in for. Especially when Karl announced that he had found a suitable yakadura, and had fixed the tovil for the following evening. As the day wore on, I felt myself becoming increasingly nervous.

'Are you sure you should go through with this?' Julian kept repeating. 'After all, if something happened, the whole Expedition would be wasted.'

I tried to reassure him, arguing that since I did not subscribe to the beliefs underlying exorcism, *ipso facto* I could not exhibit the symptoms associated with possession. Strictly speaking, I was lending myself to this rite on outwardly spurious motives; but I felt that the insight it would afford me would more than justify my pretence at taking the thing in earnest.

'Well, I still think you're crazy,' he sighed. 'But let's get a move on; it's time to go.'

We made our way to the yakadura's cottage. It was a stormy night and the palms swayed in the gusty wind. The cottage was set amidst a grove of coconut palms close to the seashore, and as we drew nearer we heard the crash of breakers. The palm trees seemed to assume strange shapes as the fitful moon hid behind the heavy stormclouds.

The yakadura stood solemnly at the door, bidding us enter. A strange array of equipment confronted us inside. Two improvized tables, one higher than the other, supported offerings of coconut and sprays of areca palm, together with the five so-called 'flowers', all neatly laid out on banana leaves. (Apart from some red blooms, these consisted of jasmine, white mustard, panic-grass, rice grains, betel nuts, limes and other offerings.) Evidently the high table represented offerings for the gods, the lower one the demons' fare.

I wriggled out of my wheelchair and sat down self-consciously on a sheet spread out on the floor. Two youths took up position on either side, to guard me spiritually against the demons and evil spirits. A pungent odour rose from the pots and sticks of incense. As my smarting eyes grew accustomed to the smoky gloom, one of the four acolytes present placed a cockerel by my feet. I sat for some minutes gazing at the cockerel, which was alive but trussed up, while the yakadura and the others fell into silence and prayer. Then he motioned me to light the nine earthenware lamps lined in front of me, dedicated to the nine planets of Hinduism.

At about half-past eight the ceremony began in earnest. Two more acolytes emerged from a back room and began to dance. With bare, glistening torsos, close-fitting white pants and anklet bells, they beat a spirited tattoo on double-sided drums strapped to their waists. As the tempo rose they began to make threatening gestures stepping right up to where I sat, the drums deafening my ears, their faces distorted into angry grins. When they had worked themselves up into a fearful crescendo, the sorcerer himself surged forth, dressed in similar tights and bells, but wearing a sumptuous red jacket. Clutching a torch in his right hand, he flung handfuls of powdered resin into the flame. Plumes of flame shot up as the dancers whirled around shrieking and howling. The incense bit into my eyes, and the scene turned into a lurid blur. After about forty minutes, the fury abated and I opened my smarting eyes to see Karl looking at me solicitously.

'Yakadura says no evil spirit in you.'

'Well, thank goodness for that. Any more of that and I would have passed out.'

Thankful to have been spared the flagellation, I relaxed as best I could on the hard floor, while the sorcerer started reciting incantations in an archaic Sinhalese. For two hours he chanted on without faltering, and I marvelled at his prodigious memory which allowed him to retain whole chapters of these arcane texts. Meanwhile the assembled company watched my reaction closely. As the prayers and incantations flowed over my head, I listened attentively, intent on taking in every detail of this bizarre atmosphere, trying to picture what effect this would have on a disabled villager. Small wonder, I thought, that under such conditions a susceptible person might be driven into a fit. Given faith and superstitious fear, the effect must be traumatic indeed. It might well trigger off powerful auto-suggestive processes, which with certain complaints might make the patient get better or at least feel better.

It was nearly four o'clock in the morning when the yakadura embarked on the final ceremony. One of his assistants brought in a small bucketful of coconut oil and stood it in front of the old man; another produced twenty lemons and a sharp knife. Chanting incantations all the while, the yakadura solemnly cut the lemons, one by one, and dropped the halves into the oil.

Karl, sitting beside Julian across the room, explained solemnly that this was some kind of divination, that it was most important that the lemons float with the uncut end uppermost. Alas, almost all fell the wrong side up. Evidently this was an ill omen, for they all frowned and cast furtive glances at me, like doctors who had just established the patient's incurable condition. I consoled myself with the thought that it seemed more likely for cut lemons to float with the broader end up, but wondered uneasily whether such grim portents wouldn't prompt the sorcerer to take some drastic action. But since I had failed to froth at the mouth or to give way to spasms or hysterics, my disability had been judged to have arisen from natural causes, and accordingly no harsh treatment was called for. Instead, the sorcerer proceeded to perform a spirited dance. Then, sweating and breathing heavily, he lay down in line with my own body, so that his head rested between my knees. One of the acolytes handed him over a pale green ash pumpkin, at least a foot long, which they both placed just above the yakadura's head, between my thighs, and the assistant spread a sheet to cover my legs, the sorcerer's head and the pumpkin. Fumbling under the sheet, the sorcerer picked up the knife. Still in his prone position, he stretched his arms; holding the knife by the handle and end of blade over the pumpkin, he directed me to place my hands over his. While he muttered sacred *mantrams* and imprecations, we slowly pressed the knife down, gradually slicing the monster into two equal parts; any malignant spirit that might have still lingered within me was now well and truly exorcised. As a final gesture, after more resin had been thrown into the torches by the acolytes, the oil into which the lemons had been cast was rubbed with strong rhythmic motion into my legs.

We all emerged, breathing deeply, into the grey dawn. It had been an uncanny experience. Few travellers have ever experienced, let alone participated in, such a rite. Far from being exhausted, I felt gloriously alive. When we eventually re-assembled around midday, Karl looked anxiously for signs of improvement in my legs. 'You rub more of the oil?' he asked. 'Oh, yes,' I grinned. 'It's bound to do me a power of good.'

Good friend that he was, Karl was also invaluable with the basic purpose of our visit, helping to locate cripples in the villages, and translating our interviews. One day, as we motored in the central part of the island, we noticed a disabled child squatting beside a roadside cottage. Karl immediately pulled up and helped us get acquainted.

There were eight children in all, sharing the mud hut with their parents. They had no possessions of any kind, except a few pots and pans and three tattered rattan mats. 'Sometimes we eat, sometimes we don't,' the father commented with long-suffering resignation. He had a gaunt, furrowed face but a ready smile. 'Occasionally I get some work on the farms, for three rupees a day. But not often. People here are poor especially now, with the drought.'

When I asked him about Gunawadana, who was sitting hunched by the doorway, it appeared that he was not really a child at all, but nearly twenty. It was the old, old story; he had been stricken by fever when he was a baby. The parents had done what they could, but neither the incantations of the *bhikku* (Buddhist monk) nor the herbs of the ayurvedic doctor, nor even the Lady Ridgeway Hospital in Colombo had helped. Gunawadana had withered away on the mud floor, developing extensive contractures, unable to join his brothers and sisters in play or at school.

'The school is little more than a mile away,' the father added, sighing. 'But the boy cannot get there, and so will never learn to read or write. But at least he has his violin.'

When I expressed surprise, Gunawadana shuffled off into the back of the hut, produced a crude, village-made violin, and accompanied himself to a song he had composed. His voice came soft and firm; there was a note of challenge in it, as if he was trying to defy the world that had never given him a chance.

> Darling, to the music I am singing
> To the sweetest music you dance
> While I am alone
> With your beauty may I get
> The powers to come and dance with you.

I was deeply moved, and asked Karl to congratulate him warmly on the beauty of his song. He smiled faintly, looking up at his father. 'Soon he might be able to earn a little,' sighed the father with a distant look in his eyes.

As we turned to leave, each of us remained silent. It was Karl who spoke as we got into the Chevrolet. 'Poor people . . . ' he murmured, 'but the need here is so very great.'

As we drove away I gazed at the meagre crops parched by the drought. Most of the stalks were stunted, the spikes depleted of seed; yet, given the lifeblood of the monsoon, the promise locked in this soil was clear to see. As they faded into the distance the Gunawadana family seemed rooted in the same earth, their brown bodies clustered by their brown hut. There was a quiet strength and peace, almost a contentment, about them; a rich potential hidden in the family's fortitude, in the father's earnestness, the son's wind-sown talent, which poverty was unable to suppress. I wondered, silently praying for that other monsoon of social and economic uplift, to unlock the promise that had retreated before poverty's onslaught, retreated down into nature's immutable core, to lie dormant in the souls of the Gunawadanas of Asia.

Karl was keen that in the interest of my health we should attend the three great festivals of Ceylon: the Hindu one at Kataragama, the Buddhist Candy Perahera and the Roman Catholic festival in the jungle shrine of Madhu. Of these the Hindu one at Kataragama was the most fascinating. When we approached this remote jungle clearing in the south-east of the island, the climax was still two days off. But as we joined the files of cars, buses, bullock-carts and vast crowds of pilgrims converging on foot towards the modest-looking temple of Kartikeya, the divinity worshipped at Kataragama, the air was already charged with excitement and religious zeal. We edged forward amidst the faithful. 'Haroo, hara,' they chanted, raising their voices to beseech the deity for his indulgence. 'The parched land is crying,' Karl muttered, hooting as he weaved around the bulging clusters of pilgrims that marked the procession like knots in a rope. 'The land is crying because it's poor and hungers for a better life.'

Having parked the car by the Manek Ganga river, from where we could reach the festival grounds on the other bank across a wooden footbridge, we joined the vibrant kaleidoscope of humanity. To everybody's delight, Karl insisted on tying around my wrist a white ribbon with a coin attached to signify that I too had come as a supplicant. Little did he realize how in a strange way this was later to assist me.

The fervour gradually mounted over the next forty-eight hours. The muddy lanes were flanked by temples, dormitories and temporary shacks selling food and various devotional objects, coconuts, flowers, conches, beads and penitents' skewers; at all hours of the day and night these lanes were thronged by troops of devotees, preceded by drums and trumpets, dancing the *Kavadi Attam*, a traditional religious dance of Hindu Tamils. Each dancer carried on his shoulder a colourful *kavadi*, like a segment of a circle in shape, usually made of a small board, which rests on the shoulder, with a bamboo arc above. Decorated with red cloth, tinsel and peacock feathers, these remarkable devices symbolize the chariot in which the god's effigy is carried in procession. To shoulder the kavadi whilst performing the Kavadi Attam is considered an act of piety.

For hours on end they danced, clutching the kavadis on their shoulders, sweat trickling down their thin, ebony bodies with their hair in disorder and their eyes haggard with fervour and fatigue. They danced on, their feet moving almost mechanically like those of stringed puppets. As we walked up and down the looped path of the festival grounds, we occasionally glimpsed even more resolute votaries, who walked on sharp nails driven upwards through wooden clogs, or those who had pierced their cheeks and tongues with arrow-headed skewers, symbols of the lance, the favourite weapon of the Lord Kartikeya. Most, if not all, seemed so worked up as to be numbed to pain, which was just as well in view of the awesome lengths to which some went in their determination to mortify the flesh. It brought to mind penances no less cruel during Easter week processions in the heyday of Christianity, mortifications which can still be seen in Czestochowa in Poland, in Seville in Spain and other places. We saw ascetics dragging carts by a harness of cords, the cords fixed to hooks embedded in their backs; another passed, pushed by a cluster of helpers, swinging prone from a mobile gallows, hanging from multiple strings attached to hooks passing through the flesh. As the crowd divided respectfully, we wondered silently at the lengths to which man's desire to gratify his God will take him.

Wishing to conserve some energy for the climax, which was due to take place in the small hours of the morning, we returned to the car early in the evening of the second day, intent on snatching some sleep. We dozed fitfully until roused at 2 a.m. by one of the sadhus whom we had met amidst the pilgrims. Rubbing the sleep out of our eyes, we pushed slowly through the crowd, across the wooden footbridge, past gaudily caparisoned elephants that lumbered in procession, to the arched gateway of the main temple.

The climax at Kataragama involves a long procession of the faithful walking barefoot over the embers of a huge log fire. Karl had been at his most eloquent earlier in the day, describing the fifteen-foot pit, and how the embers reached over 800°C. With pride he had announced that next year he would return, to walk through the fire.

Before we entered the temple courtyard, we paused to remove our shoes. Karl promptly trod with his bare feet on a discarded cigarette end. He leapt high into the air, hugging the sole of his foot. This was too much for Julian. 'Come on, Karl, you'll have to do better than that next year!' 'Oh yes. But when I walk through the fire next year I won't feel a thing, because I'll be sure of Lord Kartikeya's protection.' He answered solemnly, with childlike conviction.

The simple white gateway led into a courtyard of hard earth, scarcely more than a hundred feet across. The temple was a modest building, looking rather like a barn from the outside, low, elongated, built of stone and masonry without much artistic merit. Only the first hall, a dark cramped pillared area, was visible; a wall and heavy curtain separated this from the holy of holies, to which only a few of the high priests had access, the contents being a closely guarded secret.

Although it was still dark, the courtyard was already crammed with votaries, spectators and over a hundred devotees waiting to walk through the fire. A long trench full of viciously glowing embers led directly to the temple entrance, a few feet away, the frame outlined by flickering oil lamps. As we took up a position alongside the pit, as close as the intense heat would allow, I felt my throat tighten. Julian was staring incredulously at the embers, shimmering blue and red in the darkness. 'But no one could possibly walk through that lot!' he gasped. 'They'd be stepping into their own cremation.' 'Ah, but the God protects those who believe in him completely.' Karl murmured. 'Here comes the first.'

The grisly old *kapurala*, or priest, seemed quite unconcerned, strolling through the pit of fire as if he were going on some errand. Next came an elderly man, head and shoulders drawn back as if he were marching on a parade ground; with his eyes fastened on the temple ahead, he walked through the pit without a qualm, treading deeply in the embers. As he reached the other end, he threw his arms forward and rushed into that mysterious doorway with a half-strangled cry of love, triumph and longing, like a lost child rushing into the outstretched arms of its parent. Others followed at intervals of fifteen or twenty seconds. A young man, his wide-open eyes glowing like the coals, danced through, still carrying his kavadi, scattering showers of sparks. They came thick and fast, almost every one crossing in a distinctive manner, according to their personality. Deep faith was evident in a wizened old woman, exultation in a long-haired sadhu; some ran through taking giant strides, like coursed hares, fear widening their eyes; a few lost their nerve completely and ran parallel to the pit. 'He's the one likely to get burnt!' whispered Karl, as a terror-stricken man bounced through the pit like a ball. An emaciated sadhu stepped resolutely into the coals; he stopped half way through, bent down to scoop a handful of the glowing embers, and rubbed them on his back before calmly continuing towards the temple.

As far as I could make out, none of them seemed to suffer burns.

It is often said that the thick callouses of the habitually bare-footed villagers give them protection, but I am inclined to think that they survive unscathed due to a psychological condition induced by absolute faith and a state of semi-trance – an uncanny control of some deep powers of the subconscious over physiological processes. There was certainly an uncanny atmosphere about the place, as if some strange Power had taken hold of it. It made us squirm and shudder, ill at ease; I have visited many churches and temples in my life, witnessed many strange ceremonies, but have never encountered anything so 'present' and all-pervading as that lurking Power at Kataragama.

Long before the fire-walking had started I had made up my mind to see if I could gain a more direct experience of the ceremony, and had made discreet enquiries about being carried across. The temple authorities had agreed rather reluctantly, provided I could induce one of the walkers to carry me over. When *Swami* Gouribala, a German convert to Hinduism and one of the leading priests of Kataragama, came to talk to us, I realized that it was now or never; I explained my ambition, seeking his help. 'Perhaps one of them could be prevailed upon to carry me across?' I suggested, pointing to a cluster of fire-walkers waiting in the shadows. The Swami frowned, pursing his lips. 'I've studied fire-walking very thoroughly since I first came to Kataragama fourteen years ago,' he said looking at me searchingly. 'I certainly never heard of anyone being carried across. But if those in charge have no objection, I'll ask around for you.'

A few minutes later he returned with a young man, a Buddhist. Apparently two had volunteered at first, but custom demanded that only one person could cross at a time. As the Swami was talking with him, I sat in my wheelchair gazing wistfully at this earnest young man. He was just over five feett all and not too sturdily built. The pupils of his eyes were already visibly enlarged in the early stages of trance. He came from a remote village, and had an open, sincere face. I felt I liked him.

The Swami turned to face me. 'Are you quite sure you want to go through with this?' he asked me gravely. 'It is a serious decision. For one thing, do you realize that if he carries you across your karmas will be twined together for the rest of your lives?'

I looked at the young man's plain, honest face. 'So we will become brothers in fire?' I said thoughtfully. The idea appealed to me enormously. 'We come from such different worlds. The threads of our destinies mingled in this extraordinary place, in this strange night . . . What a fitting climax.' I thought. The more I warmed up to the idea, the more Swamiji pressed me about my true motives. When asked what I knew about Lord Kartikeya, I answered as best I could, relying on my studies of Hindu religion and mythology. He was quick to point out that this was academic knowledge, not that of a faithful believer.

'Are you sure that you would have walked across if you were able-bodied?' he asked. 'Have you complete faith that nothing will happen if you touch the fire?'

'Well, I think so, but one can never be quite sure . . . ' I replied lamely.

'You haven't gone through the rigorous preparation, the months of fasting and inner preparation. Nor have you taken a dip in the sacred river . . . That we could still arrange, but the devotees walk across the pit in a state of high excitation or semi-trance.' He pointed to another votary who was just stepping into the pit, as if sleep-walking. 'You'll notice how little conscious control he has over his actions. You should be well prepared in case our young friend here drops you into the embers, or squats there with you to ensure that you take full part.'

This was getting too much. The Swami was gently shaking his head. I looked questioningly at Julian, who was frowning at the ground. 'I should give it a miss, if I were you,' he said. 'Think of the Expedition. If anything were to happen to you, it would all come to nothing.'

Naturally, I felt disappointed; it was a near miss. I console myself now with the thought that, had it not been for Swamiji's grave and well-meaning dissuasion, these lines might have been more exciting – or not written at all.

A few days later we were back in Colombo, and I picked up the threads of press interviews, radio talks and hospital visits. One of the last hospitals we visited in the country was the Victoria Home for Incurables, situated on the outskirts of Colombo. A rather stiff, elderly matron piloted me around the wards, explaining that in all there were a hundred and ten inmates in the home.

She admitted that there were no medically qualified people on the resident staff; and that the mental cases shared the same wards with the cripples, the children with the senile. As we were leaving a ward, I noticed a girl in the far corner obviously having a fit.

'Is she an epileptic?' I asked innocently.

'She has been bewitched.'

'But what is *medically* wrong with her?'

'As I said, she has had the evil eye cast on her.'

The warmest and most vivid impression that I took away from the Victoria Home was of a crippled old woman resting quietly on her bed, with her decrepit, grey-haired husband sitting at her side. She was paralysed from the waist down and incontinent, her crumpled face deathly white, dribbling from her toothless mouth. The husband had undone her long, grey hair and was engrossed in combing it, his forehead knitted in concentration. Utterly oblivious of their surroundings, he combed with long, slow, gentle strokes, until the comb slipped out of his gnarled fingers and fell on the bed. She picked it up; as she handed it back she looked up at him with a tender radiance in her face which broke through all the ugliness and suffering. He bent over her and with a shaking hand carefully wiped the dribble off her chin. Their hands clasped, and for a long, silent moment they gazed into each other's eyes with an expression of pure rapture. I felt an intruder, but couldn't help watching out of the corner of my eye, certain in the knowledge that never had I seen love so pure and so beautiful.

CHAPTER 15

Fansa, Melkote and other Indian Rehabilitation Projects

*

HEADING south across Bengal and Bihar, we were motoring over a particularly lonely stretch of road when we encountered a man 'measuring his length'. When we pulled level we saw that he was holding a stick in his outstretched arms; each time he lay down flat on the ground he would mark the spot. Then he would get up, move forward until he stood on that spot and lie down again. We stopped to ask the reason for this penance, and he told us that he came from Sambalpur, a district in Orissa, about three hundred miles away. 'My two brothers have died, our crops have been blighted and I have these bad sores on my thigh. So I do this to attract the Almighty's benevolent attention and implore His pardon for whatever we did to offend him. It has taken me over three months to come this far. In another month I shall reach Prayag and the Kumbh Mela.'

Prayag is an old Hindu name for the city of Allahabad, near which the Kumbh Mela is held. Every twelve years millions of pilgrims from every corner of India gather on a sandbank where the Jamuna meets the Ganges.

According to the legend, once upon a time the (still mortal) gods and demons combined to bring up from the ocean a jar (*kumbh*) containing the elixir of immortality, but the moment the jar appeared above the waves they started fighting over it. As they flew over India trying to wrench the jar from one another, a few drops of the precious nectar spilled down on to the earth. One of the places on which drops fell was the confluence of the two rivers at Prayag, for which we were heading ourselves, along with about eight million others.

Miles before reaching the two thousand acres of field and sand-bank that contained the main camp, we had to slow down to walking pace. A sea of humanity, milling over road, path and field was converging on Prayag; they made up a vivid cross-section of the width and breadth of India. Parties from the same village came in single file, each firmly gripping the one in front for fear of getting lost. Bright turbans bobbed beside Gandhian caps, gay saris alongside the strange headgear of Bhil tribesmen, stuck with peacock feathers. Portly sadhus walked on resolutely, while the emaciated hermits from caves in the Himalayan wilderness staggered along, their matted hair often so long that it trailed on the ground behind them.

We arrived to find that the multitude stretched as far as the eye could see. The vast majority of the poor cooked over little oven-like burrows in the ground called *choolas*, and slept on the sand or under scanty awnings improvised from saris and dhotis. The barbers were doing a roaring trade on the mud banks by the Ganges. Beside them were huge stacks of hair; many pilgrims, men and women, were having their heads shaved in fulfilment of vows. Others went further in their zeal to mortify the flesh, lying almost naked on beds of thorns, or standing in one position for days on end, so that their legs became swollen with the strain.

We lived much like the pilgrims, eating with our fingers off 'plates' made of dried leaves, at food stalls that served rather basic and gritty curry meals for tenpence. 'You must also take a dip in the holy Ganges,' they kept urging me. 'Its waters always remain pure and health-giving. It might help you.'

Sometimes we got a little more than we bargained for. At one point an alley was half blocked by an enormous elephant enjoying its lunch. There were numerous elephants around, brought as status symbols by sadhus or wealthy landowners. Reversing the Gypsy was out of the question. 'Come on, we'll just squeeze past.' I said to Julian.

Unfortunately, the hulking beast chose this moment to develop a nasty itch. As we edged past, it pressed against the Gypsy's side and rubbed vigorously, with each gleeful scrape heaving the car right off its side wheels. Having been rocked violently about a dozen times, I decided that enough was enough. 'Put your foot down – NOW!' I yelled. Spinning on two wheels, the Gypsy managed to escape the unwelcome embrace, leaving the elephant waving a disconsolate trunk.

Close to the sadhu camp there were large *pandals* (enclosures), often with tents and marquees, occupied by some sect or sage with followers. Some were quite wealthy, feeding several hundred poor of the pilgrims each day; others were more modest. We visited many of these enclosures. Eventually, driving to the very end of the encampment, well away from the multitude and the clamour, we noticed a hut built on four stilts. A man sat on an elevated platform in front of it, talking with the people gathered below. From my enquiries, I understood that his name was Deoharwa Baba, and that his hermitage was in Badri Narayan, Uttar Pradesh State. We were told 'He is over a hundred and fifty years old, though through the power of yoga he doesn't look it. He never touches the ground, always lives on a raised platform. Whenever he wishes to move, he is carried.'

I gazed at the man as he blessed those who approached him, answered their questions and threw oranges which were reverentially picked up by those below. His face did not seem particularly wise or noble, but there was an extraordinary magnetism and depth to it. Both of us felt deeply moved and I heard myself saying 'Please help me'.

For a moment his penetrating, almost wild gaze fell on me. 'There are no short answers or panaceas in this world. But there is God. Seek not to reach him through wisdom or knowledge, but through love. Sing him in love, inebriate yourself with the love of his name, and within you you'll realize him in love.'

A chauffeur-driven limousine stopped beside our Gypsy and the driver sprang out to open the back door. Somebody from the crowd murmured 'A Minister of State and the Vice-Chancellor of Patna University.' Both men got out, took off their shoes and tiptoed with folded hands to kneel in humility before the hut. Close by squatted the driver, with the same expression of humility as his master. Minutes ago an unbridgeable gulf of worldly power and status had separated them.

To help keep order amongst so many millions, over five thousand police were on duty, not counting auxiliaries and the army had laid eight pontoon bridges to take the pilgrim flow from one bank to the other. In addition, there were compulsory inoculation centres for everybody, at least in theory. 'We just keep our fingers crossed that no epidemic breaks out,' a police officer told me. 'But as it is, bodies are floating down the river to where the millions are bathing and drinking the water.' In India those who die of contagious diseases are often thrown into the Ganges. The doctors observe this with trepidation, praying that their fears should not be proved right, but the people have a blind faith in the purifying waters of the Ganges. Another policeman told me how during the last Mela in 1954 part of the crowd had stampeded when a section of the river bank subsided. Several hundred – some say thousands – were trampled to death. 'This time we've got observation towers with closed circuit TV and can rush reinforcements in. The cynics say that at least a hundred villages could be reclaimed with the money this has cost. But who can say that the pursuit of God and salvation is less desirable than that of material progress?'

As the main day of the Mela approached, the authorities were tense but well prepared. Between five and seven million people were expected to take a dip during the morning. All non-police traffic was barred from the Mela grounds. 'We'll put you on one of our control towers and pick you up in a jeep. Please be ready at 1 a.m.,' said our policeman friend.

The two-mile drive in the dead of night was indescribably weird. The air was heavy with dust kicked up by countless feet, as the blurred mass of hulking silhouettes trudged in the starlit night towards the river. Visibility was restricted, but the dull rumble of the multitudes, hundreds of thousands abreast, sounded eerie and alarming. We saw detachments of helmeted police, jogging at the double, despatched down cordoned passageways to sensitive spots. In the dim light the scene looked like something from a journey into the underworld.

When they had heaved me up to the topmost platform of the tower, we huddled against the chill January air as we waited for dawn. As the first rays of the sun broke through the dust-laden air, we saw a sea of bobbing heads spreading far into the horizon. The bathers filled the shallow areas of confluence tightly from bank to bank – the river was broad rather than deep in this dry season. Farther up stream thousands of small craft, laden with brightly dressed pilgrims, reminded me of a painting by Canaletto of a Venetian aquatic feast.

Close to our tower was an alley-way reserved for the religious dignitaries, the swamis, yogis, Nangas, and sect leaders. Obeying a strict order of precedence according to their relative spiritual merit and sanctity, which must have taken much subtle if abstruse argument to decide, they proudly marched in tight formations. Julian and I were particularly keen to observe the Nangas, because of an encounter we had had with them on the previous day.

We were driving along in our usual way, when we had noticed a clump of huts some three hundred yards apart from the encampment, and Julian nosed the Gypsy onto the hard crust of sand. After fifty yards the ground suddenly gave way under the back wheels and he jumped out. 'There's mud or quicksand under this crust,' he shouted. I got out. The huts forgotten, our only wish was to get back on terra firma. Julian tried ramming planks under the wheels and managed to pull her out in four-wheel drive. But as soon as he began to turn back towards the track, I noticed the ground rippling under the car. The crust gave way and the Gypsy settled down up to her undercarriage. Gradually but surely she began to sink further. Julian opened the back door and started to jettison the gear. It almost, but not quite, arrested the sinking; he raced off towards the camp to get help.

I sat there helpless, unable to move an inch in the sand. A couple of hours more of this at the rate she was going and not even the roof would be visible. With the spare springs and heavier equipment that Julian was unable to remove, the Gypsy must have weighed over two tons. She needed lifting up rather than pulling out. Elephants might do it but then they too would probably flounder in the morass, and anyway, it would take hours to organize help. Then I saw a group of about fifty Nangas walking along the path. The Nangas – literally the 'naked ones' – are regarded as the holiest of Indian ascetics, having uncompromisingly rejected everything connected with the world. Their ideals do not allow them so much as to touch money; apart from a G-string, which in fact they often do away with, they possess nothing material. Whenever they went on the Kumbh Mela grounds, crowds closed in behind them to kiss their footprints and gather some of the sand as sacred mementoes.

Now a band of them was in sight, shouting and waving their hands in the air. They swung round, and led by a grey-haired elder who disdained even the G-string, jogged towards the car, bawling fiercely. Whooping and yelling they did a little war dance around the Gypsy, then picked it up, a row of rotund buttocks straining with the effort, and carried it for about forty yards to safe ground. Thereafter they did another dance and went

Crippled beggars at Ramdehora Fair, Rajasthan

off ignoring me as I gaped at them dumbfounded. It was an un-
forgettable spectacle.

The procession pressed on for seven hours, group after group,
including almost all the religious leaders, sages, sadhus and
hermits of India. Some were carried on fabulous thrones, others
rode elephants, preceded by dancing jugglers, whip crackers,
trumpeters, and insignia carriers. Other groups, whose founder
or particularly eminent member was dead, carried empty palan-
quins encrusted with gold, topped by sumptuous parasols,
emblems of rank and containing some holy scripture or relic of their
saint. By midday our policeman friend was looking more relaxed.

'Everything seems to have gone without a hitch. India has
always marched her best towards God and the things of the spirit
– therein lies both her greatness and weakness.' As we thanked him
for his hospitality, I thought he had summed it up perfectly.

The Expedition was now drawing to an end. As could be
expected, the picture emerging in my mind from almost two years
of travel was a complex one. We had met many instances of
indomitable courage and fortitude amongst the handicapped, of
quiet dedication and untiring effort amongst doctors, social
workers, philanthropists and members of the general public. To us
such encounters were like sudden shafts of sunlight on a lowering
day, bringing hope and faith to a situation otherwise so dismally
grim and sad. For apart from the pervading sense of tragedy and
sorrow, the most frequently recurring feature of the scene was
apathy, an acceptance which dogged us right across Southern
Asia; apathy on the part of the disabled, apathy to the problem
of disability on part of the public at large and apathy among many
of those in authority. In Thailand it was 'Mai pen rai', (Never
mind, who cares?). In Pakistan 'Jo ho, so ho', (What will be, will
be). The Hindus say 'Bhagwan ki khel', the Muslems 'Allah ki
doah.' In Persia and Baluchistan where we went on the way back
to England, they say 'Har cheh Khoda bekhad', or simply
'Ghismat', which, roughly translated, means that it is all the Will
of God, or Fate.

All the same, the seeds of change are beginning to bear fruit;
with conditions improving in virtually every sphere, people's
minds are gradually being prized out of the grip of hopelessness
and torpor. The Indian achievement is characteristic of this
trend. It has been estimated that the country has progressed more

in the brief span of its independence than during the two hundred years of British rule. The proportion of literates has more than trebled and today over a hundred million young people go to school and college. Thousands of miles of road and railway have been built, countless miles of irrigation canals dug and supplied with water which is trapped by several hundred new dams and many more tube-wells. Vast areas have been electrified. With the development of heavy industry, cars, jets, locomotives and nuclear fuel for industrial use are being produced. All this is being done under democracy, the world's largest democracy in which over 250 million people voted at the last general election.

The problem of disability has its root in the rural districts. Despite some migration into the urban areas generated by industrial growth, eight out of ten of the population continue to follow a traditional way of life geared to the village, a life that has hardly been ruffled, as yet, by the winds of change. To the majority of the first and even second generation city dwellers the ancestral village still remains the true home, to which they return for peace and security, especially when overtaken by sickness or misfortune. There are about 550,000 such villages in India alone; to form an intimate picture of what it was like to be disabled in an Indian village, we felt that we should take as broad an interest as possible in all aspects of rural existence; by the time we returned, we had visisted many schools, colleges, training institutes, rural co-operatives, development projects, temples, prisons and police stations, small factories and cottage industries, in addition to talking with the disabled. We attended *panchayat* – village self-administration – meetings, birth ceremonies, marriages, cremations, hoary festivals and quaint rituals, sharing their joys and sorrows with the villagers. We observed the round of sowing, tending and harvest, watched how the village hut-wife cooks, launders, looks after her husband and family, how the family go to sleep and get up in the morning, how they wash, eat and look after their cattle.

Time spent in this way was by no means wasted from the standpoint of our study: the more we learnt about the way of life of the Indian peasant, about his outlook, fears and hopes, the more vivid the picture of the village handicapped became to us.

We took special care not to miss any institution, however small or insignificant it might seem. Many of them I recall vividly for their pioneering work, or the dedication of their staff. In India there was the Army Limb Centre in Poona; the Christian Mission Hospital in Vellore, the All-India Institutes of Physical Medicine in New Delhi and Bombay; the Sheltered Workshop for the Physically Handicapped in Bangalore; the Home for Disabled Children and the Aged in Nagpur; The Iswari Prasad Dattatreya Orthopaedic Centre in Madras . . . each of these impressed us deeply. But, though inspiring in themselves, none of these had quite the mixture of ingredients I was searching for. What I was mulling over was the idea of a village-based project aimed at adapting rehabilitation to rural conditions. I decided to go over the landmarks of my journeys – recall and revisit those people who seemed to have a bearing on my project.

The first source of inspiration was the remarkable school at Fansa where the blind are taught farming. Fansa is near Bulsar in southern Gujerat, two hours of bumpy driving off the Bombay–Ahmadabad trunk road. The full name of the school is the Tata Agriculture and Rural Training Centre for the Blind, since the Tata Trust of Bombay had helped set it up in 1960 and was financing it jointly with CARE, the US Office of Vocational Rehabilitation, the Royal Commonwealth Society for the Blind and other agencies. When I had first visited Fansa in November 1964, I had been enormously impressed by what was being attempted there and by the care taken that the wide range of activities being taught should be closely relevant to village life. So in February 1966 I decided to pay another visit, partly to find out what progress they had made, but mainly to cast a more searching eye over the place in connection with the ideas fermenting in my mind.

Fansa's situation is ideal for the purpose; quiet, typically rural, with good soil and enough water. Alerted by the sound of a car, uncommon in this serene place, Mr B. H. Upadhyaya, the recruitment and resettlement officer, came out of his bungalow and shook us warmly by the hand. He led us to the relative coolness of the porch, which opened onto a lush vista of palms between whose dark, pencil-straight silhouettes I could glimpse the foam-edged brilliance of the ocean.

As we sipped cool coconut milk, I heard how fifty-two trainees had now completed a two-year course in subjects ranging from agriculture, vegetable-growing, horticulture, to market-garden-ing, poultry and dairy farming, as well as various crafts and trades.

We then wandered about the 240 acre estate and I observed with mounting wonder, totally blind trainees engaged in digging, weeding, tending and watering flowers, brick-making, milking cattle and other activities. From a distance one would have never guessed that they were blind. Julian asked our friend Mr Upadhyaya by what secret means this had been achieved.

'There's no secret,' he said smiling broadly. 'We give each trainee a small plot, 105 by 10 feet. From that moment they are responsible for everything, preparing the ground, sowing, transplanting, irrigating the crop while it's growing, right up to the harvest.'

'But if a man is blind, how can he do all this?'

'It's not as difficult as you might think. We always break the operation down into basic steps which are easy to learn. In fact we carry out a sort of time and motion study before we try teaching the trainees any operation. You'd be surprised how fast they learn once they grasp the process in this way, step by step.' He pointed at a man working by some large cannas with big luxuriant red blossoms. 'Watch this man watering his flowers. He knows the position of every plant so well that he invariably waters each one without having to grope or risk trampling. Now see him go to the tap to fill his can. The path is narrow and winding, but he doesn't hesitate.' 'Shankar, pull out those weeds!' Mr Upadhyaya called out. It didn't take Shankar a minute to find the weeds. 'Now pick a couple of the nicest blooms for our guests, please!' Unerringly Shankar stretched out for the largest flowers which he brought us, smiling.

One of the most positive things about Fansa is the emphasis placed on team work, encouraging the trainee to develop his initiative within the context of the group. Apart from his personal responsibilities for the individual plot or bench-job, with all the pride and confidence which this gives, everything else is shared. We were shown how the trainees live in small, modest two-roomed dwellings, two to a room. Meals are taken communally, which encourages the sharing of hopes, fears and experiences. In this way the whole personality is covered in the process of rehabilitation. Whereas many institutions believe that a basic skill is enough, and cheerfully send a blind man back into the wide world to fend for himself, Fansa has attempted to rehabilitate the whole man. To me this aspect was of the utmost importance. All too often I had met hard-working, well-meaning people who had rationalized rehabilitation down to its narrowest physical aspect. 'A fellow has no legs? Give him some artificial ones and he's rehabilitated!' I knew too well from my own experience that disability involves more than a limb or paralysed muscles. The experience reverberates through the entire personality like an earthquake. Some things it destroys outright, others it cracks or undermines, things which may not be obvious to the eye, but are no less vital for being hidden in the recesses of the personality. Such damage can usually be mended, but it requires a sensitive touch and perception on the part of those who attempt the healing. It should always be borne in mind that, at least initially, disability affects the entire person, including his attitude to life, to society as indeed it also affects society's attitude to him. Without help to guide him back towards self-confidence and the rough-and-tumble of daily life, even the most elaborate artificial limbs will be so much scrap metal.

Such total rehabilitation is expensive, especially where hospitalization and artificial aids are concerned. Expensive enough by Western standards, let alone Eastern ones. For example in Britain where the average annual income per capita comes to £1,262 (men) and £644 (women) it costs £47 weekly at present to keep a patient in hospital. With physiotherapy and other specialist services the cost for a paraplegic (disabled in two limbs) amounts to £50 weekly, while the average time spent in hospital is six months, or twelve months in the case of a tetraplegic (disabled in three limbs). The total cost, which in Britain is fully borne by the state, thus comes to £1,300 and £2,600 respectively. To this should be added about £55 for a double full length brace, £50 for a wheelchair, and about £600 for an Invacar. In India where the average annual income per capita is only Rs 447 (£25) the weekly costs of hospitalization, also borne by the State, come to between about 84 and 140 rupees. But for a number of reasons, most of which have emerged in the foregoing pages, only a small proportion of those in need benefit in a timely and effective manner.

When I asked Mr Upadhyaya about costs at Fansa, he told me that the basic cost worked out at around 4,000 rupees per trainee, but that in addition, every trainee received upon the successful completion of the course about five hundred rupees' worth of implements, seeds, or even a bullock, to help him get started. 'But you should bear in mind that we are chiefly engaged in research work here,' he added. 'Against these costs you should offset the work we are doing in developing agricultural techniques, implements and tools for the use of blind farmers everywhere.'

The cost was unavoidably high because of the experimentation. In fact it rose to about the average annual income of ten Indians per trainee, but it was apparent that the techniques being developed in Fansa were proving effective. The biggest hurdle was that of village prejudice, once the trainee had returned. What would the rest of the village say when a blind man expressed the unprecedented wish to work in the fields? How would the family react when a man, long accepted for a physically useless cripple, arrived home with his head full of strange and new-fangled ideas, and, hesitantly at first, made his way out to the fields, groping to memorize each tiny detail of the lie of the land, each tree or boulder along the path? Mr Upadhyaya reported that of the fifty-two that had successfully completed the Fansa training course, thirty were working their land happily; contact had been lost with nine; thirteen (twenty-five per cent) had fallen by the wayside, having surrendered to the pressures of prejudice and discouragement.

Despite such problems I found Fansa a highly imaginative pioneering institution, and throughout the time I spent there I observed everything I could. I remember how we stopped in the cowshed to admire the way Jaydev was milking his buffalo cow. As he squatted by the flank of the slouching beast, he told me how he had been blinded when he was nine years old by smallpox, and how heartbroken his father had been. He had four sisters; how could they be provided with dowries when the time came, now that he, the only son, had been stricken? Until he had come to Fansa, the future had looked bleak for them all. 'But even if the darkness remains in my eyes, things are brighter now,' he said cheerfully. 'Perhaps the evil has finally burnt itself out. When I go back next year, not only shall I be able to help my father work our land but we will farm it much better than ever before, thanks to what I have learnt here. My sisters will be provided for, and my father will be able to spend the rest of his days in peace. The continuity of our family and our land will be preserved.'

When we left Fansa the following morning, my ears were still echoing with Jaydev's words. If only something like Fansa existed for other handicapped villagers! Come to that, if only there were more Fansas to cater for the village blind! For the number of totally blind in India alone is in the region of two million; of these it is reasonable to assume that 1,600,000 live in villages. Yet virtually all the institutions for rehabilitating the blind I had come across were firmly centred on towns, and catered in their training and outlook for urban life.

The question of costs was a recurring nightmare. All around me I saw a crying need, but I was determined to keep both feet firmly on the ground. To be widely effective any training centre for rehabilitating the rural disabled had to be geared, like Fansa, to village conditions and to self-help. My idea was not for some home, where the chosen few might be helped, but to try and establish a research scheme where a constructive approach could be evolved towards tackling the problem as a whole. If, because of its cost, and the need for highly trained personnel and sophisticated techniques, medical rehabilitation could not at present be made available for the millions of rural infirm, then its role would have to be reduced or even sidetracked in favour of vocational and social rehabilitation, where costs and skills would be less onerous. Such a process would be truncated, no doubt, but infinitely more effective than nothing at all.

The more I travelled, the clearer it became that the first step should be to set up a pioneering research centre, where disabled trainees could work these problems out in practice, not only for their own benefit, but for all their afflicted brethren.

The blind were being taught farming at Fansa; why not the orthopaedically handicapped? It was essential to determine exactly what was possible – and how. Could, for instance, a farmer with useless legs hoe and cultivate a small plot while moving on his seat? And if so on irrigated land, could he cultivate dry-farming land, where the parched soil gets as hard as stone, and the supply of rain-water is erratic? What soil, what crops, would prove the most suitable? What simple aids, what tools would assist him best? Of such questions there were hundreds, but they had one thing in common: no thorough effort had yet been made to find the answers.

What about the reservations of the families back in the villages, which was the bane of the Fansa project? Perhaps part of the answer lay in involving them too in what their relatives were doing. Let the trainees have their own plots; let them grow what they please, drawing freely on the guidance of the centre's agronomist; let them sell what they grow, on the earn-as-you-learn principle; let them invite their families to see for themselves, to admire the crops which they were growing; let the family see the money which their 'helpless' relatives have earned from the sale of their own produce. To what extent was this practical? Would it really work out? Only experimentation would tell. As to the costs involved, I felt that since I had raised enough money to mount the Expedition, perhaps I could raise more. Of one thing I was sure: I would just have to try, try harder than ever before.

Naturally the medical aspect of rehabilitation could not be entirely ignored. Techniques would have to be simplified. In this connection I thought of Dr V. Marwah, the ingenious orthopaedic surgeon at the Medical College Hospital in Aurangabad. When I had met him a few months previously in his workshop, he had described to me how his first effort, confronted with the shortage of orthopaedic appliances, had been to arrange fortnightly clinics, in which several disabled people at one end of the surgery faced various local notables or businessmen at the other. 'I examined each case before them so that they could see each patient in the flesh. A confrontation like this is much more effective than charity in the abstract.'

But this only helped a few. Next, the doctor became increasingly concerned with the number of lightly handicapped who for lack of appropriate treatment became as helpless as the severely afflicted. 'These are the ones we should be assisting as a matter of priority,' he said, warming to what was obviously a subject near to his heart.

'I racked my brains, trying to think of cheap, simple gadgets. But this wasn't only because of the shortages here. Give a hill-billy rustic one of those fancy, expensive braces, and more likely than not he'll just hang it up on the wall! But fit him up with some simple, crude appliance without any trimmings or shiny chromium to alarm him, and he'll take it in his stride, and make good use of it.'

He went on 'I had a patient called Rambhau, who was a classic

Amte (left) and his
family in Somnath

'Gift of Labour': women
carrying earth for a new
road in Anandwan

case. Owing to a railway accident in his childhood, he had lost both legs below the knee; a simple appliance would make all the difference and give him the chance of working and supporting himself. One day I was leaving the hospital for lunch when someone arrived on a bicycle. He got off and kicked the stand attached to the rear wheel. Suddenly I had it! If that stand, a simple, everyday item, was strong enough to support a bicycle, why not a person? The spring, with a little modification, would act as a knee lock, allowing Rambhau to move his 'leg' through a right angle, to stand or to sit. I bought a bicycle stand that afternoon for eleven rupees, and Rambhau is now working happily as a farmer, about twenty-three miles away from here.'

Over the last eight years, the cost of Dr Marwah's bicycle-stand peg leg had risen to about twenty-four rupees. But it worked well, as I could see for myself from patients exercising outside his workshop on the hospital verandah. It was not the fact that it cost about two per cent of the Western equivalent that was so impressive; what was really significant was that the cost was within reach of those who needed help, that the materials were always available at the nearest cycle shop. What was more, such a peg leg was tough and simple enough for bad road surfaces, and wouldn't fall to bits after a week.

The peg leg was only the start. In the course of my brief visit, I was fascinated to see how the doctor had extended this principle to making artificial arms out of bamboo and scrap iron (thirty-five rupees: a Western model would cost about fifty times as much). The brace was perfectly serviceable, in that whoever used it could move around, carry small objects, even scratch himself if need be. Leather sockets for amputated stumps, do-it-yourself physiotherapy exercises – the range of his ingenuity seemed endless. In his modest way he made it all sound simple, even obvious; but like most things that sound or look simple when they have been worked out, I knew that a formidable amount of time must have gone into each one. To me, Dr Marwah was revolutionizing the whole concept of medical rehabilitation in India. I said so, as I was saying good-bye, and he smiled modestly.

'Well, you could say "Indianizing" it, perhaps?'

The science of medical rehabilitation has been evolved over the years by Western doctors of merit, dedicated to the alleviation of the pain and sorrow that attend disability. Brilliant in their own fields, their profound knowledge of the human body is matched by their concern for perfecting techniques, medications and prostheses which will make life easier in the highly sophisticated and predominantly urban societies in which they and their patients live and work. Whilst such techniques are wholly admirable within this context, it does not necessarily follow that they are ideally suited for export. In the East the tendency is to copy and to adopt Western techniques, all geared to a way of life, scales of preference and socio-economic conditions vastly different from the Eastern ones. All too often the grafting proves ineffective. In the West, for instance, the design of prosthetic appliances takes for granted that the person concerned will use chairs, tables, beds, sitting lavatories; also that walking surfaces will be smooth and hard. In Indian villages, however, people usually eat, sit and sleep on the ground; they use squatting latrines, if they don't use the fields or open spaces; walking surfaces are usually unpaved and stony and muddy in the rains. But even if these factors were allowed for, what of the welter of beliefs such as those of karma, or dharma, or possession by evil spirits, or of other quaint traditions, prejudices and thought processes? Patently, these should also be taken into account.

Dr Marwah mentioned the sophisticated brace being left to hang on the wall. I remember seeing just that. I also remember what happened when a friend of mine brought from England a large box of toys for distribution to the children of an Indian village. The inconspicuous wooden ones were played with immediately; but the large dolls in pretty frilly dresses joined the wedding saris and jewellery in the family trunks, to be preserved reverently for generations to come, and carefully taken out once in a blue moon on special occasions. I felt that these frilly dolls wistfully languishing in coffers had a valuable lesson for the sophisticated braces.

Amazing results can be achieved on a shoestring. Perhaps the most outstanding example of this we encountered was a small boarding school for severely handicapped boys aged between ten and fifteen in Melkote, in the Mandya District of southern Mysore. I heard of it fortuitously, when visiting an agricultural training project (Vidyapith) in southern Mysore in September 1965. Julian and I spent a most stimulating day watching the way in which they manoeuvred themselves about, with quick, agile movements. We discussed the school with its founder, Mr Surendra Koulagi. There was something about him which impressed me deeply. The school was lacking premises, equipment, almost everything normally associated with a school; and yet the boys were happy despite their terrible handicaps. In March 1966, as the expedition was drawing to an end, I decided that we should pay another visit to the Karuna Gruha, or the Home of Sympathy.

After a long weary drive across mountains and jungle from Kerala, we reached the sleepy little town of Melkote at dusk. As we drew up by Koulagi's house I wondered for a moment if we should have camped nearby and come at a more convenient time in the morning. But we had been spotted. A small figure was sitting on the veranda wall of the school opposite.

'Arthur, Julian back!' he cried, as he jumped down, arms first, like a cat. Paralysed below the waist he pushed himself on his seat over the rough cobbles of the narrow alleyway. Within seconds he had flung the car door open and was looking up at us with a huge grin.

Roused by the commotion, the boys were pushing themselves fast on their bottoms and in no time we were surrounded by a sea of upturned faces, all firing questions at once. 'Where you come from?' 'How long you stay with us?'

By the time Julian had extracted my wheelchair from the back of the Gypsy, Koulagi had joined the welcoming party. Joining his hands in the namaste greeting he called out 'Welcome to Melkote again. While my wife prepares food, I'll take you across to the school. The boys have been longing for you to come back.'

Julian backed up the Gypsy so that it wouldn't block the narrow alley, and we set off down the gentle slope of the lane. Many of the cobbles were missing or depressed, and it took the combined efforts of Julian and Koulagi to push and heave the wheelchair. Meanwhile the boys around us chattered excitedly as they shoved along on their seats with no apparent difficulty. 'There's a moral somewhere in this,' I said as I breathed hard with the effort of turning the wheels. 'I am as helpless as a babe sitting in this, while these boys who have never seen the inside of a physio gym, seem to move with uncanny ease.' 'I know,' grunted Koulagi. 'The parents of one of the boys saved up for months to buy him a wheelchair. On the fourth day it crashed down the slope into a wall. Luckily he was only slightly hurt.'

We reached the school, a low, single-storied structure of adobe, roofed with the local tiles, shaped like narrow drains cut lengthwise in half. Adapted to the tropical climate, the entrance was doorless, and the small windows without panes. When Julian had hauled me up the three front steps, the boys followed on their bottoms.

The inside consisted of one fairly large, rather dark, room. There was not a stick of furniture to be seen. Part of the floor was beaten earth smoothed with a solution of water and cow-dung, the rest flagged with greyish stone. There was no ceiling and the underside of the tiles were visible above the rafters. On the walls there hung a large map of India, posters of Gandhi and Nehru, an illustrated calendar and gaudy pictures of Hindu divinities. Another door at the rear led to a small garden, where the boys took great pride in growing flowers and vegetables, which they sold to help bolster the school's minute budget.

The room served, depending on the hour, as schoolroom, canteen, living-room and dormitory. It was time for the evening meal; the boys had already washed under the tap by the garden and made ready the circular steel trays, called *thali*, for a meal of rice, with *brinjals* (egg plant) for vegetable and some milk.

Afterwards they crowded around with so much delight in their soft eyes and happy smiles that I felt almost embarrassed. Their faces expressed not only the bond that united us but their wonderment at the strange wide world which I represented, a world which to them seemed full of gadgets and opportunities to help overcome a handicap. Yet, to judge from their confidence, joy and lust for life, their own rehabilitation was no less thorough. None of the boys who were plying us with questions could raise himself more than about two feet off the ground. All were badly handicapped, mostly for lack of timely treatment, but even if they lacked material possessions they were rich in enthusiasm and the things of the spirit.

The Karuna Gruha was no mere school for them – it was a home, a family. They did not feel the lack of desks and furniture, or toys which few village children ever possess. In rural India schoolchildren sit cross-legged on the ground and chalk their exercises on slates (slates are normally used up to the fourth year and exercise books thereafter), while the teacher sits on a chair in front. Villagers usually eat squatting on the ground and sleep on mats on the ground. What they lacked desperately was more room, so that this single room would not have to cater for everything. Whilst they were eating, Koulagi told me of the other priorities, which he would dearly love to provide: more elementary textbooks, equipment, teachers for different age-groups, more craft training courses where the boys could be taught a trade through which they could later make a living.

Mrs Koulagi brought us a potful of the strong, aromatic Madrasi coffee, and we went outside to sit in the evening coolness of the lawn. An almost full moon had just risen. The little town below was in a deep shadow, punctured here and there by faint lights. Conscious of its beauty we went on talking quietly. It was now my turn to ask questions, how did the 'family' work, how did they manage their finances, how organize the rota for cleaning and washing clothes. They answered eagerly, displaying an urge for service not merely to their own small fraternity but to all the disabled they could reach and the society of the able-bodied at large. The faith and innocence that pervaded the constitution they had drawn up in no way detracted from its fitness for daily use. Their guiding light and inspiration had been the Gandhian ideal of *Sarvodaya* or community service by which they tried to live. The lucky few who received the occasional rupee from their parents, immediately paid such windfalls into a common fund to be spent on the whole group. The orphans, who most likely had never received anything in their lives, now have their share of the fund, as presents or minor luxuries such as stationery, soap and hair oil.

Talking freely in this way, I began to capture a vivid impression of their everyday lives. This fascinated me not only because of the contrast with what they had suffered previously, but particularly on account of the ideas and guidance their experiences offered for the project maturing in my mind. I tried to discover the extent to which lack of treatment, braces, chairs, etc., was impeding their return to a fuller life. They conceded readily that the larger appliances such as wheelchairs were more likely to hamper than assist in these surroundings – they pointed out my own difficulties in the lane outside as an example. Yet this made little difference to their urge for such aids. Puckering his eyebrows thoughtfully, Kumaraswamy, whom Koulagi described as the school's brightest pupil, was quick to express his feelings. 'I'd like a chair or brace to lift myself up; not so much because of what it might do for my mobility, but because it would raise me from the indignity of shuffling in the gutter. Also, when you spend your life so low down, you begin to associate normality with height, the ability to look at others face to face. If I were four feet off the ground instead of two feet, I think I'd feel less disabled by half. But now that we are in the Karuna Gruha and able to do so many things well – this matters less.' From the discussion that followed, it was clear that wheelchairs and braces were of great value as morale boosters. Moreover, as could be expected, the individual's urge for the trappings of physical rehabilitation seemed in direct proportion to his intelligence, and the extent to which his outlook and personality were emancipated. Since, unlike Kumaraswamy, the majority of villagers are simple souls, of strictly limited needs and ambitions, I felt confident that I was on the right track: that the more expensive, sophisticated side of medical rehabilitation could be side-tracked in favour of the vocational and the social sides. This was bound to make the process harder, the results imperfect; but the Karuna Gruha was a living example of how infinitely better this was to nothing at all.

Kumaraswamy's quiet, studious face was in striking contrast with his paralysed, withered body; his legs at the ankle were hardly thicker than a man's thumb. 'He has the greatest admiration for Gandhiji, and with a true Brahmin scholarship, has memorized large portions of his speeches and writings,' Koulagi explained proudly. 'He also teaches reading and writing to some of the illiterate citizens here in the village, and writes himself.'

'Well, that's excellent,' I said. 'Could you show me something that you have written?'

While Koulagi fetched a lamp, Kumaraswamy shuffled off towards the school, smiling self-consciously, his legs bouncing lifelessly over the cobbles. In a minute he was back with a neat exercise book tucked in his shirt. 'I wrote these some years back,' he said. As I flicked through the pages, I noticed long essays on the Indian constitution, the meaning of education, an impassionate plea for the brotherhood of man. Some of the essays were in English, some in Kannada (the language of Mysore State), all neatly set out in purposeful, rounded hand-writing. As I leafed through the pages, I found what I was looking for – an essay about himself, how he came to the Karuna Gruha.

'Once I felt sad,' he wrote, 'unwanted and angry at the cruel fate that had made a cripple of me. But after I joined the Karuna Gruha I felt as if I had been born anew. I began to realize that my disability could be a blessing in disguise, an ennobling experience, since it led me to a greater concern and love for others. No more do we boys of the Karuna Gruha feel inferior to our able-bodied brethren, but equal to them.' I closed the book and looked at him in admiration. From behind his black-rimmed spectacles he was gazing at his companions with obvious affection. Then he glanced at me. 'We're a happy family now,' he said simply.

When I asked him to tell me a little more about his life at home, he described his parents' sorrow that had gradually turned to bitterness; how he had sat for days on end with nothing better to do than listen to the radio. His mother had tried to help him, occasionally teaching him to sew and knit. 'But deep down they regarded me as a visitation, a cross that they were destined to bear. I lived in a limbo.' Now his parents had been won over and were proud of him. 'They are confident that I will become a breadwinner, like my brothers.'

Whilst Kumaraswamy was telling his story, the others sat around in a circle, listening attentively, those who understood English nodding their heads in agreement. Some had endured worse. Kingaya, a thin, crumpled twelve-year-old, deformed by untreated polio which prevented him from sitting upright, propped himself up with his hand on his chin, and told me how his father tried to abandon him on the village refuse pit soon after he was born. 'My mother had to hide me. I never had anybody to play with. The other children used to tease me all the time . . . ' he said quietly without bitterness.

'How d'you feel about your father now?' I asked.

'I love him, of course,' he replied without hesitation, looking at me wide-eyed. I had asked a stupid question.

As nine o'clock approached the boys drifted away for their tap wash and to spread their sleeping mats. For us the night was still young and bright as the moon that outlined the huddle of roofs and tiny backyards of Melkote. When Mrs Koulagi came to say that dinner was ready, we made tracks to their house. Tied to a rope from two hooks fixed into a beam, hung a traditional baby's cot of ornately chiselled wood. It was empty now, for the younger of the two Koulagi sons had just grown out of it. At the rear, there was a little stone-walled backyard with a shed occupied by a buffalo cow and her calf, and a well and a mango tree. 'There are also a couple of cobras living somewhere in the wall, but they don't harm anybody.'

Over a meal of rice, curd, lentils and egg-plant, I asked Koulagi about his own story. He told me of his background, of his father who had been a postmaster in various small towns in northern Mysore. From an early age he tried to help others, looking after younger children, escorting them to school, helping them with their homework. This instinct matured in time, and began to crystallize whilst he was still at college in Bagalkot. When he found that a degree course in politics and social science could not be taken in Mysore, he decided to leave, much to his parents' dismay, and try his luck in Bombay.

There he met Jayaprakash Narayan, the great statesman and social worker. Narayan liked the unassuming dedication of the twenty-two-year-old Koulagi, and offered him a job as his secretary and general assistant. He would help him in carrying on the work of rural improvement in which he was currently engaged with Vinoba Bhave, another venerated social worker and torch bearer of Gandhian ideals and rural policies. Characteristically, Koulagi refused a salary. 'My needs were simple. All I required was my basic keep, some food and clothing. I believed in the cause; what I wanted was to serve, not to profit.'

For five years he had walked the length and breadth of India with Narayan. Eventually he felt sufficiently experienced and self-confident to strike out on his own. With Narayan's encouragement, he decided to see what he could do in Melkote. At first, the work was of a general social nature, such as assisting the local weavers to organize themselves into a co-operative, to by-pass the moneylenders and middlemen. Eventually, with the help of a few friends, he had set up the Janapada Seva (Community Service) Trust, with the object of helping neighbouring villages to become self-reliant and self-supporting.

'In a sense, this was preparatory to what I wanted to do most: to help the physically handicapped. For years I had been troubled by the problem of disability, especially in the villages. So one thing led to another, and I founded this small school – the rest you can see for yourself!'

The lights of Melkote flickered and went out one by one. But my thoughts were not on the hour; I was eager to find out more. I asked about the future, about plans for expansion? Koulagi said they had recently started a sewing course, a weaving course and a poultry farm, and hoped soon to have a section for disabled girls. 'But funds are always the problem. The school is barely self-supporting, and I'm never quite sure how we are going to manage next week. I have sixteen boys now, and a long waiting list. All one can do is to try and try again – and sometimes succeed. But you have travelled far and wide in India and beyond, looking into this problem. Tell me about your findings.'

I told him briefly about the Expedition and about the plans maturing in my mind; about Bob Wulff's work in Thailand, about Fansa, about Dr Marwah in Aurangabad, how all had impressed me and given me valuable leads to what I wanted to do. Koulagi listened attentively but said nothing. I went on, describing how I saw the basic need for social and vocational rehabilitation, possibly by playing down the physical side, which was too costly and required more sophistication and technical know-how than the country could spare at present. In a developing country such as India, I argued, where the bare earth still remains a close reality, the first priority should be to adapt rehabilitation to the facts of rural life, and afterwards to concentrate resources where the 'cost : effect ratio' was greatest, and go all out for schemes most likely to prove feasible and effective.

I explained that in the West it would be unthinkable for someone like myself to be seen dragging along the street on my bottom. It would be intolerable for the passers by, no less than for myself. I could never go to an interview for a job in that fashion. But for villagers here, who are so close to nature, who eat, live and sleep on the ground, things are rather different. Let medical rehabilitation go on in the towns and teaching hospitals. But until the country progresses sufficiently for the full, comprehensive process to be available to all, let's have a curtailed one, well adapted to the village realities. As a result of my fact-finding journeys my conclusions are that the greatest need is undoubtedly in rural areas, where about eighty per cent of the handicapped are located but receive virtually no help of any kind. In view of this I should like to help set up a rural pilot research project aimed at evolving patterns of rehabilitation in all respects related to village conditions, reducing costs and techniques to a level that would be consistent with the budgets and other limitations of handicapped villagers. The brunt of the research in this centre would be directed at social and vocational rehabilitation; the physical side should be limited to simple appliances which a village cobbler, smith and carpenter can make.

When I had finished, Koulagi sat silently for several minutes in the darkness. 'It must be the hand of God,' he said eventually. 'You may make what you like of this, but I have worked for many years trying to help people who are wretched and suffering, people who are faced with no hope. Now I have been led to this kind of work that you have seen with my boys. What I have always hoped to do was to set up some sort of project for handicapped people in the villages, along the lines you have described. It truly is the most amazing thing that you should come here and voice my own ambitions like this.'

'Perhaps we could join forces one day.' I cried, wheeling myself over to him and grasping his hand.

'Perhaps we will.'

CHAPTER 16

Anandwan: Amte's Miracle

*

I F you stick a pin in the centre of a map of India, the point will probably fall near the town of Nagpur. When we arrived at the large modern complex of the Medical College Hospital on the outskirts of the city, I introduced myself to Doctor V. N. Wanakar, the orthopaedic surgeon. After touring the wards, this cheerful doctor insisted that we should accompany him home for lunch. To my delight, he not only showed the greatest interest in my project, but had wide experience of working with the disabled, particularly those living in rural areas.

As we were finishing our curry he said 'If you would like to meet somebody who has done really remarkable work in this field, you should meet Amte at Anandwan.' 'What does he do?' 'Well, I think the best thing for you would be to go there and find that out for yourself.'

Anandwan lies sixty-six miles south-south-east of Nagpur, off the main trunk road to Hyderabad. As we passed through a few drab villages of mud-brick, country-tile and thatch, the only signs of activity came from the sporadic herds of small, bony cattle kicking up the dust over the parched land and lethargic buffaloes being washed by little boys as they wallowed in the meagre streams. Now and then we passed a straggling group of women in colourful saris carrying their *lotas*, or large brass water pots, on their heads and occasionally a gang of road repairers, the women working the hot asphalt with their bare hands, while monkeys sat by the trees, chattering to themselves.

Suddenly I caught sight of a field of cotton bushes that stood waist high, flaunting their robust health. This cotton was in marked contrast to the miserable, straggly crops that usually flanked the roads we travelled. Beyond the cotton I glimpsed a cluster of modern buildings, their roofs red tiled, their white walls gleaming in the sunshine. From a green notice board we saw that we had arrived at 'ANANDWAN, Warora, founded 21st June, 1951.'

As we turned into the drive, I saw to my left a large brick building being built, and on my right, a huge stack of gleaming tin-cans, standing outside a small workshop. A few yards farther on there was a flourishing vegetable plot, flanked by papaya trees overburdened with fruit. Then we met a big herd of healthy, well-fed buffaloes standing outside the farm dairy waiting to be milked, and finally a group of people in the shade of a *gul mohur* tree, clustering around a tall, thickset figure dressed in a white cotton shirt and shorts. Hearing the car, the man turned and strode over. 'Welcome to Anandwan,' he said, a smile spreading over his broad, forceful face.

While I was busy introducing ourselves, Julian began to heave my wheelchair out of the back of the Gypsy and before I could stop him, Amte had seized the handles. 'Let me show you around.' We began by visiting the printing shop; here he showed us the composing room, where half a dozen of his patients were squatting on the ground before trays of type. They were type-setting two books by hand: one in English and the other in the local script, Marathi; the pages they had just finished setting were being 'locked up', and Amte showed me where another patient was pulling proofs for inspection. 'Signatures' of this book, sixteen pages at a time, were being printed and folded in the press room; while at the far end of the building, they were busy binding. 'Look,' said Amte, grabbing the clawed hands of one of the binders. 'All leprosy patients.' I could hardly believe my eyes. The man who was gripping these signatures and binding them in cloth had no fingers.

'All . . . ?' I stammered.

'Yes, all. Come, I will show you where we do most of our work when they arrive.'

He seized my chair and I found myself outside the hospital, a simple one-roomed block close to the printing shop. As we came into the room, a woman was bending over a patient in a string cot. 'Nailini,' Amte cried, 'come and meet our guest.' She finished giving the injection, and came forward to greet us.

'Auntie', as she was usually called, was the eldest of five daughters; when their father died, she was only eight, but she vowed that when she had completed her education she would renounce marriage, and concentrate on helping her mother. 'In fact,' said Amte, 'she was working for the post office until 1961 when she came here, and she was doing this so that her younger sisters could have dowries and get married.'

They had a school for the children of leprosy parents on the campus at Anandwan, and when she first arrived Nailini taught there. 'One day her mother came to visit her,' he continued, 'and straightaway I realized that she was showing the early symptoms of leprosy. I broke it to her as gently as I could, but to no avail: mother and all five children made a suicide pact. Nailini stole some poison from a drug-store and was the first to take it. Luckily we got to her in time, pumped her out, and prevented the others from swallowing theirs.' Amte then described how he had taken the whole family on a tour of Anandwan, and how when they left they were determined to fight back. 'I'm glad to say they're still fighting, despite having been thrown out of their home. The other girls all have good jobs, and they all congregate here from time to time for a reunion.'

As we were leaving the hospital building, I asked how long on average the patients stayed. 'It depends,' Amte replied. 'This hospital also serves as home for those who are too old or too crippled to fend for themselves in the colony, but we also admit the lepromatous cases, that means those in the infectious stage. It usually takes about three years to check the pro-gress of the disease, but this varies widely. Here in the colony we offer them a home, the right atmosphere to help them regain confidence and a place in society. To those that need it, we also offer training, so that they can eventually support themselves, and become rehabilitated back into their community life. Often, of course, they have no homes to return to, in which case they join one of our co-operatives and stay put. The patients you saw in the print shop were all under training. Let me now show you others in the tin-can workshop.'

This was a building similar to that of the print shop, made of plain cement-faced brick with whitewash and a tiled roof. 'They spend six months on average here,' Amte said, shouting to make himself heard above the clatter of machinery. 'Afterwards they can either stay or go back to their homes. If they go back, it is usually after having saved enough money to buy basic tools and equipment to set themselves up on their own.' He paused. 'There is always a good demand for these things in villages. Not one has failed to make a living out of it yet.'

I watched a patient with badly clawed hands sitting at a foot-pedal guillotine, as he worked on empty cans that had once contained motor-oil or American Aid soy-bean salad oil. 'But what about their hands?'

'Oh, you mustn't swallow all that stuff,' he replied, with a hint of impatience. 'We don't believe in the impossible here, we just try and find a way around it!'

Much of the equipment was of home-made origin, ingeniously put together. Simple hand or foot operated machines for cutting, pressing, bending, grinding – the welding was electrically operated. Handles were usually adapted to afford an easier grip to deformed hands, and there were protective devices wherever there was risk of cutting on the sharp edges. Amte beckoned to one of the women, who fetched a set of three canisters, meant for sugar, salt and other condiments. It was crude, with the brand name of the motor-oil still showing, but obviously useful to a villager, proof against insects and the weather. Other products included spouted containers for edible oil, larger ones for storing grain, sieves, mirror-frames. 'This is what we sell in the market for things like rice, flour, or lentils.'

As I stood there, I couldn't help noticing the look of trust and veneration on the woman's face. She followed us outside, away from the noise, and stood beneath a large notice board with various chalk markings. 'What's all this about 200,000 rupees?' I asked.

'That's the turnover of the tin-can co-operative since it started five years ago. Patients like Radha here pay me twenty rupees a month for their keep. Once the cost of raw material has been deducted, the rest is theirs – they divide the profits amongst themselves.'

As I looked at this shy, smiling woman standing proudly under the sales chart, the vision of a thousand handicapped people flooded through my mind, staring hopelessly at me from their ramshackle beds and street corners. If only there were more such workshops, more smiling faces.

When I asked Amte what Radha did with her money, he told me the outline of her story, how when she first showed the symptoms of leprosy she was thrown out of her village, and found herself alone in the jungle, in the heavy monsoon rains, foodless and friendless. No-one in her family or the rest of the village wanted to set eyes on her again, for fear of catching the dreaded disease. She had never left her village before; for three years she wandered from place to place, begging the odd crust, submitting to the shouts and curses that a leper must expect.

'Radha, tell our guests how you came here,' Amte said. 'I will translate.'

'Well, when I first heard of Anandwan,' she said shyly, staring at the ground, 'I didn't think anyone would want to have anything to do with me. So I hid in the bushes. But then some patients saw me, and brought me to Baba.' She paused, looking up into Baba Amte's face uncertainly. He nodded. 'But instead of shooing me away, he welcomed me, and told me that I was going to be like another daughter to him. Now I am happy! My illness has been cured!'

It was a simple story and all the more moving for its simplicity. Amte grasped one of Radha's stumps. 'Look, Arthur, the clawed hands!' he said. All that remained of her fingers were short stumps about an inch long. 'And yet she is one of our best workers and teachers now for sheet metal work!'

As we walked away, he told me that Radha had been too shy to tell me more about her family. But from time to time she sent them two hundred rupees from her savings – a colossal sum to a landless labourer, the equivalent of six months' wages. By this time we had reached a vineyard, where we stopped for a minute to admire the vines.

'Everyone told me that it was impossible,' Amte remarked. 'They said that we could never grow grapes on this soil. Here, taste these,' he added, thrusting into my hands a bunch of large, juicy grapes. 'The vineyard is small, but we now have one of the highest yields per acre in the State of Maharashtra. What's more, this is another way in which we break down prejudice. When the villagers hear about our vineyard, they come to have a look. Then they ask my patients for help and I encourage them to accept the invitations. Have you ever heard of leprosy patients going back to the villages as advisers, as experts?'

'I certainly have not,' I replied.

Moving on, we came to a group of semi-detached bungalows, the housing units in which the patients live. When I admired their construction, Amte commented that in the battle against prejudice, the patient has always to do that much better than the able-bodied: the house has to be better built, the crops have to be of better quality, the factory product has to be better made and finished. Without a trace of arrogance, he described how the produce of Anandwan usually swept the board in district exhibitions and competitions, winning first prizes for anything from the biggest radish to the best stud-bull, from the largest egg to the heaviest pumpkin. Likewise the children of the Anandwan school usually came first in inter-school competitions. 'Of course, they have built all these houses themselves.' They were simple four-roomed units, one room per family. Simple, even primitive to a Westerner; yet with their electric light and tap water, they represent a Hilton style of living to an Indian villager. I watched as one of the women finished her washing. Instead of wasting the soapy water, she carefully emptied her pail into an irrigation channel that led to the vegetables in their small plot. 'All this construction has been done by your patients?' I exclaimed. 'Oh, yes. We never employ outside contractors. We don't have that kind of money, anyway. Come and see our latest project.'

When we had first turned in the drive I had wondered about the building that was going up nearby. 'This is our own college,' Amte said, waving his arms in an expansive gesture. 'The leprosy patients have built it for the able-bodied. It cost 250,000 rupees.' I was unable to believe my ears. 'You really mean that the patients have built all this for the able-bodied?' 'Yes, and we have covered most of the running costs too. We have 570 students now. The college has close ties with Nagpur University, with courses in art, science, commerce and agriculture.' 'This has nothing to do with leprosy?' I asked, still unable to take it all in. 'Oh, no, only a minute percentage of the students are connected in some way, through their parents. The majority come here from the surrounding area, just as they would to any college. In fact, it works well, because the students often help out with odd jobs on the colony and in this way, they'll never be tempted to harbour prejudice against a victim of leprosy.' He paused, surveying the bustle of activity in front of us. 'They're finishing the staff accommodation now. It's been a long haul, but it's been worth it.'

'But how on earth did you achieve all this?' I asked. 'Well,' he replied with a shrug, 'I suppose you could say that is the story of my life.'

'That is what I want to hear, more than anything else,' I said. 'When will you tell me the story?'

He looked at me for a moment before replying.
'You'll stay the night, I hope?'
'We'd be delighted.'
'Very well. I'll tell you something tonight.'

When we returned to their house in the centre of the colony, Mrs Amte was performing her evening devotions in front of her small domestic shrine. 'Let her finish!' Amte chuckled, 'she prays for both of us!' Wondering how I was meant to take this, I remained silent. 'She exerts a calming influence wherever she goes,' he added. 'I remember that at her old home, when I first met her, there was a vicious aggressive cow. The moment the cow entered the lane there would be a commotion, but Indu merely had to go and stand in front of the beast and it would become docile and quiet. Now she has to tame the jungle hurricane!'

A moment later Mrs Amte came in to welcome us, and enquired gently what had brought us here.

Later Amte began to tell his story. He came from an orthodox Brahmin background. His father was a landlord and government official, quite well off by local standards. His mother had never received any formal education, but was a good teacher and had the ability to explain the most difficult things to a young boy in a vivid, imaginative way. He was very close to her.

By contrast his relationship with his father was similar to that between a heavy Victorian father and his son. 'From my earliest childhood, I think I was a puzzle to him. For instance, a good Brahmin is supposed never to take life, any life, or to indulge in "menial" pursuits such as fishing – especially repulsive since it involves killing. But I loved to go fishing, and one fine Sunday afternoon I was seen by neighbours walking through our Brahmin quarter in Nagpur whistling gaily, with a fishing rod slung over the shoulder of my red school blazer and a tinful of worms in my hand. This was duly reported to my father. "You are no son of mine," he said, more in sorrow than anger. "I wish you had never been born!" To me, the ideas and conduct of my father and his class, seemed not merely rigid but downright petrified. For one thing, I soon developed a sympathy for the "poor and down-trodden" and a distaste for respectability. This was made plain during the Holi Festival in which everyone took part with great fervour and ribaldry. In the course of the celebrations, a man was tied to a bier and taken around the town, to be abused at random by everyone in the procession. I got the chance of playing this role. I had to wear a garland of broken slippers and various other peculiar accessories. As I was carried on the swaying shroud, I was thrilled that I'd finally broken out of the sphere of respectability. I was scared, however, that somebody might go home and tell my parents what I was up to. But at least I was sure now that I'd been accepted by the people whom I loved.' 'That makes two of us,' I interrupted. 'I was elected Chief Fool last year in Mathura.' 'You were?' Amte laughed. 'Maybe we have a lot more in common?'

As we sat around the small dining-table, with Mrs Amte hovering discreetly in the background, I asked Amte if he could recollect any major turning point at this time of his life. 'Several! One happened when I was about thirteen. I remember that day well: it was sunny and hot, and we all felt happy and excited because it was Diwali. My mother had saved lots of small change from her shopping, and gave this to me to buy myself firecrackers. Stuffed full with sweets and feeling that life was grand, I ran towards the market. Then I saw a blind beggar. He was sitting in the hot sun by the edge of the unpaved street, while gusts of wind raised clouds of dust and rubbish over him. "Andhalyala paisa de, Bhagwan," he kept calling plaintively – "give one paisa to this blind man, oh God!" Beside him lay his brown stick with a little bell, and his thin and mangy dog. In front of him a dirty old rag was held down against the wind by four stones on the corners, and in its centre stood his begging bowl, a rusty cigarette tin. My bright, happy world came crashing down. I rushed across and started putting such handfuls of coins into the tin that he held out to me, that it almost fell from his hands with the weight. "I am only a blind beggar, young sir, don't put stones in my bowl." "These are not stones but coins. Count them if you wish!" I said. He sat and counted and then recounted, sorting the coins into little piles on that tattered cloth. He just couldn't believe it. He went on feeling and counting those coins. It made me so sad that I ran home in tears.'

Amte's wish to become a doctor provoked a major clash at home and this was one of the few battles that Amte lost. But before he joined the law faculty at Nagpur University, he attended the Mission College.

During university vacations, he spent long periods in the jungle with Gond tribesmen, hunting with them and sharing their life.

In 1936, after Amte had successfully sat for his BA, his family began to press him to choose a wife. 'But I preferred my vagabond life. I grew my beard and hair long, matting it as the sadhus do, and rubbed my body with ash. This put a stop to matrimonial advances, but it also gave me an added introduction to the hearts of ordinary people.'

After taking his Bachelor of Law degree in 1938, Amte practised for a couple of years in Chattisgarh. When his father retired in 1940 to his house in Nagpur, he prevailed on him to come and practise in Warora. The place needed a competent pleader; the family estate, 450 acres of good land by Goraja village, was only five miles away and Amte could keep an eye on things. Thus in 1940 began his momentous connection with Warora, a sleepy little town with a population of fourteen thousand.

Gandhi had established himself in the Sewagram Ashram, only fifty-seven miles away, and Amte met him frequently. The non-violent Satyagraha movement made a profound impression on him, even if he felt a sneaking bias towards more drastic methods. Determined to put his legal practice to good purpose, he organized lawyers to represent, free of charge, the mounting numbers whom the British were arresting and often condemning to death. The British police had been suspicious of him for some time. In August 1942 things came to the boil with the launching of the Quit India campaign. The British arrested Gandhi, Nehru and all Congress leaders they could find down to the District level; the leaderless masses responded with riots and processions. Amte was arrested, allegedly for singing the National Anthem, and flung into jail in Chanda, where he remained for twenty-one days.

Whenever he visited Goraja, the plight of the untouchables moved him to the core. 'They were desperately poor, often starving and virtually naked. Worse than that – they were like cowed animals. There was a good well a few yards from where they lived; but owing to prejudice and the fear of ritual pollution, they were forbidden to draw water from it. They were not even allowed to touch my feet in greeting – they had to touch the dust several yards away.'

Amte hadn't been ignorant that such conditions existed, but now for the first time he was experiencing them at first hand, and in his own family village. Against bitter opposition, he opened the well to the *harijans* (the 'untouchables'), helped them build better dwellings, and ate with them. 'I made a special point of joining them at their prayers, singing *bhajans* (devotional songs) with them, for I believed that it was particularly through a shared worship of God that the fundamental identity and fellowship of all men would reassert itself.' Most of Warora was outraged; yet his outstanding personality and integrity were respected, and he was elected vice-president of the municipality, a post roughly equivalent to that of deputy mayor.

'Bread is the supreme truth, Arthur,' he went on. 'I pledged myself to obtain a better return for the manual workers. Work purifies and ennobles the spirit. Gandhi, Tagore and Vinoba Bhave were like beacons that lit my path.'

'But what about your legal practice?'

'I was charging fifty rupees for chattering for fifteen minutes, while a labourer was not getting even three quarters of a rupee for twelve hours of toil. That was what was eating into me.'

It was in 1946 that he first met Indu Ghuleshastri, the daughter of a well-known Pundit; her family had been Sanskrit scholars for seven generations. A friend of Amte's was arranging the marriage of Indu's elder sister, and had also been entrusted by the widowed mother with the task of finding a suitable match for Indu. The household was crowded with guests; the old maid-servant was struggling in the scullery to wash an ever-growing heap of clothes; every few minutes someone would toss a few more in.

Amte observed that Indu invented numerous reasons why she should keep leaving the guests, and the moment she stepped inside the scullery, she pitched in to help. 'Not a word of this to my mother,' she would whisper to the old servant. Amte strolled about keeping a discreet watch on the scullery and the big sloping concrete block on which the two women were pounding the clothes. 'I thought no ordinary Brahmin girl would stoop to wash other people's dirty garments, when she could have been enjoying herself, and suddenly something within me stirred.'

A few days later, Amte saw Indu's mother, and announced that he was about to give up his vow of celibacy. When she asked why, he replied that he had found a bridegroom for Indu.

'But what has that got to do with your vow?'

'Because I am the candidate.'

The poor woman received the shock of her life; the preliminaries

Mealtime at Anandwan

for an Indian marriage are invariably more indirect and circum-spect. Besides Amte's past, his notoriety and now his manner of proposal: all were radically wrong.

Ultimately Indu's mother gave her consent and the day of the marriage was fixed. Three weeks before the celebrations were due to begin, when the bridegroom was staying at the Ghuleshastri's house, two thieves broke in during the night. 'One of them went off to ransack the house, while the other stood with his dagger poised over me, thinking I was asleep. Suddenly I got him in a leg scissor lock, and we rolled over the bed and floor. His friend came running back but I managed to hit him in the testicles. Then both of them set on me with their knives and I remember the gleam of the daggers in the moonlight and their hot, panting breath as we rolled over and over. They stabbed me repeatedly, including just above my right eye. One would have got me in the throat had I not caught the blade, almost cutting my fingers off.' The thieves eventually ran away. With sixteen wounds on his body, Amte was rushed to the Mayo Hospital in Nagpur, where at first he was not expected to last more than a few hours.

When in December 1946 Amte stepped up to the marriage podium, he was swathed in bandages.

The following October their son, Vikas, was born. With the support of a courageous and devoted wife, Amte no longer had to face his self-appointed task alone. He gave up his legal practice, shaved off his beard and most of his long hair, and went to Goraja to wind up his connection with the estate.

In December 1947 he set up the Shrama (labour) Ashram, an experiment in communal inter-caste living. The number of participants varied between twenty and twenty-five; there was one poor Brahmin family who knew something about agriculture, but the rest were harijans, one of whom brought his three wives. R. K. Patil, a local politician and notable, loaned them seven acres of scrub on the outskirts of Warora; living in fraternal harmony they cultivated the land in common, cooking and eating in one kitchen, pooling their incomes. To secure some of the capital they required for manure, seed, implements and the like, Amte invested the little money he had saved up from his legal practice in buying job lots in Nagpur of anything from cheap fountain pens and teapots to stationery and millet; these he re-sold in Warora or wherever there was a prospect for a good sale. But no land yields immediately; until they harvested their first crop, they lived on two small meals a day, mainly coarse millet *chapatis* and *dhal* or pulses.

'I had spent my boyhood enjoying myself, so I knew nothing about preparing a seed bed or drawing water from a well,' he remarked. Nevertheless the little community grew a bumper crop of vegetables. Having chosen a site in the heart of the Warora bazaar, Amte took the produce there and deliberately left the prices unmarked. The buyers were free to pay any sum and take away any quantity according to their conscience.

When he first came to the market, the other vendors looked askance at him, thinking that he represented cut-throat competition. 'But after a few days it was they who got up on their own accord to attack a rich man who took away the whole basket for a few annas. "Have you no shame?" they said. "Don't you feel a swine, taking for such a sum the things that have cost a man's sweat?"'

Indu took to wearing the rough, cheap fabrics that cost a few rupees in the Warora bazaar and distributed the silk saris of her trousseau amongst the harijan women of the Shrama Ashram.

While her husband worked in the fields, she cooked with the other women and to help the budget, made reed brooms, baskets and even leather sandals. This involved handling dead matter, often from cows, which the orthodox regarded as the lowest and most despicably outcaste job of all. This was the limit, so far as her relatives were concerned. 'Nobody came to see our Vikas. But you should have seen what lovely little brooms I made! I was an expert!' she added with a twinkle. 'It wasn't easy though. The three wives quarrelled incessantly. They were all indescribably dirty and stank. I used to spend hours tending their sores and de-lousing them. I nursed them when they were sick, gave them lessons in reading and writing and taught prayers to the children.'

Amte went on 'The area was extremely unhealthy, and eventually almost all the members of the ashram went down with malaria. The place was also full of cobras; Indu used to kill up to fifteen a day. Weeks later, she was stricken by typhus. To make matters worse, she was pregnant again.' Now, on top of Amte's work in the fields, he nursed Indu himself through forty days and nights of high fever, cooked for the family and took on all the household duties. In December 1948 their second son, Prakash, was born.

Although he had resigned from his other offices, Amte was still vice-president of the Warora municipality. When the night-soil carriers went on strike, claiming that their quota was excessive, he decided to do the job himself, to find out exactly what was involved and whether the claim was justified.

Outside the big towns, few Indian latrines are of the flush type; the cleaner has to go down into the pit under the latrine, shovel the excreta into a round wicker basket and carry it on top of his head to the place of disposal. Amte found that he could clean the forty latrines in about four hours. One day as he was struggling home he saw a bundle at the side of the road and with a shock realized that this heap was not only human, but alive. Moreover the creature was shivering with unbearable pain and cold, and breathing heavily. 'When I looked closer in the failing light, I saw that it was a man in the ultimate stages of leprosy, a rotting mass of human flesh, with two holes in the place of a nose, without trace of fingers or toes, and with worms in the sores that had once been nostrils and eye sockets.' For the first time, he ran away, terror-stricken. For Amte, this was his life's climacteric. 'That sense of revulsion made me loathe myself: from that moment onwards, I was out to conquer fear.' He forced himself to return. He gave the leper food, and put up a bamboo awning to shield him from the pouring rain, and cared for him until he died.

This experience brought home to him that others needed help even more desperately than the 'untouchable' harijans. For some time past he had wanted to launch out into some permanent field of social work. In fact he and Indu had virtually decided to go to the jungles of the Gond tribal area, where, in his youth, Amte had burnt and cut patches in the jungle with them, shot boar and lived in their leaf huts, until he had become accepted as one of them.

'I knew a lot about the Gonds,' he said, 'nothing about leprosy. But the image of that dying leper was burning me like a branding iron and wouldn't give me a moment's rest.' He paused for a moment, looking across at his wife. She took up the story. 'We had two small boys, and talked for hours about the chances of contracting leprosy. I assured Amte that he must follow the dictates of his heart, that I would find my happiness in helping him.'

Prejudice was rife about leprosy; it was believed that it was sufficient to pass close to a leper to contract the dreaded disease. Neither Amte nor Indu knew the truth about the low contagion rate of the disease.

'Finally we made our decision. We vowed to dedicate ourselves to work amongst leprosy victims. For the rest, we just entrusted ourselves into the hands of God.'

Once they had reached their major decision, Amte acted fast. Having read all the books about leprosy that he could find, he went to work in the Warora leprosy clinic. This was run by the local government doctor, but only two or three patients were attending it weekly.

The news spread like lightning over the local grape-vine, 'Amte has thrown his lot in with the lepers!' The healthy shuddered before the 'reckless vagary of the mad lawyer'; the lepers flocked to the weekly clinic – twenty, fifty, hundred. two hundred. 'It's wicked! It's monstrous! He'll have all of us contaminated with leprosy!' the cry went up.

To gain further experience, Amte started commuting twice a week to the leprosarium at Dattapur, which was run by a respected Hindu missionary and disciple of Gandhi's, Manohar Diwan. He learned fast. After a few months, Diwan realized that Amte now needed more technical, medical knowledge and advised him to attend a specialized course at the Calcutta School of Tropical Medicine.

In August 1950, Amte stepped into a lecture room of that faculty. At this time the discussion was raging about the artificial breeding of leprosy germs. Leprosy is a contagious disease, almost certainly caused by a tiny germ, *Mycobacterium leprae*. Seen under a microscope, this resembles a slender rod, about one five-thousandth of an inch long (and a tenth as broad), so that ten of them could be laid, end to end, across the thickness of this page. For many years, doctors, scientists and research workers had been labouring to prove that this micro-organism was the culprit, responsible for the disease.

But before a scientist will admit that a disease is caused by a specific micro-organism, he has to satisfy himself on at least three counts: that he can find the germ in every case of the disease; that he can grow the germ in a 'pure culture' in the laboratory; and that he can reproduce the disease by transferring the germs grown in the laboratory into a human host, and collect the germs again at a later stage. So far as leprosy is concerned, the first proved easy; the germ was found in every patient, but once the germs were placed in a pure culture, with no contaminating organisms, they proved impossible to cultivate.

The lecturer described how numerous attempts had been made to grow the leprae germs in the usual animal hosts, monkeys, Russian hamsters, rats, rabbits and others, and how all these attempts had failed. 'Perhaps man is the only likely laboratory "animal",' he concluded. The remark was not meant to be taken seriously, but it preyed on Amte's mind. Such an experiment would be highly dangerous. If it proved successful, the human host would make medical history, and in all probability an enormous contribution to the battle against leprosy, but he would also become a victim, with the prospect before him of social ostracism and disfigurement.

Two days later Amte stood up in class and raised his hand. 'I wish to become a guinea-pig. I shall do this for the advancement of science and for the benefit of leprosy patients.' The class stared at him. 'There are animals . . . ' the lecturer pointed out. But Amte had made up his mind. He injected himself with an emulsion obtained from smears taken from positive cases of leprosy, that is with the live virus. The experiment failed.

However, about the time Amte left Calcutta, having finished the course, the whole basis of leprosy treatment was revolutionized by the discovery, and subsequent cheap manufacture, of the sulphone drug diamino-diphenyl-sulphone, also known as DDS, or dapsone. Provided that the patient was 'caught' early enough, and the tablets were taken every week, it effected a cure in well over ninety-five per cent of cases and brought relief to millions.

But dapsone takes a long time to act. Once the disease has been recognized, treatment with the drug is necessary for a minimum of two years, longer in more serious cases. There is also the problem of prejudice, and the problem of highly infectious patients running around in their villages, spreading the disease. The more Amte thought about these problems, the more he realized that DDS was only a beginning. What was needed were centres to which infectious cases could come for treatment. Once they were in such centres, those who had no stable source of livelihood, or could not be expected to return to their former one, could be trained in some basic skill whilst under treatment, and through selling their products, the colony could be made less dependent on public or private support. Late in 1950, he started negotiating with the State government for the grant of a piece of land on which to set up the farm-cum-leprosarium he had in mind.

On the 21st of March 1951 he stood on fifty acres of rock-strewn scrub, surveying the scene around him. He could not see far, for the place was dense with bushes, trees and bamboo. The nearest well was two miles away; the soil, the little there was of it between the stones and boulders, was poor. 'I looked at it with profound emotion and perhaps a tinge of dismay. It was more than just a patch of disused quarry; it was like glimpsing into my own future, a new volume of my life. Perhaps it was symptomatic that there was nothing but a tangle of boulders, roots and creepers there. Outcast land for outcast men. This is our lot from now on, I thought.' Around him was gathered a small group: Indu and their two small boys, and six highly positive male patients, two old and four young.

'Friends, we must dig for water. We want to transform this forest into green fields. But we are not going to beg for help; as you know to your cost, beggars receive more insults than gifts. Charity destroys – but work builds! Are you going to join me?'

For a moment the lame and ugly, the deformed and ailing patients kept quiet, visualizing the enormity of the task ahead. To clear the jungle meant years of back-breaking work, moving the stones by hand, carrying them away, tearing out trees and scrub. Such work would be almost impossible for the able-bodied; but most of these men suffered from crippling deformities of their hands or feet. Their total assets numbered one lame cow and fourteen rupees in the bank. How could they attempt this? Yet such was the respect in which they held Amte that with one accord they shouted 'When can we start?' Anandwan, the optimistic 'Forest of Joy', was born in that moment.

The task here was more formidable than that at the Shrama Ashram. They did not even have a cottage to return to in the evenings. Two shacks of bamboo matting and grass were erected. The lepers occupied one hut, the Amtes set up home in the other. If the huts kept out the worst of the monsoon, they afforded little protection against other hazards. 'Scorpions and cobras were everyday visitors,' Indu commented. 'Once when I lifted the top off my flour jar I discovered a huge king cobra in it. It looked like a monster! But it must have thought I was an even bigger monster, because it slunk away leaving a floury path behind it.'

The first priority was to dig a well. They possessed four shovels, two hoes, three pick-axes, two crow-bars and five axes. It was not so much a matter of digging, since there was no earth to speak of, as cutting and breaking and burrowing through the rock. Sharp chips flew as the men grunted and the pickaxes bit into the stone. Amte dressed, ate, worked and lived exactly like his patients; he kept a sharp lookout for splinters for he knew that if they hit the lepers the smallest piece of rock chipping could remain, unfelt and undetected in a sandal and cause ulcerating sores. Once a large thorn pierced the sandal of one of the patients and buried itself in his sensationless foot. As he extracted the thorn and tended the wound, Amte realized that one small difference still remained between him and the others: the men wore sandals cut from worn-out automobile tyres, while he wore safer and more comfortable sandals made of leather. That same evening he cut himself a pair of sandals from a threadbare tyre, vowing that never again would he wear any other type of shoe; to this day people discreetly raise their eyebrows, baffled by his curious footwear.

Amte vividly described the sinking of the well. 'After about six weeks, when we were about thirty-four feet down, the rock was becoming a little moist. It was May: the temperature outside rose to 118°F – inside that hole it was fearfully hot. Then a bee, followed by a butterfly, came down to the moisture. Two days later, when we arrived in the morning, we found a frog sitting happily in a tiny puddle between the stones. Three days later water came through in abundance; we worshipped that water with wild flowers and milk. Then for the rest of the day we sat by our well, just staring delightedly at the water.'

To clear the jungle in the immediate vicinity of the well, they broke up stones and huge boulders with their flimsy tools, carrying the pieces away in their arms, stone by stone; then levelled the ground, spreading thinly what soil there was, 'bunding' the little fields to preserve the precious water from the impending monsoon and protect the soil from erosion. They possessed no plough, much less bullocks to pull it. These first patches they cultivated entirely by hand, growing their first crop of maize, chilis and brinjals (egg plant).

On the 21st of June 1951 they held an opening ceremony in Anandwan, presided over by the famous national leader and champion of rural development, Vinoba Bhave. As he cut the tape across the bamboo entrance to the hut, he said: 'Another Ramayana is being lived and enacted in this jungle. One day, I feel, it will be no less famous than the story of Sita and Rama we all revere.'

Water is so rare in this parched area of Central India that it soon attracted visitors. The human variety were welcome, the others less so. It was nothing unusual for a tiger to come now and then hoping to quench its thirst. Panthers, scorpions and cobras, kraits and pythons (the longest they killed measured seventeen feet) were a continual bane. Yet rats were the most dangerous, for they soon discovered that they could gnaw at insensitive hands and feet with impunity while the leper was asleep. 'I remember one morning a patient ran to me screaming in terror,' said Mrs Amte. 'His arm had been chewed from elbow to wrist, so that the bone and tendons were showing in places. I had to steel myself not to faint as I dressed the wound before sending him off to hospital. After this, we put mosquito nets over their beds, bandaged the insensitive parts for the night and even made them wear shoes in bed, but the rats chewed through the lot! Finally, we spread poison everywhere, but it took a long time to get rid of the rats.'

Word about Anandwan spread quickly, how this was a place where leprosy victims enjoyed self-respect, and worked for themselves. Before many months had passed, a steady trickle of patients began to arrive from the surrounding area. Many were 'active', so Amte built a modest hospital hut near his own shack, where Indu together with some of the ambulant patients could take care of them.

The lonely lame cow that they had started with was replaced in time by two others from the local *Gorakshan*, the home for lame or old cows. 'Up to the end of 1952 we had only male patients, and they all felt rather lonely. The rat poison made it difficult to keep pets. The cows were a great help. It was not only that the little milk was appreciated, but the patients now had something to dote on.' Because of the risks of contagion they could not milk the cows, so Indu helped with this. When Amte ploughed, she scattered the seed.

One day a police constable arrived bearing a small child he had found abandoned in the bushes outside the colony. Amte described the scene; 'Without a moment's hesitation, Indu took it in her arms. The poor mite was covered with eczema, but she never shrank from touching or fondling it. For six months she tended that child as if it were her own. But then the poor little thing died, and I shall never forget how she wept.'

By 1954 there were about sixty patients and they had dug six wells. All fifty acres had been cleared of jungle and were under cultivation. They had been given a pair of bullocks, and large crops of grain and vegetables were being harvested. Loading his bullock cart with potatoes, beetroot, cauliflowers, brinjals, the likes of which had never been seen in Warora, Amte went to the Sunday market and spread out the tempting produce. Admiring glances were cast at the quality. His prices were very reasonable, but buyers were scarce. 'How can we eat those vegetables?' they said. 'Do you want us to catch leprosy?' Hearing this, Amte invited contractors to bid for the vegetables on the root, per plot. Now nobody could say that the vegetables had been handled by lepers. The quality was matchless and in consequence there was no shortage of bidders.

The next priority was the construction of permanent and more comfortable dwellings. Help came from an unexpected quarter, from 'Service Civil International', an organization based on Western Europe, which sponsored parties of young volunteers for work on projects in India and elsewhere. Under the leadership of a Swiss, Pierre Oppliger, a group of fifty volunteers of both sexes who had been engaged on construction work at Gandhi's ashram at Sewagram, sixty-two miles from Warora, came along, and so in January 1954, the jungle around Anandwan resounded to the cheerful noise of fifty workers, speaking twenty-three different tongues. Before the young people left in the following April, six gleaming white-washed buildings stood ready in a quadrangle. The volunteers had also effected a change of heart amongst the local people. 'There must be something about the place. All these foreigners coming from far away to give their labour for it!' they exclaimed. Towards the end of their visit, the volunteers ran short of food and the citizens of Warora came bearing potfuls of rice and dhal. Diffidently at first, they looked around and noticed with some surprise that Anandwan appeared to be like other farms, except that it was better run.

After this the colony became almost self-generating. More brick buildings were added as patients flocked in by the hundred, many from Bengal, Andhra, Madras, a thousand and more miles away. Later in 1954, Amte, as secretary of the trust set up to run Anandwan, bought six cows. The following year a proper dairy herd was started with twenty-five head of cattle. More land was made available by the State government. The account books no longer resembled a child's entries for pocket money, but registered six figure numbers.

The initial battle had been won, but there was no resting on laurels. Amte set out to survey the incidence and nature of leprosy in Warora and sixty surrounding villages, working systematically from the detailed maps kept by the *kotwal* in each village. For the best part of two years he was away from Anandwan. During this time he had many strange and moving experiences. One of the fundamental conclusions that he drew was that it was impractical to treat more than a fraction of leprosy victims, perhaps twenty per cent at most, in institutions. There could never be room for all of them, nor indeed did most of them wish to be in institutions. As a result he developed a 'Trace and Treat' campaign. By 1957 he had set up eleven weekly clinics, within a radius of about thirty miles from Warora, with a total of about four thousand patients. Many of the clinics were held by Amte himself, while others were managed by a dedicated group of trained ex-patients.

By this time there were about three hundred inmates and fifteen permanent buildings at Anandwan; by the early sixties both figures were to double.

As vice-president of Warora Amte had set up a number of co-operatives, amongst teachers, fishermen, stone-cutters, sweepers and others and these ventures had proved a great success, giving him the confidence and experience for organizing co-operatives in Anandwan. With the help of Swiss Aid Abroad, a voluntary organization whose representative in India was now Pierre Oppliger, (earlier the leader of the voluntary builders), the tin-can workshop was built in 1960. This was the beginning of a fruitful co-operation; the pioneering work at Anandwan and Amte's personality caught the imagination of the Swiss. Once a year an appeal went out through the French-speaking Cantons, and many people gave up a meal, to give the proceeds through Swiss Aid to Amte.

The co-operatives multiplied. Whereas up to this point they had concentrated almost exclusively on agriculture, the time had now come to branch out into tailoring, weaving, printing, leather-work. 'I've always been a strong believer in letting things take their own course, without soul-destroying rules and regulations. The patients began to run their own affairs, which left me free for developing my interests elsewhere!'

Amte paused, the hour was a very late or rather early one, for he had talked till it was nearly dawn. So far I had said nothing about my own project though all the time I had been thinking that Anandwan was unique, that the potential it represented was enormous and that somehow I must tap this well of experience for other handicapped people. But by now Amte was off on a description of what he hoped to do with the 1,300 acres of jungle land the government had just given him in a place he called Somnath.

'Baba,' I interrupted him most unceremoniously, 'you have simply got to do something for the orthopaedically handicapped.'

'Go on,' he replied 'why should I do this?'

'Because you have achieved something unique here and what you have done for the leprosy patients, you can do for other handicapped people. No-one has ever tried to set up even a pilot project. No-one has tried to adapt rehabilitation to the village level, to suit the needs and pockets of ordinary villagers. You alone have the experience to tackle what I call the "Asianizing of rehabilitation in Asia"!'

He looked at me long and hard. 'In many ways I think you are right. I know that there is a tremendous need. But alas there are only twenty-four hours in a day. My health is not good. And I have a number of projects in mind. How can I possibly take this on as well?'

Apart from the gigantic project at Somnath, there was the extension of Anandwan for training villagers in better methods of cultivation, a campaign for a family planning programme in the area, a new cattle breeding programme, a central hatchery for poultry breeding, damming the nearby Wardha river for irrigation purposes! As he ticked them off on his fingers, my hopes began to falter. Yet, I knew that my instinct was right, that I had never met anyone better qualified to set up the kind of pilot project for the handicapped I had in mind, so I began to tell Amte a little more of our Expedition, of the cases that were typical of the problem. As I talked, I felt as though I were pleading on behalf of all the hundreds of pathetic cripples that I had met, pleading with the one man who had the ability and experience to lead them out of the wilderness of their hopelessness and despair. It was not until I saw Amte grinning at me that I realized I was shouting at the top of my voice and banging the table to emphasize the points that I was trying to make. 'You know,' he said, 'I can never resist the enthusiasm of others and I don't expect others to resist my enthusiasm either!'

I was slightly abashed. 'So you will do something?' I asked, hoping and praying he would say yes. 'I will try,' he said.

For the next two hours we sat at the breakfast table, discussing in broad terms how this new project could shape up. When we said good-bye, we embraced warmly and Amte said 'Something will come of this, Arthur, we will work together one day.'

As I waved farewell, I felt in my heart that at least the foundation of the project had been laid, even if the walls were not yet scheduled.

CHAPTER 17

Sandhi-Niketan: the End of the Track

*

London. January, 1970.
WHEN we docked at Dover, having clocked up 63,386 miles
since the Expedition left, not to mention 25,000 miles by ship and
plane, and a further 5,000 by train, raft, horse, elephant, bus and
sedan chair etc., I felt that I was riding the crest of the wave. The
Gypsy looked surprisingly fit, despite the treatment that we had
given it. The seats were a little threadbare and several irritating
rattles had developed, resisting every effort to trace and treat
them; but we had lost nothing of real consequence, and the body-
work was still in fine shape. We had visited 134 hospitals, 47
institutions and other places for the handicapped right across
South Asia, and interviewed some 500 disabled persons, over 150
of them 'in depth'. As I sat down to draft our report, I realized
that I could say with complete honesty that the Expedition had
'successfully completed its mission, without serious illness, accident
or mishap . . . '

'Most of the hospitals and other institutions concerned with the welfare
and rehabilitation of the disabled have been visited in all the countries
on the Expedition's itinerary. Numerous case histories of handicapped
persons were collected . . . Every effort was made to bring the condition
and needs of the handicapped further to the attention of the local
authorities and public opinion. These ends were sought by means of
press interviews, public addresses, radio and television, discussions with
government ministers, industrialists, and other officials. But the most
important were the numerous personal contacts with the disabled
themselves and their families, when it was possible for a measure of
comfort, encouragement and hope for the future to be given. . . .' The
report was concluded with a mention of further plans: 'There is one
specific project with which I hope to be associated. It will involve the
setting up in India of a rural settlement where disabled villagers could
be assessed and trained, so that they could eventually be re-integrated
as useful members of the community within the context of their
villages.'

My personal affairs, however, were in a less happy state. Before I could start raising funds for the projected settlement, I had to take drastic action over our house in Queensborough Terrace. My mother's death had dealt a shattering blow to Tadeusz. Having cared for her right up until the last with the devotion of a saint, her death had left him utterly alone. Eventually he had left the house, unable to bear the weight of the loneliness and the silent memories. I was only too delighted, incidentally, when he subsequently remarried, feeling that he more than deserved the love and comfort of his present wife.

The house now belonged to me, but was in such an appalling condition that it represented a liability rather than an asset. Having been left more or less unattended for over a year, the walls were peeling, the roof was leaking, everything was falling to pieces. The local authority was banging on the door, demanding that I put the place in order, threatening to slam an order to foreclose if I failed. To make matters worse, some of the tenants were disagreeable characters who not only refused to leave when I asked them, but threatened me repeatedly with physical violence when I met them. The situation was a mess; to cut a long story short, it took me several years of highly expensive litigation to evict them. Eventually I managed to raise enough money to tear the house apart from the inside, and to re-build it into a block of modern flatlets.

Apart from my worries on this score, I lost three of my oldest friends in quick succession. My beloved Scooby had died as well, back in 1965; I was now totally alone, and the experience was not one that I would wish to repeat. What kept me going in these dark days was my hope for the future. Fortunately, I had the challenge before me of writing this book. When I look back now, I am horrified to see how little I have managed to include; my note-books are still crammed with unmarked material, people that I met and would have loved to write about. Having expended so much blood and sweat in collecting material, it was galling to find, over and over again, that I simply could not include everybody without writing about five books. No doubt many others have experienced this, but I often felt like a father contemplating infanticide, when I realized that one of my precious 'children' would have to be cut out.

As the book began to take shape, various friends and interested parties decided that a quick, flying visit to Anandwan was called for. Little progress had been achieved with the plans for the projected settlement, because Amte had been busy with other schemes, and because I had been preoccupied with my personal affairs. To set the ball rolling, we decided that I should hammer the plans out on the spot.

Arriving at Anandwan, I drove through a cluster of new, modern buildings – the place had expanded beyond recognition since my last visit. My arrival coincided, as it happened, with the settlement's annual reunion. As the jeep drew to a halt, people were streaming from all directions towards a group of new houses, formed around a square. Eager hands grasped my wheelchair, and propelled me towards a large marquee, where I noticed Amte talking volubly to a cluster of people. 'Hallo, Baba!' I shouted. He came over, looking a bit more grey and drawn than I had remembered, and I noticed that he was wearing a cervical collar; but the familiar energy and sparkle were undimmed. 'Welcome home!' he said as we embraced. 'Come on, no time for talk now. Time for the fun!' Before I could protest, unseen hands had hoisted me and the chair bodily up on to the dais, which was surrounded by wheat, eggs, grain, millet, grapes, lentils, cotton – in true Harvest Festival fashion. As we sat facing the crowd, sitting cross-legged on the ground below us, he talked as if I had only been away for a couple of days. 'See those children over there?' he said, pointing to one of the groups below. 'They're all blind. We have a blind school now, a new experiment. And there are the College students. We've got 695 at the college now.'

As the first speaker rose to his feet, we all grew silent. P. L. Deshpande, the eminent Marathi poet, welcomed us in the name of the Friends of Anandwan. Explaining the background to the newly built Sukha Sadan (Abode of Bliss), where we had assembled, he said that since leprosy victims continued to flock to Anandwan from far and wide, further developments had been necessary to accommodate the growing family. Sukha-Sadan had been designed as an independent, self-supporting co-operative aiming at rehabilitation through small-scale industries – weaving, spinning, printing, and making useful objects out of old tin-cans. There were twenty-six five-roomed houses, each accommodating two families and two old or severely crippled leprosy victims, who would be looked after by the relatively able-bodied families. Thus the problem of old age, of loneliness, of worry and fear of the future, was resolved in a happy community of compassion and self-help. 'What a beautiful, what a unique concept has been materialized here! What a shining example to a world where the rising numbers of the old and helpless are becoming a "big problem"!

'But this new project is intended to do more than merely bringing back self-respect and the means to a decent life. It is above all an experiment in social integration, crashing through the barriers of caste, language and nationality, a brotherhood forged on the anvil of pain that has been shared. Our task here is to wipe away the tear from the heart, to bring back joy into life.'

The second speaker was Pierre Oppliger, the representative of Swiss Aid Abroad. Speaking quietly and modestly, he expressed his joy on behalf of his fellow countrymen at having been associated with Anandwan for almost a decade. They had been proud to assist financially again in this project, as a contribution to the war against suffering. As the applause was dying down, I suddenly felt a sharp dig in my ribs.

'You're next,' Amte hissed.

'But I can't . . . I haven't prepared . . . ' I stammered. Protest was useless. As I searched desperately through my mind for something to say, I gazed down at the sea of faces below. Their corporate expression was not one of curiosity, or even expectancy; it was more an expression of brotherly affection. Grasping the microphone, I found myself describing without a moment's hesitation how wonderful it felt to come home again to my own family. The words came pouring out as I told them how I had longed for this moment when I had sat in my cold, damp bed-sitter in London. Without daring to look round at Amte, I launched into a brief description of why I had come. 'So, my friends, I hope very much that I shall return yet again, very soon, to work alongside you all, to strive with you for a better life for all of us who have been struck down by misfortune.'

As I replaced the microphone on its stand, I glanced apprehensively at Amte. To my relief, he was grinning mischievously, his eyes twinkling.

After a hurried breakfast the following morning, we piled into Amte's jeep, bound for the Manpower Training Centre at

The beginnings of Sandhi-Niketan

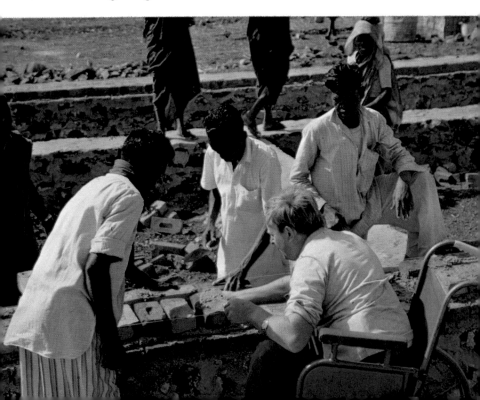

Somnath. As we bowled along, I caught up with some of the news, how the crops on the Anandwan Farms were now yielding twice the local average, sometimes even more; how they were pulling in more and more prizes for agricultural produce. I also realized, watching Amte, that he was in constant pain. The cervical collar was necessary because he was suffering from cervical spondylosis of the upper vertebrae. It was quite plain that this caused him agony; every few minutes he would sigh quietly, raising his left arm so that one of his sons could massage the muscles. The doctors had forbidden him to travel, and above all to avoid jolting; but he had been too sick to visit his patients at Somnath for some months, and felt that he must now make the journey at whatever cost. When I asked if the collar really achieved anything useful, he parried the question in typical Amte fashion. 'All my life I have never looked back,' he shouted above the engine noise. 'Now I can't even look sideways!'

When we left the narrow strip of asphalt, we began to bump alarmingly over a cart track, with bamboos and tree branches scraping the sides. After about a mile, we suddenly saw green fields of thick, lush millet, with a row of simple huts down one side; beyond was thick jungle. Amte gazed at the crops with visible emotion. 'This is the first time that this land has been sown, the first time ever that it has yielded productively. The cycle of sowing and reaping has always been like a creed to me. The mystery of life is all around us – right here, for anyone who has eyes to see or heart to feel. Where many Christians associate Christ's Resurrection with Easter, with going to church or attending to their devotions, I see it in each plant that dies in the autumn, or in the dry season, and is born again in the spring or with the rains. God can only come to life when you discover Him in everything around, in the seeds, in the fertilizer, in the chorus of the birds, the march of the seasons . . . '

We stared in silence at his beloved fields. His was a real faith, virile and earthy, not something to be acted out in a ritual between four walls. It reminded me vividly of the stories that I had heard so often in my childhood of the dusty paths and hills of Judaea. There was the same hot, burning sun, the same sort of rugged existence to be snatched from a stony land. I thought how similar it all was, down to the aphorisms and parables culled from wayside trees and birds. This too was the world of the simple, the poor, the humble, those in pain. 'The meek shall inherit the earth . . . '

There was a pioneering atmosphere about Somnath that you could almost reach out and touch. He insisted on showing me everything, bumping my wheelchair over the rough paths, explaining they had already held two student camps, such as he had foreshadowed back in 1966. In May 1968, about 1,200 college and University students and teachers from all over the country had come; the camps had been a great success, and the idea was already catching on, with more student work camps being planned in other parts of the country.

Dusk had drawn in by the time we returned. As we sat down to eat under the stars, I noticed that a large log fire was blazing outside the hut in which we were to sleep, to keep predators from approaching too close. The food was served by a charmingly shy girl who had accompanied us from Anandwan in the jeep; I leaned over to my neighbour, Mr Pandit, and asked who she was. 'Oh, Madhu is a PhD,' he replied. 'But she likes it better working here. She is one of the family now, like the rest of us.' When I questioned him more closely, he told me that he himself had been a stockbroker in Bombay. 'But this life has its rewards,' he added rather disarmingly.

It was not until the following morning that I succeeded in tackling Amte about the project. He cut short my carefully prepared preamble with an expansive wave of his arm. 'You have come a long way to talk to me,' he said, 'but I have a surprise for you. I have worked out most of the details already!'

The smallest 'viable' unit, he suggested, was one of twenty-five trainees, with workshops and hostel accommodation. These twenty-five would be trained primarily in agriculture, with complimentary courses in tailoring, leather-work and cotton spinning. Each course would be supervised by an instructor, while a physiotherapist would keep the trainees in trim and help in the development of simple aids. The whole unit would be administered by a superintendent, assisted by a liaison officer for field work, contact with relatives and 'follow-up'.

'But how ever much will this cost?' I asked apprehensively, only too well aware that it was I who had the task of raising the money.

'Well, I haven't quite finished my calculations,' he replied. 'But if we use the same designs for workshops and hostel accommodation that I have developed over the years at Anandwan, I would think about £9,500 for construction. On top of that we must add equipment and running costs for the first three years, at least. This would bring the total to about £20,000; but since dry farming for the severely handicapped is problematical, we should bring water to irrigate the experimental training farm; that should cost another £14,000 . . . '

'You realize I have no money yet. It's a great deal to raise!'

'I have never had money, but that has never stopped me!'

'I agree with you entirely,' I said. 'All I can offer now are the royalties from a book. This should help to get us started, at least.'

He paused, and gave me a searching look. 'If you contribute the royalties from your book, I will give the land. I have ten acres at Anandwan already cleared. I had thought of using it for something else, but now I have changed my mind!'

Within a couple of hours we had discussed the basic plan in detail, modifying details, pruning everything that was not absolutely essential, arguing fiercely about the nature of the courses. I found myself agreeing in the end about virtually everything. Despite his apparent pre-occupation in the preceding three years with a host of other projects, Amte had evidently spent a good deal of time studying the needs of the handicapped, turning over in his mind how he could make some practical contribution to their problems. Naturally I never mentioned this, but I like to think that somehow my own enthusiasm had communicated itself to him, and sparked off a chain reaction. Perhaps my brief visit brought to a head all the plans that he had been turning over in his mind.

When I returned to London at the end of 1968, many people thought I was crazy to launch out on this project with inadequate funds. But I had spent years sitting in a wheelchair, organizing the Expedition and then playing around with words; for years I have been itching to get up and do something concrete to help create something with my own hands.

Perseverance has paid off once more, in that I have now received an advance in connexion with my book. My bags are now packed. The labels read 'Anandwan, District Chanda, Maharashtra, India.'

*

Anandwan. March, 1970.

I reached Anandwan a month ago, late in the evening of the 1st of February after a cramped and jolting ride in the public bus from Nagpur. 'You look dead-beat Arthur,' Baba said as he escorted me to the modest guest-room I knew so well. 'But please be ready by seven o'clock tomorrow morning. I've got a surprise for you.' I pleaded with him to tell me, but he was adamant. 'Tomorrow will show,' he said firmly as he helped me lower the mosquito net and wished me a good night. The low roof of red tiles threw off the warmth caught during the day's heat; but I slept soundly until the sparrows began to chirp on the rafters above my bed. I jumped out of bed and washed hurriedly under the tap at the back of the room.

The project site lay half way between Anandwan and its extension, the agricultural co-operative of Mukti-Sadan. The *kharif* (monsoon) crops had been harvested back in October and November; the parched fields were now the colour of bitter chocolate. I peered eagerly across the stubble, as we bumped over the quarter-mile dirt track; two pairs of willing hands pushed from behind, but my wheels kept sinking in the dust, which made progress exasperatingly slow. At last we sheered off to the left over a ploughed field; the going became even harder across furrows that had dried into sharp ridges. Suddenly I saw two parallel rows of trenches, two lovely rows flanked with banks of excavated earth and heaps of broken grey stones. 'You've already started the foundations!' 'Yes, my little surprise,' Baba grinned. 'We thought we'd celebrate your return with something concrete!'

I stopped my chair between two furrows and wiped away the sweat that was trickling into my eyes. I had visualized this scene on innumerable occasions; years of planning and work, of hope, and sometimes despair had led to this. Incidents in my life that had seemed disjointed at the time, like so many leaves swept by the heedless winds of fate, now seemed to fall into a pattern, as if guided all along in God's wisdom.

As we bumped over the furrows, my eyes drank in avidly every detail of the scene. Where the trenches stopped, pegs marked the shape and extent of the buildings. From the outline, I saw that they formed three sides of a quadrangle of an area of one and a half acres, which would leave about eight and a half acres for the experimental farm plots. Across the fields to the north and south the red-tiled roofs of Mukti-Sadan and Anandwan respectively were outlined in the bright morning sunlight. The view to the west was cut short by a row of bushes and a scrubland outside the Anandwan lands. To the east, the direction which the Sandhi-Niketan buildings would face, the ground sloped gently down, allowing a distant sweep across brown fields, with patches of scrubland splashed by the vivid orange of flowering palas trees, with the shimmering dark green of the jungle beyond.

At the edge of this flank, there was a small cashew-nut tree, heavy with sprays of little waxy flowers. I watched as Amte strode over and pulled out a roll of stiff paper from a canvas bag that hung from one of its lower branches. He was joined by a man with a square, open face, wearing a rough collarless shirt and blue cotton shorts. 'Arthur, come and meet Bhau, our master builder.' The ground was more level here, so I wheeled myself over and folded my hands in namaste. 'He doesn't know any English, but he's a very able craftsman. He's already helped build most of the dwellings both in Anandwan and Somnath.' Bhau returned the greeting, smiling stiffly.

Baba unfolded the sheet. 'Look here!' The blazing sunlight made me screw up my eyes. After a moment I realized that it was the complete plan, with rooms for twenty-five trainees, craft training halls, physiotherapy gym, kitchen, storerooms, quarters for staff, bathrooms, everything.

'Baba, you've even had an architect to do the drawings!' 'Architect? An architect here? We drew them ourselves!' I looked up at him in amazement. As I scrutinized the plan, I marvelled at the precision and neatness with which each dimension had been inscribed. 'But how do you determine the size of these walls? This one facing the cashew tree for instance,' I pointed, 'it's shown as being twenty-two feet ten inches. Why the ten inches?' 'Tiles and certain timbers come in standard sizes,' he replied. 'Cutting them would involve waste in both labour and materials. Our building costs come to twelve rupees per square foot, all told; this is not for a mud-hut either, but for proper single-storied dwellings in brick, plastered and tiled.'

In 1966 I had seen a similar dwelling being built for a village headman in Gujarat; I was told it was cheap at twenty rupees per square foot. But Amte applies the peasant's knack for finding use and value in everything; nothing at Anandwan is wasted. The plans allowed for waste water from the kitchen and bathrooms to be channelled to irrigate the vegetables and fruit trees. The stones that had been extracted while digging a well were neatly piled up, to help build the foundations.

The following day I woke up at five-thirty, eager to get started. Working hours on site were from eight to twelve, and two to six. Having enlisted the help of two sturdy pairs of arms to push and heave me through the dust, I arrived at seven-thirty, along with the first workers. Bhau, unmistakably the boss with his sun glasses, his tape measure and his spirit level, waved me a friendly greeting. By eight o'clock, the rest of the fifty-strong work force had assembled.

Apart from Bhau and myself, the work force was drawn from the leprosy patients of Anandwan. The eight masons or brick-layers receive a small wage, in addition to their board; the others get full board, maintenance, medical care, but no wage. As I smiled at them, hands folded in the namaste greeting, they smiled back shyly, and I noticed that all bore the tell-tale marks of leprosy disfigurement. Thrown out of their villages, shunned and despised, they had come to Anandwan to find hope and a purpose in life again. Along with the walls of the project, we were help-ing to re-build men and women. The resignation and despair of their former lives was being buried along with the foundation stones.

Communication was something of a poser, since none of them spoke a word of English. So I manoeuvred myself out of the way, to watch without disrupting the rhythm of the work. The building art in rural India has jelled over the centuries into a set pattern; everything, of course, is performed by muscle power without mechanical aids. The women do all the heavy labouring work, trudging steadily to and fro with the brick, stone or mortar balanced on their heads, with silhouettes like Greek goddesses; while the men retain the more responsible jobs, mixing the mortar and laying the bricks. Stone, sand and lime were now arriving, the bullocks grunting and straining as they hauled the two-wheeled carts over the rough ground.

My first attempts at lending a hand were a disaster. Although some of the women were thumping the coarse uneven surface inch by inch, with heavy pounders, the result was still something of a nightmare for a Western-type wheelchair. Owing to the bumps and the sharp stones, I still needed two or three strong men pushing from behind; within a short time my solid rubber tyres were chipped and cut, and starting to part company from the rim. Mindful of Koulagi's boys, and their astonishing agility on the cobbles of Melkote, I tried abandoning the wheelchair. But paralysed muscles waste away, and my seat is little more than skin and bone; in no time at all I had cut myself on the sharp chippings, and had to retire back to my chair, bloody but unbowed.

After a while I found that I could help unload some of the stones from the bullock cart. If I positioned myself right up against the back of the cart, and hooked one arm firmly around the rear hand-grips of the wheelchair, I could stretch the other arm about half way into the cart. The stones came from a local quarry, already broken into relatively small chunks weighing anything from five to twenty pounds apiece. Owing to my wasted trunk muscles, I had to keep holding on firmly with one hand; but my arms are powerful, and after a while I was unloading my end with one hand as fast as the driver was unloading the top end with two.

In four days we unloaded all the stones for the foundations of the first half of the north wing. As my hands grew steadily more sore and calloused, I comforted myself by thinking of the plans rolled up in the cashew-nut tree. Three rooms for female trainees, bathroom, ten small rooms for male trainees, bathrooms, latrines, kitchen, dining hall, scullery and stores – nearly 225 feet in all. Morale shot up to a new high.

My attempt at brick-laying was not a success. The masons usually work in pairs, starting a course of bricks from one corner and working away from each other along the walls, until they eventually meet up again and start the next course. Trowelling accurately but fast, they lay between a thousand and fifteen hundred bricks daily per pair; since my trowelling was neither accurate nor fast, I merely slowed everybody down. But by watching closely over a period of time, I have now found at least three other jobs that I can do effectively. There was always a small group sifting the sand; one would load up the rough sand, two or three would carry the sand across to the sifter in the *ghamelas*, the metal bowls about fifteen inches in diameter; another would pour the rough sand from the ghamelas on to the top part of the wire mesh, which was angled at about forty-five degrees; and two more would rub away with wooden slats, so that the sand fell through the mesh and the gravel slid harmlessly to the bottom.

If I got out of my chair and scooped away a hollow by the base of the sifter, I found that I could rub at the rough sand provided I held on with my other hand to the wooden frame of the sifter. I also found that if the ghamela was emptied from too high up I would get covered in dust. Every grain of dust would be trapped in the sweat, and I would begin to wriggle and scratch all over; if the sand was poured from too low down, it would bounce off the wooden cross-piece in the middle, and get mixed up with the stones by my feet. There is a right way and a wrong way for every job. We use a lot of sand, and we sifters have to keep at it. As soon as a pile of clear sand builds up underneath the mesh, the sifter is moved round a few feet with the main heap of unsifted sand as the centre of a circle.

Bricks have to be moistened before they are laid: a dry brick takes moisture out of the mortar and does not bind well. I found that if I manoeuvred myself in my chair between the pile of dry bricks and the water drum, I could take them, one by one, from the stack on my left, dip them into the drum on my right, and reach round far enough to pile them neatly in threes, so that the women could load them on their head. After a while I made a number of signs to them that if they let me get ahead, until the pile was about four feet high, they could load without stooping. This is much appreciated, and speeds up the work. Even so, work still has to stop every three-quarters of an hour or so, while the slimy red fluid is emptied and the drum refilled. I had no idea that bricks suck up so much water. Luckily we have tap water on site, since Amte laid on a pipe from one of the Anandwan wells before I arrived.

For brick mortar, one part of lime is mixed with three of sand in a shallow pit, about fourteen feet square by a foot deep. The two are mixed slowly, with water being added frequently, and great care has to be taken that the correct proportions are used. The mixers stand around the pit, churning the mix with a kind of hoe fixed to the end of a six-foot bamboo, until it is all sufficiently soft and doughy for the masons to trowel. (Lime is relatively cheap. Cement is only used for pointing, plastering and certain features that require greater strength or durability.)

At first I was content to watch the lime hiss, bubble and steam as water was poured on to slake it, and to watch them pushing and pulling on their heavy bamboos. The mix turns gradually, once more water and sand has been added, into a thick gravy-brown goo. Then I discovered that if I twisted sideways, with my chair parallel to the edge of the pit and leaned with my chest hard against the armrest of the wheelchair, I could use both arms to heave and push the bamboo. This was fine, except that the pressure on my chest became so intense that I had to shift my position every few minutes. Practice makes perfect however, and I find that I can now heave away for reasonable periods at a time, usually working with at least one other. This makes life easier, in that I can concentrate on the edges while my companion tackles the centre part. Of the three, I would say mixing mortar is now my favourite job, despite being the most strenuous.

My fellow workers are a source of unfailing fascination, and I keep watching them out of the corner of my eye. Virtually all are simple souls and illiterate; only a very few of them know how old they are. But there is something timeless about them, as they tread with the splayed toes of feet that have never worn shoes. The men wear coarse cotton shirts over their dhotis or baggy pants; the women hitch up their bright-coloured saris at the back, pulling the bottom end forward between the legs and tucking it into the waist at the front. Small and wiry, with thin, streaky muscles that never bulge, they seem capable of carrying the most amazing weights on their heads without showing a sign of fatigue. All day long they walk to and fro with their loads, their firm, measured gait never faltering: truly the salt of the earth.

Attitudes and beliefs engrained across the centuries run deep. The masons, all leprosy patients trained by Bhau, are very conscious that their status is a high one, immediately below that of the master builder himself, and would never expect to undertake the more menial tasks of preparing or carrying materials. Everyone is well aware of his place, his rung on the ladder, believing it to be predestined and their due lot. As for me, I represent something quite outside their experience and comprehension: a foreign sahib, with useless legs into the bargain, sitting in a strange (and rather useless) contraption, who insists on performing tasks that no normal sahib would dream of undertaking. Yet I doubt if they would be particularly interested, even

314   THE UNBEATEN TRACK

if I found some way of conveying the nature and purpose of my working here. Such things are to be accepted, not questioned.

Yet as the days pass I am beginning to sense a subtle change in our relationship. Communication is still at a premium, in that my Marathi has not improved as much as it should have, and their English remains nil. But I feel that some of the initial remoteness has disappeared. I can offer no proof, but I think that a subtle affinity is evolving between us, a bond of the heart. With misfortune in common, we are joined together in the task of raising the walls, brick by brick, of the project, for which we have now chosen the name of Sandhi-Niketan. Roughly translated this means Home or Opportunity. In fact it is not quite so simple, since *Sandhi* has several meanings in Marathi. It means a treaty, or an alliance, for one thing; I have always felt that the disabled need an alliance to bring them back into the mainstream of life, to help them regain their rightful place in the community. But Sandhi also means the faint outline of something on the horizon, a beacon in the far distance that is perhaps a little vague and shimmering in the haze, but is a sure guide to a brighter morrow. At Sandhi-Niketan we aim to reach out for the skies.

One of my fellow workers expressed this sense of fraternity to me today in a strangely moving manner. She smiled at me shyly, as she finished loading her ghamela with some of the mortar I had been mixing. I smiled back, and we wiped our foreheads simultaneously with the back of the hand. Her fingers, reduced to gnarled stumps by leprosy, were now a sandy-grey colour from the mortar; placing her left hand over her right, she rubbed the palms together, and pointed with her stumpy finger first to me, then to herself, and then to the wall beside us that had been built that afternoon. Her face broke into a happy smile. 'Yes, I understand,' I said. 'We are building Sandhi-Niketan together, and this is a happy thing. Soon, very soon, Sandhi-Niketan will bring smiles of hope to the faces of sorrow.'

*

Anandwan. April, 1970.
Sometimes I have to pinch myself as I watch the walls go up. But we have been pressing on with the construction of Sandhi-Niketan. My own work, like that of the others, fell into a routine: sifting sand, mixing mortar, dipping and piling the

bricks. How fast or for how long I can do any of these at a stretch, depended partly on the heat. The thermometer soon registered 103°F in the shade, while we laboured in the scorching sunlight, where I guess it must have been some 20°F hotter. My problem was still with me, and is likely to remain with me in that I could not bend forward without the help of my arms, and had to work twisted sideways, leaning with my full weight across the edge of the side arm. It soon felt pretty painful, as if a burning but blunt knife were being pressed across my chest.

On Sunday mornings everyone in Anandwan gathers for *Shram-dan*, literally the Gift of Labour, which Gandhi first introduced as a concept to nurture the dignity of labour and community service, through the co-operation of all, irrespective of caste. Since I returned here last February, the weekly Shram-dan has been concentrated on building a better road between Anandwan and the agricultural co-operative, Mukti-Sadan. At the stroke of six o'clock in the morning, the whole place becomes deserted, except for the sick and the old and those too ravaged by leprosy for work, as about 250 men and women converge on the new road, bearing shovels, pickaxes, crow-bars and ghamelas.

Shram-dan in full swing reminds me of the feverish activity of an ant-heap. Lashed by nothing more ominous than the stentorian voice of whoever is in charge, the party divides into two groups, one to dig the earth, the other to carry the ghamelas, two, three or even four at a time, up the hundred yards or so to the embankment of the new road. The earth is easy enough; but once we take off the topsoil at our loading end, we have to tackle the *muram*, a flaky conglomerate in the early stages of formation. This is quite soft, as stones go, but tough if you are shovelling with your rib cage pressed against an armrest. But nobody minds if I work slowly. The aim is not to beat records but to do your best.

In fact these Sunday morning workouts serve a number of purposes. Leprosy patients are grateful for the new fellowship, and rejoice in their regained ability to work; the Mukti-Sadan co-operative is getting a better road; Sandhi-Niketan is getting a road that will pass within twenty yards of the nearest building, instead of the present sixty yards. Furthermore, the ground on which the west wing will eventually stand is being levelled, the hump being removed ghamela by ghamela to form the embankment for the new road. The cost of erecting the plinth for the west wing will now be considerably reduced. The embankment grows a further forty yards every Sunday; a mechanical earth-mover could probably carry in one gulp what 250 men and women carry by ghamela in three hours. But earth-movers are expensive, and do not bind people together in the joy of fellowship and shared effort.

Self-reliance is a motto at Anandwan. No labour is brought in from outside, except for highly specialist work like electrical installations. Apart from salt and sugar, it grows its own food; having fed between 800 and 850 patients on average, the surplus is sold, to the tune of about 150,000 rupees per annum. It has its own tailors, shoemakers, printers, smithy, even its own post office, all staffed by leprosy victims. I often stop off to watch the small balding figure of Daulat Mistry, the carpenter, at work with his son and two apprentices, planing door and window frames, preparing roof trusses, sawing posts for the verandah. Stocks of poles for the scaffolding, frames in various stages, the end grain blackened with tar, lie scattered around the shed near the Sandhi-Niketan site, the golden-yellow of fresh teak glistening in the sun. The great merit of teak lies in its resistance to termites; the cost of the logs, which come from Chanda, varies according to size and quality, but averages out at sixteen rupees per cubic foot.

We are making excellent progress with the building. By the 8th of March, five weeks after the foundations were dug, the walls had risen beyond the door and window openings, and were being taken up again in a solid line above. Water, of course, is a must on a building site, particularly in such torrid heat. Water for drinking, water to slake the lime, to mix the mortar, water for dipping the bricks or for the women to pour over the rising walls so that the mortar dries out slowly and doesn't crack. For this, they carry the water in large, bright five gallon tins emblazoned with a pair of clasping hands and a caption in seven languages 'Donated by the People of the United States of America'. The tins originally contained soy-bean salad oil, used in the Anandwan kitchens. But true to the principle of 'never a wasted product', the patients never dispose of the empty tins, but take the tops off, screw in a wooden crosspiece for a handle, and put them to good use again.

I was intrigued at first – even slightly alarmed – by the scaffolding. Reasonably straight saplings and branches are secured in the ground at about ten-foot intervals and roughly two foot away from the wall. Other pieces, about five feet long, are secured at regular intervals at right angles through the wall, a brick being removed for each piece. The platforms are made from lengths of bamboo cane lashed together, which look rather precarious, but support the weight of the masons. The first level is fixed about five feet off the ground, and as the wall is built up additional levels are secured at similar intervals. No ladders or pulleys link these platforms: the masons clamber up between the walls and poles. A woman is posted underneath where a mason is working, to take bricks and mortar brought by other women and lift the stuff to the platform above. If there are more platforms, the women form vertical human chains, passing materials from one level to the next.

Even if most of the work is routine, a day seldom passes without excitement of some kind. The other day one of the workers went to the bushes a mere twenty-five feet away to mind his own business. Presently he shot out holding his pants down by his knees, yelling 'Snake! snake!' Fortunately he had taken a spade with him, which he had thrown at the brute, scoring a hit. The other worker-patients came running, wielding whatever they could grab, and returned with a six foot cobra. The cobra was very dead, thank goodness.

On the 21st of March, the first day of spring, the brickwork on the first section of the building was virtually completed. Unfortunately I was no longer able to do much to help, but watched as teams of men, some standing on the ground, others on drums, slowly heaved the beams to support the roof's timber superstructure. First they lifted one end up onto the wall, then the other, and fixed them in position. By the same process, relying entirely on sheer manpower, they hoisted cumbrous triangular trusses into position amidst a pother of hhhmmm! odha! (pull) ghya! (take) paha! (look), hhmmm! Once this main framework was fixed, the rafters were added, each notched to grip the beam along the wall. Three more courses of brick were laid, embedding these beams safely into the structure of the wall, while the carpenters were busily hammering the laths.

The men could now start on the tiling. By the 6th of April the entire section was tiled, and the long verandah faced with wooden pillars to support the overhanging roof. A great deal still remained to be done before the main work was over on this section, filling the floor-space with hard muram and tamping it down solid with heavy pounders. The entire structure had to be plastered, inside and out. Even on the roof there still was work to be done, on the cornices on either side of the dining-hall. But since there were no more bricks to be washed, and hardly any mortar to mix, my own work became lighter. I was frankly relieved; the heat is now becoming torrid. The thermometer has already registered 112°F in the shade and continues to rise; to sit in a metal wheelchair is rather like keeping one's bottom in a red-hot oven. All the metal parts are scorchingly hot, and I have to take care not to touch them. Heat reigns supreme and insinuates itself into everything. The sky has turned a whitish colour, like a shroud of seething lead. Most of the trees have shed their leaves. The temperature is bound to pass the 118°F mark soon; this area is notorious as amongst the hottest in Asia, and even birds, particularly crows, will often fall dead of heat exhaustion. Everything sucks up the heat; if I happen to touch the wall by my bed, its heat wakes me up immediately. My midday tap wash has turned into more of an ordeal than a pleasure, for the water spouts out close to boiling. The body never stops sweating, even during sleep, and is permanently coated with a moist, sticky film.

But nothing can detract from my joy as Sandhi-Niketan comes to life. The big day arrived on the 21st of April, and all Anandwan gathered dressed in their best dhotis and saris. I was reminded of the vodka drinking and the festive mood that invariably accompanied the completion of a house in Poland.

In Anandwan the ceremony was a blend of old and new. The religious rite represented tradition and tradition permeates every aspect of life in India. The hoisting of the flag, emblazoned with the words Shrama Sanskar Chhaoni (Work Oriented Camp) and showing a tree with many branches, portrayed the new; it also symbolized integration amid diversity.

The religious ceremony was to take place at four-thirty and the afternoon had been declared a holiday; the morning was filled with feverish activity. Men were threading mango leaves, which are believed to be auspicious, on strings to be stretched round the roof and over doorways. Strips of blue and yellow cloth were wound round poles that had been set up to support the marquee, itself resplendent in shades of blue and orange. Cloths of the same colours were spread on the ground under the marquee, where those who could find no room in the dining-hall would take their place.

For the convenience of disabled trainees a gentle slope, made of concrete, led into the dining-hall.

Inside the hall women had drawn a beautiful *rangoli*; it was made of ground quartz tinted to vivid blue, green, white, red and orange (this is regarded as an auspicious pattern). A six-inch high wooden stool, a *chourang*, was placed nearby. On it was set a tumbler filled with water with five leaves of the betel-nut tree stuck into it (five is a lucky number); there were five other kinds of nut including tumeric and walnut and, finally, there was a *shaligram* stone which is sacred to the God Vishnu the Preserver.

In the afternoon men and women began to gather expectantly. At last a Hindu priest strode up the ramp into the hall wearing a white shirt and baggy trousers. Almost everyone was there (except Amte, who had had to go to Somnath), Mrs Amte, the blind boys, all the children of Anandwan and all its workers; men and women squatting on opposite sides of the hall. The priest sat cross-legged, a little to the right of the chourang. A recently married couple (their presence being deemed lucky) squatted by his side.

A hush fell as he began chanting in a low tone from a Sanskrit text which lay open on his lap. The couple then threw handfuls of rice over the chourang, also flowers and garlands of roses, hibiscus and *mogra*, which resembles white jasmine. Then the priest motioned to them to place a coconut on the flower-laden chourang and to light a tiny oil lamp. This was placed on a small round metal tray which was then passed round, each person extending their palms towards the flame and then putting them against their cheeks. A girl came to apply the red tikka mark to my forehead.

When the propitiation by fire ended everyone rose and shouted Vishnu's attributes: 'Maker of Happiness', 'Destroyer of Sorrow', 'Remover of Bad News'. The distribution of holy water (water in which the statue of the diety had been bathed) followed, a few drops being poured into the hands and drunk. Finally a sweetmeat made of wheat flour, clarified butter, sugar and milk was offered. Then everyone walked three times clockwise round the chourang and the ceremony was over.

I am writing these last lines in the relative coolness of the Sandhi-Niketan verandah. As I look down the verandah, I can see the foundations for the next section. The trenches are carefully marked out on both sides with string, the dark brown muram heaped like a parapet alongside. Bricks are being stacked up in readiness, a fresh mortar mixing pit has been dug alongside, and sand is being unloaded from bullock carts in soft, golden heaps. Amte has just arrived and is talking to Bhau. The masons have just started building the corners of the plinth. I shall join them presently.

In another two months this section too will be completed, by which time the money will be exhausted. More, much more will be needed to complete all the buildings, equip them, provide for the maintenance of the trainees, pay the staff, buy a van, irrigate at least part of the fields. Where the money will come from I do not know. Yet I feel that since Providence has helped and guided me so far in this task, it will not fail me now. However, Providence seldom works on its own, so I shall have to try harder than ever before. Because soon, very soon I hope, there will be crippled trainees on this verandah, regaining their hope, their rightful place in society.

Another cartload of stone has just pulled up by the foundations, the bullocks breathing heavily from their exertion. I know that this small plot can achieve little in terms of the massive human problem we confront. But we have made a start. God willing, the journey will continue, ascending over obstacles and into rising planes of achievement, and none of us will be alone in this arduous path.

> I sought my soul, my soul I could not see;
> I sought my God, my God eluded me;
>   but when I sought my brother, I found all three.